Three Splendid Little Wars:
The Diary of Joseph K. Taussig

NAVAL WAR COLLEGE *HISTORICAL MONOGRAPH SERIES NO. 16*

The historical monographs in this series are book-length studies of the history of naval warfare, edited historical documents, conference proceedings, and bibliographies that are based wholly or in part on source materials in the Historical Collection of the Naval War College.

The editors of the Naval War College Press express their special gratitude to all the members of the Naval War College Foundation, whose generous financial support for research projects, conferences, and printing has made possible the publication of this historical monograph.

Three Splendid Little Wars:
The Diary of Joseph K. Taussig

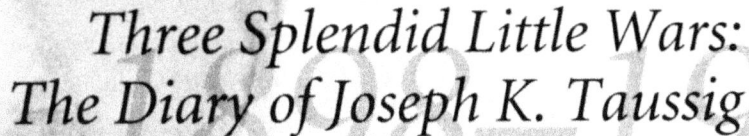

Edited by Evelyn M. Cherpak

NAVAL WAR COLLEGE PRESS
NEWPORT, RHODE ISLAND
2009

The contents of this volume represent the views of the authors. Their opinions are not necessarily endorsed by the Naval War College or by any other agency, organization, or command of the U.S. government.

Printed in the United States of America

Historical Monograph Series

Library of Congress Cataloging-in-Publication Data

Taussig, Joseph K. (Joseph Knefler), 1877-1947.
  Three splendid little wars : the diaries of Joseph Knefler Taussig, 1898-1901 / edited by Evelyn M. Cherpak.
    p. cm. — (Naval War College historical monograph series ; no. 16)
  Includes bibliographical references and index.
  ISBN 978-0-16-082792-1 (alk. paper)
  1. Taussig, Joseph K. (Joseph Knefler), 1877-1947—Diaries. 2. Spanish-American War, 1898—Personal narratives, American. 3. Spanish-American War, 1898—Naval operations. 4. Admirals—United States—Diaries. 5. United States. Navy—Biography. 6. Philippines—History—Revolution, 1896-1898—Personal narratives, American. 7. China—History—Boxer Rebellion, 1899-1901—Personal narratives, American. I. Cherpak, Evelyn M. (Evelyn May), 1941- II. Title.
  E729.T38 2009
  973.8'9—dc22
                                                2009021051

NAVAL WAR COLLEGE PRESS
Code 32
Naval War College
686 Cushing Road
Newport, R.I. 02841-1207

TABLE OF CONTENTS

Editor's Note..ix
Foreword, by *John B. Hattendorf* xi
Introduction xv
    Part 1: The Spanish-American War, 1898 1
  I. Tampa: Waiting for War 3
 II. At Sea 13
III. Daiquirí, Siboney, and Santiago 19
 IV. Battle of Santiago Bay 27
  V. Surrender at Santiago 39
 VI. War's End 45
VII. Letter to Charles Taussig 61
    Part 2: The Philippine Insurrection and the Boxer Rebellion, 1899–1901 65
VIII. At Sea in the Caribbean 67
 IX. South America 77
  X. The Philippine Islands and China 103
 XI. The Boxer Rebellion 131
XII. Duty in USS *Nashville* and USS *Culgoa* 157
    Index 167
    Titles in the Series 175

EDITOR'S NOTE

The Spanish-American War, the Philippine Insurrection, and the Boxer Rebellion occurred over a hundred years ago. Scholars have produced a spate of books treating the Spanish-American War, the Philippine Insurrection, and the Boxer Rebellion. Personal accounts of service in the Spanish-American War have been published as well, yet fewer for the latter two conflicts.[1] The unpublished diaries of Joseph K. Taussig, who participated in all of these conflicts, are therefore a uniquely valuable personal account of his wartime experiences. The documents add to our knowledge of these events as seen through the eyes of a young naval cadet who was thrust into battle even before graduation from the U.S. Naval Academy. They also reveal his feelings about war, with its boredom alternating with terror.

The diaries are located in the Naval Historical Collection at the Naval War College, where they form part of a larger collection of Taussig Papers that include family correspondence; journals of service in USS *Wadsworth*, USS *Little*, and USS *Trenton*; fitness reports, photographs, subject files, newspaper clippings; and miscellany, including certificates, citations, and imprints for the years 1884–1947.

Taussig's Spanish-American War diary is divided into five sections of penciled, dated entries on notebook paper. They were written under wartime conditions and, no doubt, in haste and under some stress. Imprints of officers, ships, and views of Cuba, taken from magazines of the period, were tipped in later. His journal of the USS *Newark* covers the Philippine Insurrection and the Boxer Rebellion; it is a legal-size bound volume, written in ink, and also dated. The present volume reproduces ink drawings of parts of the ship and other views done by Taussig at the time.

I have followed standard editorial practice in editing these documents. The original spelling, punctuation, and capitalization have been retained. Footnotes identifying ships, people, and places have been supplied, and the spelling of proper names is corrected there.

The editor wishes to thank Mr. George Philip of South Freeport, Maine, grandson of Vice Admiral Taussig, for donating to the Naval War College in 2005 the two diaries published here. Mrs. Joseph K. Taussig, the admiral's wife, donated his letters and personal papers to the College through the good offices of her children, Mrs. Emily Taussig Sherman of Newport, Rhode Island, and the late Captain Joseph K. Taussig, Jr., USN (Ret.), of Annapolis, Maryland, in 1988. Mrs. Sherman made subsequent deposits of her father's papers in 1989, 1992, 1996, and 1997.

I am indebted to a number of individuals at the Naval War College for their help and support with this project. John B. Hattendorf encouraged and supported the publication of this work, while Pelham Boyer of the Naval War College Press oversaw the production process. Melissa Cameron of Intekras and her staff set the type and prepared the book for printing. The Naval War College Foundation, under the executive directorship of Rear Admiral Roger Nolan, USNR (Ret.), provided the funding for printing.

Elsewhere, the staffs of the Harvard University Archives; the Redwood Library in Newport, Rhode Island; the Blunt White Library at Mystic Seaport, Connecticut; and the U.S. Naval Academy Library provided assistance. Dr. Norman Friedman, independent scholar, identified several foreign vessels. I alone am responsible for any errors in this work.

EVELYN M. CHERPAK,
Portsmouth, Rhode Island

NOTE 1 For personal memoirs of the Philippine Insurrection and the Boxer Rebellion, see John W. Ganzhorn, *I've Killed Men* (London: Robert Hale, [1940]); A. B. Feuer, ed., *America at War: The Philippines, 1898–1913* (Westport, Conn.: Praeger, 2002); Frederic A. Sharf and Peter Harrington, *China, 1900: The Eyewitnesses Speak—The Boxer Rebellion as Described by Participants in Letters, Diaries and Photographs* (Mechanicsburg, Pa.: Stackpole Books, 2000).

FOREWORD

The study of the history of naval warfare is an integral part of the Naval War College's educational programs. The importance of the discipline was firmly established at the foundation of the College in 1884, with the initial contributions of both the College's founder, Stephen B. Luce, and his successor as the school's president, Captain Alfred Thayer Mahan. Historical research and analysis have continued as recognized elements of the academic life of the institution for the 125 years since. Nowhere, in fact, has the history of warfare at sea been more thoroughly investigated and analyzed for the professional purposes of the U.S. Navy than at the Naval War College. Nowhere is there a more logical requirement for a corpus of relevant source materials and for an academic research department devoted to new research in naval history. On 1 January 2003, a Maritime History Department was established at the College, as part of the Center for Naval Warfare Studies, to carry out this function. Predating this, a program for the publication of books and source materials on the history of naval warfare was formally established by the College in 1975—a series known as the Naval War College Historical Monographs. In order to encourage and make more widely known the College's extensive collections for historical research, including its archives, historical manuscripts, and associated materials in the Naval War College Museum's collection, the series has been restricted to publications of book-length works that deal with the history of naval warfare and that are based, wholly or in part, on the College's rich historical source materials in the Naval War College Library's Naval Historical Collection and the Naval War College Museum. As the series has developed over the past thirty-five years, these works have taken a variety of forms, including bibliographies, conference proceedings, and many edited historical documents. This series is now managed by the Maritime History Department, in collaboration with the Naval War College Press and the head of the Naval War College's Naval Historical Collection.

Consistent with the earlier books that have appeared in this series since 1975, Dr. Evelyn Cherpak, the current Head, Naval Historical Collection, has edited the present volume from materials in Manuscript Collection 97, The Papers of Vice Admiral Joseph K. Taussig (1877–1947), which were donated to the Naval War College Foundation in 1988, with subsequent additions from family members. In 1996, Dr. William N. Still, Jr., edited another diary from the Taussig papers for this series, which appeared as *The Queenstown Patrol, 1917.*

In this new volume covering the years 1898 to 1901, Dr. Cherpak has made a significant contribution to American naval history with the publication of these diaries. Vastly different in approach and sophistication of observation from those of more senior officers, these diaries capture the viewpoint and growing professional understanding of a young man during his very first experiences of wartime operations. In the years between 1882 and 1902, the U.S. Naval Academy did not use the titles "Midshipman" or "Passed Midshipman" for officers and naval engineers in training, employing the term "Naval Cadet" until the more traditional title was restored on 1 July 1902. During these years, the Naval Academy's academic program lasted six years. The first four years were spent at Annapolis, the next two at sea.

In part 1 of this book, Taussig writes while still in the first phase of his education at Annapolis. Taussig's very rough and impressionistic notes of his first experiences of naval operations during the Spanish-American War, in 1898, are interesting for the manner in which they document some of the typical attitudes and interests of a novice, while also providing the modern reader with a fascinating viewpoint on the war.

In part 2, Taussig has already finished his Annapolis years (in early 1899) and is beginning his two years of required sea duty before returning to Annapolis to take his final examination and to await a vacancy for promotion to ensign. During the entire period recorded in part 2 Taussig is still a naval cadet and has yet to take his final promotion examination. He does that, but only in mid-1901, after the commanding officer of USS *Culgoa* (in the final entry printed in this book) allows him to proceed to that step, with the words, "An Excellent Journal. Approved." In part 2 Taussig's journals for 1899–1901 contrast with his first journal for 1898, as he records his observations of two more wars, the Philippine Insurrection and the Boxer Rebellion, observations that document his growing professionalism and his increasing interest in and understanding of the naval profession.

Taken as a whole, Taussig's diaries in this volume provide a valuable glimpse of the initial stage of a naval officer's professional military education just a little over a century ago. When compared and contrasted with the diary that the same man was to keep in 1917, in command of a destroyer during World War I *(The Queenstown Patrol)*, Taussig's early journals and diaries can be seen as substantively marking the first stages of the development of an officer's professional understanding.

Taussig built on these initial experiences and developed his professional understanding when, as a captain, he became a student at the Naval War College in 1919, staying on for two years as an instructor in tactics in 1920–21. Returning to Newport after two additional periods in command, he became head of the Naval War College's Strategy Department in 1923–26 and chief of staff to the President, Naval War College, in 1927–30, before becoming a flag officer in 1932. In the light of these further experiences and the advanced professional education that Taussig would eventually acquire, the diaries published in this volume provide insight into the basic professional military education at the entry level in the early twentieth century.

JOHN B. HATTENDORF, D.PHIL.
Ernest J. King Professor of Maritime History
Chairman, Maritime History Department

INTRODUCTION

The United States began preparations for war with Spain over Cuba after the sinking of the USS *Maine* on 15 February 1898.[1] The battleship had arrived in Havana to protect American interests and citizens after riots occurred in the city. Since 1895, the Cuban *insurrectos,* whose goal was an independent Cuba, had been at war with the Spanish, who hoped to retain the last vestiges of their empire in the Americas. Prior to the sinking of *Maine* there had been little public interest in the conflict in the United States, but after the incident there was overwhelming support for war with Spain.[2] At that time, Joseph K. Taussig was in his final year at the U.S. Naval Academy in Annapolis, Maryland, where he was a football and track star and president of the Academy's Athletic Association. Once hostilities began, he, then a naval cadet (in today's terms, a midshipman), was assigned to the battleship USS *New York,* on board which he took part in the bombardment of Aguadores and Santiago and saw action at the battle of Santiago Bay on 3 July 1898, where the Spanish fleet was decimated and Admiral Pascual Cervera taken prisoner.[3] After this first taste of war, Taussig returned to the Naval Academy.

He was assigned to the protected cruiser USS *Newark* after graduation and commissioning. The ship departed New York City in March 1899 for the long voyage to the Philippines, stopping in the Caribbean, Caracas (Venezuela), Montevideo (Uruguay), and a number of ports in Chile and Peru before transiting northward to Mare Island Navy Yard, near San Francisco, California, for inspection and repairs.[4] *Newark* made port calls in Hawaii and Guam on its way down the Pacific and arrived in Cavite in November. For the next five months the ship was on station at Vigan, on the island of Luzon. During this time, Taussig and a naval party were sent to Pamplona to rescue Americans held prisoner by rebels who opposed U.S. control of the islands. Once in Pamplona, however, the rescue party was ordered to return to the ship. In December, *Newark* moved to Aparri, where it received the surrender of the *insurrectos* in Cagayan, Bataan, and Isabela provinces.[5]

In April 1900, *Newark* received orders to sail, first to Japan and later to Taku, China, where the Allied Relief Expedition was being formed to rescue foreigners besieged by the Boxers (members of an antiforeign, anti-Christian movement) inside the legations at Peking, as Beijing was then known. The joint force consisted of British, French, Italian, Austrian, German, Japanese, and Russian troops, as well as U.S. Marines and Navy personnel. The naval forces were under the command of Admiral Edward Seymour, Royal Navy, with Captain Bowman McCalla, U.S. Navy, as second in command. It was there that Taussig became acquainted with Captain John Jellicoe and Lieutenant David Beatty, who would later be First Sea Lords of the Royal Navy.[6] On 7 June the expedition proceeded by train toward Peking but was forced to stop to repair the railroad tracks that had been torn up by Boxers. The train was intermittently attacked by the Boxers, whose goal was to rid China of foreigners and missionaries in order to preserve the old ways that were now threatened by modernization and westernization. The imperial forces of the dowager empress sided with the Boxers and took part in attacks on foreigners as well.

The relief expedition was forced to return to Tientsin when the railroad bed, both north and south of Yang Tsun, was destroyed. In addition, supplies were running low. The force of 2,100 men was isolated and cut off from help just seven days into its rescue mission.[7] During the retreat, Taussig was shot in the right leg in an encounter with the Boxers. He recovered in Japan and was awarded the China Relief Expedition Medal.[8] Some forty-three years later, he would receive the Purple Heart for gallantry in the Boxer Rebellion. Within three years' time and by the age of twenty-three, he had seen action in three conflicts initiated by native groups who opposed foreign control or intervention in their countries.

Taussig faithfully kept a daily journal throughout these conflicts. In his journal of the Spanish-American War he described the situation in Tampa, Florida, as the troops prepared to embark, the landing of the army at Daiquirí and Siboney, the condition of the Cuban and Spanish armies, the battle of Santiago Bay, a visit to Morro Castle in Havana, and the fleet's return to New York at the war's end. Included in this book are his pencil sketches of the troops, ships, calculations, maps, and naval signals, as well as prints of ships and naval personnel involved in the war. A letter to his brother, Charles Taussig, that describes the attack at Aguadores and the battle of Santiago Bay appears at the end of the journal (chapter 7 of this book).

The second journal covers duty in the Philippines and in China during the Boxer Rebellion. In it he described the ports and cities he visited, his shipmates, several naval officers (including Admiral Seymour, Captain McCalla, and Rear Admiral Louis Kempff, U.S. Navy), social life, recreation, the political situation in China, and the progress of and problems confronting the relief expedition. Drawings of the boilers, tubes, valves, and suction pumps of the USS *Newark* and USS *Mindoro* and views of the urban centers of Vigan and Pamplona are interspersed within the text.

A list of the ports that *Newark* visited, with dates, and an intelligence report on the fortifications of Sydney, Australia, and the government of New South Wales complete the journal. He submitted his journal to Captain John Fremont, commanding officer of *Culgoa*, who signed it, with an endorsement that it was an excellent piece of work.

The two holograph diaries, with almost daily entries, are well written, descriptive, and legible. The unbound Spanish-American War journal consists of 125 handwritten pages, with an additional thirty-five pages of imprints. The journal of the USS *Newark* is 120 pages long. The latter was used as the basis for Taussig's article on the U.S. Navy's participation in the Boxer Rebellion published in the U.S. Naval Institute *Proceedings* in April 1927.[9]

Joseph Knefler Taussig, of German Jewish ancestry, was born in Dresden, Germany, on 30 August 1877 to Rear Admiral Edward D. Taussig and Ellen Knefler.[10] He graduated from high school in Washington, D.C., in 1895 and was appointed a naval cadet that same year, graduating from the U.S. Naval Academy in 1899. Taussig was advanced four numbers in grade as a result of his wound in the Boxer Rebellion. After recuperating, he was assigned to the USS *Nashville* in the Philippines and then to the USS *Culgoa*, a supply ship that carried meat and provisions from Australia to the U.S. Army in the Philippines. Service in the USS *Culgoa* was followed by an assignment in the USS *Yorktown*, commanded by his father. While serving in *Yorktown* he rescued a shipmate from drowning in Yokohama Harbor, for which he received the Silver Life Saving Medal from the Treasury Department in 1902. This was the medal that he was to prize the most throughout his life. He was promoted to ensign in 1901.

When Taussig returned to the United States in 1902, he joined the USS *Texas*;[11] he then served as navigator in USS *Topeka*.[12] In 1905 he was in USS *Amphitrite*, the station ship at Guantanamo Bay, Cuba, and the next year he was executive officer and navigator in USS *Celtic*.[13] In 1907 Taussig joined the USS *Kansas*, one of the ships of the Great White Fleet, which was to sail around the world to demonstrate American naval power and presence.[14] After the fleet rounded Cape Horn and reached San Francisco, he was detached and assigned as aide to his father, by then commandant of the Norfolk Navy Yard. In 1910 he was appointed flag secretary and aide to Rear Admiral Charles Vreeland, commander of the 2nd and 4th divisions of the Atlantic Fleet.[15]

Prior to the U.S. entry in World War I, Taussig took command of the destroyer *Ammen* as a lieutenant commander in 1911, followed by an assignment in the Bureau of Navigation in Washington, D.C., until 1915.[16] This duty would stand him in good stead, as he was able to expose the shortcomings in personnel after the war. In 1915 he took command of the new destroyer USS *Wadsworth* and command of Division 6, Destroyer Force, Atlantic Fleet.[17] In July 1916, he was placed in command of Destroyer Division 8. With the British suffering hardships due to unrestricted submarine U-boat activity in their waters and the destruction of merchant shipping, President Woodrow Wilson sent Division 8 to Queenstown, Ireland in May 1917. There Taussig met Admiral Louis Bayly of the Royal Navy, who queried him as to when his ships would be ready for war.[18] Taussig famously replied: "We are ready now, that is, as soon as we finish refueling." The American destroyers were ordered to search for U-boats off the coast; however, they met with little success. A depth charge fired by *Fanning* sunk *U-58* on November 17.[19] Taussig was to earn the Distinguished Service Medal for an attack on a German submarine on 29 July 1917 and receive the Order of Saint Michael and Saint George from the British government for his service during the war.[20]

In 1917, Taussig was promoted to commander and returned to the United States in December to commission the destroyer USS *Little*.[21] By May of the next year *Little* was in Europe, patrolling off the coast of France. In August, with the war drawing down, Taussig was detached; he was promoted to captain in September. He reported to the Bureau of Navigation, where he headed the Division of Enlisted Personnel. Aware of the deficiencies of manpower during the war, he became embroiled in a conflict with Assistant Secretary of the Navy Franklin D. Roosevelt over the use of paroled criminals to fill enlisted ranks to make up for the shortage in naval personnel.[22] Taussig opposed this program and decried the inadequacy of the Navy's manning in testimony before the Senate Subcommittee on Naval Affairs. Consequently, he made longtime enemies of Roosevelt and Secretary of the Navy Josephus Daniels.[23] He averred that "the Navy was far from being ready for the war . . . and the enlisted personnel was entirely inadequate for the proper manning of our already completed ships on a peace time basis, and was dangerously deficient should we be suddenly thrown into war."[24] As a result, Secretary Daniels denied publication of Taussig's Naval Institute prizewinning essay on naval personnel.

In the 1920s Taussig had a long and fruitful association with the Naval War College, in Newport, Rhode Island. He attended the senior course of the College in 1919, graduating in 1920. The following year he remained on the staff as a member of the Tactics Department. From July 1926 to June 1926, he was chairman of the Strategy Department, and from 1927 to 1930 he was chief of staff. Between these tours he took command of USS *Great Northern*, renamed *Columbia* when it became flagship of the U.S. Fleet in 1921.[25] He assumed command of USS *Cleveland* in 1922 for a period of eleven months, during which he assisted the survivors of an earthquake in Chile.[26] The Chilean government awarded him the Order of Merit, First Class for his humanitarian efforts. For the next six months, he was assistant chief of staff to Admiral Hilary P. Jones, commander in chief of the U.S. Fleet.[27] In 1926 he assumed command of USS *Trenton*.[28]

Following his last Naval War College assignment, in 1931, he took command of USS *Maryland*.[29] He was promoted to rear admiral in 1932 and served as chief of staff to Vice Admiral Richard H. Leigh, Commander, Battleship Divisions, Battle Fleet.[30] In 1933, he was appointed Assistant Chief of Naval Operations, in the Navy Department. According to Admiral Fredric S. Withington, however, Taussig never had a chance of promotion beyond rear admiral because of his earlier dispute with Franklin D. Roosevelt.[31] Columnists Drew Pearson and Robert S. Allen accused Roosevelt of racial discrimination when Taussig was not selected as commander of the U.S. Fleet in 1936.[32] Instead, in 1936 he was assigned to Battleship Division 3, Battle Force, with his flag in the USS *Idaho*;[33] in 1937 he reported to Commander, Cruisers, Scouting Force, in USS *Chicago*, still with the rank of rear admiral.[34] In May 1938, he reported to the Norfolk Navy Yard as commandant, a post his father had held some thirty years before.

Taussig again crossed swords with now-president Roosevelt in April 1940, when Senator David I. Walsh from Massachusetts asked him to testify during the Senate hearings on the plans to expand the Navy. Taussig defended the building of *Iowa*- and *Montana*-class battleships and gave evidence of the aggressiveness and expansionist tendencies of the Japanese, who in fact hoped to control China, the Philippines, and the Netherlands East Indies.[35] Taussig supported the resupply of U.S. bases in the Pacific and the defense of the Philippines. He noted that the American merchant marine was inadequate compared to the Japanese merchant fleet.[36] Admiral Taussig testified, "I cannot see how we can escape being forced into war by the present trends of events."[37] This set off a firestorm in the press that lasted for several weeks.[38] Roosevelt was furious and wanted to relieve Taussig of his command of the Norfolk Naval Base, but the Chief of Naval Operations, Harold R. Stark, urged him to reconsider, and the president took no action.[39] Admiral Stark, however, issued on 23 April 1940 a reprimand, which was entered into Taussig's record.

Taussig was forced to retire because of age on 1 September 1941, even though he petitioned to remain on duty due to the impending crisis. He was promoted to vice admiral on the retired list on 22 October 1941, owing to his service in the Boxer Rebellion. Taussig's request to return to active duty was granted, and he ultimately served on the Naval Clemency and Prison Inspection Board, the Naval Discipline Policy Review Board, and the Procurement and Retirement Board until April 1947. On 8 December 1941, Roosevelt removed the reprimand from his record when Taussig's son, Joseph K. Taussig, Jr., was severely wounded while serving in USS *Nevada* during the Japanese attack on Pearl Harbor.[40]

Vice Admiral Taussig died on 29 October 1947 at the U.S. Naval Hospital Bethesda, Maryland. His survivors then included his wife, Lulie Johnston Taussig, who resided in Washington, D.C., and in Jamestown, Rhode Island; two daughters, Mrs. Emily Whitney Sherman of Newport and Mrs. Margaret Philip Helmer of

Irvine, California; and his son, Captain Joseph K. Taussig, Jr., of Annapolis. Today, Mrs. Sherman survives.

A prolific writer, Taussig contributed forty-four articles to the U.S. Naval Institute *Proceedings,* and in retirement he wrote *Our Navy: A Fighting Team,* which was published by McGraw-Hill in 1943. He was the recipient of a number of medals, including the Distinguished Service Medal, Legion of Merit, Sampson Medal, Spanish Campaign Medal, Cuban Pacification Medal, Victory Medal, Second Nicaraguan Campaign Medal, American Campaign Medal, American Defense Service Medal, and the World War II Victory Medal, as well as those previously mentioned. The destroyer escort USS *Joseph K. Taussig* (DE 1030) was named in his honor and launched in 1956.[41]

Taussig was a staunch defender of the Navy. He was aware of the service's deficiencies in personnel and preparedness during the first and second world wars, and he spoke out against the bureaucracy and the prevailing wisdom, however unpopular that made him. As a young man, he was tried in war and not found wanting. Courageous and keenly aware of his duty, he did not hesitate to put himself in harm's way. His meticulously kept journal now brings these events alive for readers some hundred years later.

NOTES

1 USS *Maine* (BB 2), an armored battleship, was commissioned in 1895. Assigned to the North Atlantic Squadron, it was sent to Havana to protect American interests and citizens but exploded on 15 February with the loss of 252 men. The ship was raised in 1910 to determine the cause of the explosion and then sunk in the Gulf of Mexico in 1912.

2 David F. Trask, *The War with Spain in 1898* (New York: Macmillan, 1981) pp. xii, xiii.

3 See *Journal of the Spanish-American War,* in Joseph K. Taussig Papers [hereafter Taussig Papers], Naval Historical Collection, Naval War College, Newport, Rhode Island [hereafter Naval Historical Collection]. A manuscript register to the papers was compiled by this author and published in 1989.

4 The journal of the cruise of the USS *Newark* is available in the Taussig Papers.

5 For works on the Philippine Insurrection, see Richard E. Welch, Jr., *Response to Imperialism: The United States and the Philippine-American War, 1899–1902* (Chapel Hill: Univ. of North Carolina Press, 1979); Stuart C. Miller, *Benevolent Assimilation: The American Conquest of the Philippines, 1899–1903* (New Haven, Conn.: Yale Univ. Press, 1982); Brian McAllister Linn, *The Philippine War, 1899–1902* (Lawrence: Univ. Press of Kansas, 2000); and *The U.S. Army and Counterinsurgency in the Philippine War, 1899–1902* (Chapel Hill: Univ. of North Carolina Press, 1989).

6 John R. Jellicoe (1859–1935) joined the Royal Navy in 1872. He served as captain of HMS *Centurion* during the Boxer Rebellion. He was commander of the Grand Fleet during World War I and received criticism for his actions during the Battle of Jutland. In 1916, Jellicoe was named First Sea Lord but was removed from office in December 1917 by Prime Minister David Lloyd George. He served as governor general of New Zealand, 1920–24. David Beatty (1871–1936) entered the Royal Navy in 1884. Beatty received recognition for his service in the Sudan under Lord Kitchner and in the Boxer Rebellion, during which he was wounded at Tientsin. He was promoted to rear admiral in 1910, the youngest ever in the Royal Navy. He was named commander in chief of the Grand Fleet in 1916 and served as First Sea Lord from 1919 to 1927.

7 For works on the Boxer Rebellion, see Christopher Martin, *The Boxer Rebellion* (London: Abelard-Schuman, 1968); Chester C. Tan, *The Boxer Catastrophe* (New York: Columbia Univ. Press, 1955); Victor Purcell, *The Boxer Uprising: A Background Study* (Hamden, Conn.: Archon Books, 1974); George N. Steiger, *China and the Occident: The Origin and Development of the Boxer Movement* (New Haven, Conn.: Yale Univ. Press, [1927]); and Joseph Esherick, *The Origins of the Boxer Uprising* (Berkeley: Univ. of California Press, 1987).

8 See Taussig's letters to his parents in the Taussig Papers.

9 Joseph K. Taussig, "Experiences during the Boxer Rebellion," U.S. Naval Institute *Proceedings* 53 (April 1927), pp. 403–20.

10 Rear Adm. Edward D. Taussig (1847–1921) graduated from the U.S. Naval Academy in 1867. He served in the Spanish-American War, the Philippine Insurrection, and the Boxer Rebellion, and he took possession of Wake Island for the United States in 1899. His personal papers are located in the Naval Historical Collection.

11 USS *Texas* (a battleship) was commissioned in 1895 and served in the North Atlantic Squadron. It saw action during the Spanish-American War. Decommissioned in 1901, it was recommissioned in 1902 and made flagship of the Coast Squadron.

12 USS *Topeka* (gunboat) was commissioned in 1898 and served during the Spanish-American War. Much of its subsequent duty was in the West Indies, but it also served as a station ship and a training ship. It was decommissioned and sold in 1929.

13 USS *Amphitrite* (BM 2) was commissioned in 1895. It served in the Spanish-American War and was a training ship. Decommissioned in 1901 and recommissioned in 1902, it served at the Naval Training Station, Newport, Rhode Island, and in Cuba. During World War I, it was a training ship and guard ship in New York Harbor.

14 USS *Kansas* (BB 21) was commissioned in 1907 and went around the world with the Great White Fleet. In 1913, it operated off Tampico and Vera Cruz (as then spelled), protecting American interests there. In World War I, it was an engineering training ship and convoyed troops home. In 1920, it served as the flagship of Rear Adm. Charles Hughes, Commander, Battleship Division 4. It was decommissioned in 1921.

15 Charles Vreeland (1852–1916) was an 1870 U.S. Naval Academy graduate. He served in the Asiatic, Pacific, and North Atlantic stations before commanding USS *Kansas* during the round-the-world voyage of the Great White Fleet. Promoted to rear admiral in 1909, he took command of the 2nd Division, Atlantic Fleet, in 1910. In 1911, he was aide and principal adviser to the Secretary of the Navy, supporting a strong navy and a construction program. Vreeland retired in 1914.

16 USS *Ammen* (DD 35) was commissioned in 1911 and was in the Torpedo Flotilla, Atlantic Fleet, until June 1917, when it was assigned to Queenstown, Ireland. It was decommissioned in 1919.

17 USS *Wadsworth* (DD 60) was commissioned in 1915. Prior to World War I, it patrolled off the New England and Virginian coasts. As the flagship of destroyers patrolling off Queenstown, Ireland, it made several unsuccessful attacks on U-boats and may have damaged two during the summer of 1917. In March 1918 it was assigned to Brest, France. It was decommissioned in 1922 after two years in reduced commission.

18 Louis Bayly (1857–1938) served as Commander in Chief, Western Approaches, during the British-American antisubmarine campaign during World War I. He joined the Royal Navy in 1870, served in the Egyptian War (1882), was president of the Naval War College (1908–11), and Commanding Officer, 1st Battle Squadron, 1914. Promoted to admiral in 1917, he retired in 1919.

19 USS *Fanning* (DD 37) was commissioned in 1912. Assigned to the Atlantic Fleet, it rescued survivors of the *U-53* attack on merchant ships off Newport, Rhode Island, in 1916. During World War I it was based in Queenstown, escorting convoys and rescuing survivors. It successfully attacked one U-boat. Stationed in Brest, France, through 1919, it was decommissioned that year.

20 For Taussig's duty in USS *Wadsworth*, see William Still, ed., *The Queenstown Patrol, 1917: The Diary of Commander Joseph Knefler Taussig, U.S. Navy* (Newport, R.I.: Naval War College Press, 1996). Taussig's holograph journal of *Wadsworth* is in the Taussig Papers.

21 USS *Little* (DD 79) was commissioned in 1918. From May to December 1918, it was in Brest on convoy duty. It escorted President Woodrow Wilson to Paris for the Peace Conference and back to New York. It was in reserve status until 1921 and was decommissioned the following year.

22 Clark G. Reynolds, *Famous American Admirals* (New York: Van Nostrand Reinhold, 1978), p. 348. Franklin D. Roosevelt (1882–1945) was born in Hyde Park, New York. He graduated from Harvard University in 1904 and attended Columbia University Law School. From 1913 to 1919, he served as Assistant Secretary of the Navy. Prior to his years as president (1933–45), he was governor of New York (1928–32).

23 Josephus Daniels (1862–1948) was a newspaper editor in Raleigh, North Carolina. A Democrat, he served as Secretary of the Navy (1912–21) and was U.S. ambassador to Mexico (1933–44).

24 U.S. Senate, Subcommittee of the Committee on Naval Affairs, *Naval Investigation: Hearings*, 66th Cong., 2nd sess., 1920, p. 476.

25 USS *Great Northern* (AG 9) was commissioned in 1917. Acquired by the Navy from the Army in 1921, it was flagship of the Atlantic Fleet. In November 1921, it was renamed *Columbia*. It was a troop transport ship during World War II.

26 USS *Cleveland* (CL 21) was commissioned in 1903. The ship was assigned to the Pacific Fleet in 1920 but also served in the Caribbean and in South America, where it represented American interests, provided assistance in disasters, and made courtesy calls.

27 Hilary P. Jones (1863–1938) was an 1884 graduate of the U.S. Naval Academy. He served in the Spanish-American War and attended the Naval War College in 1916. During World War I, he was commander of Division 1, Squadron 1 Cruiser Force, and in 1918 was named commander of the Newport News Division of the cruiser and transport forces. In 1920, he commanded the Battleship Force, Atlantic Fleet, and in 1921, with the rank of admiral, was Commander in Chief, Atlantic Fleet (later designated the U.S. Fleet). He retired in 1927 and in 1930 was naval

adviser to the American representative at the London Naval Conference.

28 USS *Trenton* (CL 11) was commissioned in 1924. It took part in scouting, gunnery drills, and tactical exercises during the 1920s and in combined maneuvers with the Battle and Scouting Fleet. It carried out tactical exercises in Narragansett Bay during the summer of 1926. During World War II it patrolled off the coasts of South America and Alaska. *Trenton* was decommissioned in 1945.

29 USS *Maryland* (BB 46) was commissioned in 1921. In the 1920s, it made goodwill visits to foreign ports and participated in training and fleet exercises. Stationed in Pearl Harbor in 1941, it survived the Japanese attack there. During the Second World War, it earned seven battle stars for actions in the Pacific theater.

30 Richard H. Leigh (1870–1946) was a 1901 graduate of the U.S. Naval Academy. He was chief of staff to Adm. William S. Sims during World War I and graduated from the Naval War College in 1925. He was Commander in Chief, U.S. Fleet, and chairman of the General Board. He retired in 1934 due to a disability and was advanced to admiral on the retired list in 1941.

31 Frederic S. Withington (1901–82) was a 1923 graduate of the U.S. Naval Academy. He retired as a rear admiral in 1961. For the dispute with Roosevelt, Frederic S. Withington, interview by John T. Mason, U.S. Naval Institute, June 1971, p. 35.

32 Drew Pearson and Robert S. Allen, "Merry-Go-Round," *Washington Herald*, April 1940, Taussig Papers.

33 USS *Idaho* (BB 42) was commissioned in 1919. During the 1930s it was stationed in San Pedro, from where it conducted training exercises in the Pacific. During World War II, it took part in actions in the Gilberts, Marshalls, and Marianas, as well as at Guam, Iwo Jima, and Okinawa. It was present at the Japanese surrender in Tokyo Bay on 2 September 1945 and was decommissioned in 1946.

34 USS *Chicago* (CA 29) was commissioned in 1931. It served as the flagship of Commander, Cruisers, Scouting Force, from 1931 to 1940. It earned three battle stars in World War II and was sunk by Japanese torpedoes in 1943.

35 U.S. Senate, Committee on Naval Affairs, *Construction of Certain Naval Vessels, Hearings*, 76th Cong., 3rd sess., 22 April 1940, p. 188.

36 Ibid., p. 192.

37 Ibid., pp. 191–92.

38 The Taussig Papers contain newspaper clippings from April–May 1940 both supporting and criticizing the admiral's controversial statement.

39 B. Mitchell Simpson, *Admiral Harold R. Stark: Architect of Victory, 1939–1945* (Columbia: Univ. of South Carolina Press, 1989), pp. 36–37.

40 Joseph K. Taussig, Jr. (1920–99), was a 1941 graduate of the U.S. Naval Academy. He was officer on duty and antiaircraft officer in the USS *Nevada* at Pearl Harbor when the Japanese attacked on 7 December 1941. He was severely injured, losing a leg. Taussig graduated from George Washington University Law School in 1949 and retired as a captain in 1954, due to his disability. He served as secretary-treasurer of the U.S. Naval Institute and editor of the U.S. Naval Institute *Proceedings*.

41 USS *Joseph K. Taussig* (DE 1030) was commissioned in 1957. It saw duty with the Atlantic Fleet, based in Newport, Rhode Island, in 1957–58. It was sent to the Mediterranean during the Lebanon crisis and in 1959 went on a goodwill cruise to South America. In 1961, the ship was stationed in Jacksonville when the Cuban missile crisis occurred. Two years later it embarked on a goodwill cruise to Africa and the Mediterranean. During the next nine years, before it was decommissioned in 1972, *Taussig* operated mainly in New England and Caribbean waters.

Part 1: The Spanish-American War, 1898

I Tampa
Waiting for War

Joseph K. Taussig's Spanish-American War journal begins on 29 May 1898. It appears to be a continuation of a journal that he began at the U.S. Naval Academy just before going off to war. The previous few pages are missing.

Sunday, May 29.

[missing pages] see me off. The class had special arrangements made for travelling at reduced rates. Road was very dusty and hot. Were delayed at Tye River, Virginia for an hour on account of a cylinder head blowing out. Reached Danville, where we had dinner, 2 1/2 hours late.

Monday ~~June~~ May 30.
Enroute to Key West

Reached Jacksonville two and a half hours late, and changed cars to East Coast of Florida train, which had been held two hours for us. The trip down the coast was *very* dirty. It being warm the car windows were left open, and as there had been no rain along here for several months the dust was awful. There being no ladies in the car we sat around in very "undress" costume, and got *very* dirty in attempting to keep cool. We reached Miami at twelve, about an hour late and got on board an old side-wheel steamer, *(City of Key West)* which was very comfortable after the train.

Tuesday May 31.
Enroute to and at Key West

The trip on the boat was very pleasant, being cool and comfortable, the only bad ~~circumstance~~ feature being the poor breakfast and dinner we had on board. We arrived at Key West about three in the afternoon and reported to Commodore Remey.¹ We were told to come back the next morning. Key West was dirty and hot and seemed very much to me like a "Dago" town. Every room at the only hotel was

---

NOTES 1 George Collier Remey (1841–1928) was an 1859 graduate of the U.S. Naval Academy. He was appointed commanding officer of the Naval Base, Key West, in 1898. Promoted to rear admiral in 1898, he served as Commander, Asiatic Squadron, 1900–1902.

taken, but they promised to find places for the fifty-three of us, Courtney,[2] Buchanan,[3] Fenner,[4] Major,[5] Lackey[6] and I lived in one room in the annex across the street. In the evening took a ride in the mule cars, and turned in on arriving at our room. The mosquitoes had a good time in spite of our nettings, and made things very lively.

Wednesday, June 1.

At Key West

Loafed around all morning trying to keep cool. Wrote a letter home. Took a look at the *"Winslow"*[7] and saw where she had been pierced by Spanish shot. In afternoon received orders from Commodore Remey to proceed to Tampa and report to senior Naval Officer present. Left that night on the *"Mascotte"*[8] about eight o'clock. Had a very pleasant and comfortable trip.

Thursday, June 2.

En route to and at Tampa

Arrived at Port Tampa about two o'clock in the afternoon. Found the harbor full of transports, there being 23. Reported to Captain Hunker[9] of the *Annapolis*.[10] He placed one or two of the 33 who were ordered here, on each one of the transports to act as signal officers. Major and I were kept onboard the *Annapolis* and given staterooms in the wardroom. We expect to be here only until we run across the *New York*. The *Annapolis* is the flagship of the vessels which are going to convoy the troop ships. Took dinner on board and then went on shore to send trunks on board. Returned about 8:30. Have been assigned to 2d Division, under Ensign Zeigemeier.[11]

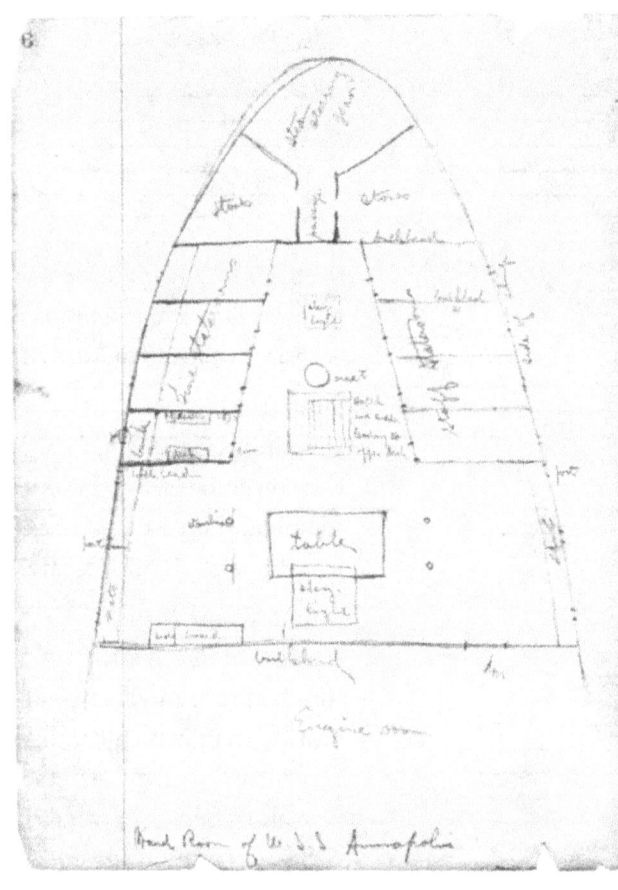

Drawing of mail room USS Annapolis

---

2 Charles S. Courtney (1877–1966), U.S. Naval Academy, 1899.

3 Allen Buchanan (1876–1940), U.S. Naval Academy, 1899.

4 Edward B. Fenner (1876–?), U.S. Naval Academy, 1899.

5 Samuel I. M. Major (1877–1952), U.S. Naval Academy, 1899.

6 Henry E. Lackey (1876–1952), U.S. Naval Academy, 1899.

7 USS *Winslow* (Torpedo Boat No. 5) was disabled during the search for a Spanish gunboat in Cardenas Harbor in May 1898.

8 *Mascotte*, a 1,097-ton steamer, was built by Ramage & Ferguson Leith in 1885.

9 John J. Hunker (1844–1916) graduated from the U.S. Naval Academy in 1866. He was commanding officer of the Convoy Fleet that left Tampa, Florida, for Santiago, Cuba, in 1898. He led the expedition to Nipe Bay, Cuba, in 1898. He was promoted to rear admiral in 1906.

10 USS *Annapolis* (Patrol Gunboat No. 10) saw action at Siboney and Baracoa and sank the gunboat *Don Jorge Juan*. It took part in the landings in Puerto Rico.

11 Henry J. Zeigemeier (1869–1930), U.S. Naval Academy, 1890.

rmy troops lining up to board transports

encil figure of soldier back ew

Friday, June 3d
On U.S.S. Annapolis off Port Tampa

Remained on board all morning. Cadets came on board from troopships to get orders endorsed by Captain Hunker. In afternoon Major and I went to Tampa which is nine miles from Port Tampa. The streets there are full of officers and soldiers on foot and horseback. Very little attention is paid to the uniform worn. Most of the men are dirty from the dust, none of them wear coats but go around in blue flannel shirts with suspenders on top. Most have belts with either bayonet or pistol, and as a rule, wear brown canvas leggins. They are a hardy looking lot of men, and seem to mean business. The officers when on duty take off their coats and are not easily distinguished from the men. I notice that at all times they wear blue woolen shirts under the coats instead of the white shirt and collar. Major and I left Tampa at 6:10 and arrived at Port Tampa at 8:10 (distance 9 miles). Read "Quo Vadis" until ten o'clock.

Saturday, June 4.
Off Pt. Tampa
Read in morning until ten o'clock, when Captain Hunker sent me ashore to find Captain McKay[12] who is in charge of the transports. Gave him a paper assigning numbers to each troop ship, and orders to have the numbers painted in white on both bows and quarters, and on both sides of the smoke stack. Read "Quo Vadis" all afternoon and evening, finishing it. The transport *"Irizaba"* of the Ward line came in during the afternoon.

Sunday June 5.
Off Port Tampa
Was on watch today as Officer of the Deck, under the supervision of Lieutenant Kline.[13] I am glad I was given this duty as it is good experience and I wont be so green when I strike the *New York*.[14] There was nothing going on, and I only had to see that the regular routine orders were executed. During the morning the Captain sent me on shore to inspect the towing hawsers of the troopships in order to find out which ones could be adapted for towing in case of a breakdown. Most of them were very poorly equipped having nothing larger than 6" hemp hawsers, and some did not have any at all. However I found several that had good 10" hawsers. We read in the New York papers of the 3d that this army is supposed to be landing in Cuba. This proves that the censorship is very strict and no news, unless official, is reliable. It is not known when the Army will be ready to start. The convoy has been ready a long time and all arrangements on the part of the Navy have been made.

"Formation of fleet carrying army of invasion"

---

12 Charles Edmund McKay (?–1918), U.S. Naval Academy, 1861.

13 George W. Kline (1864–1922) graduated from the U.S. Naval Academy in 1885. He was in USS *Brooklyn* on the Asiatic Station, 1899–1900. He was promoted to rear admiral in 1921.

14 USS *New York* (Armored Cruiser No. 2) was Admiral William Sampson's flagship during the battle of Santiago Bay. Early in the war, it bombarded Matanzas and searched for the Spanish squadron.

The transports are nearly all large passenger steamers belonging chiefly to the Merchant and Miners Transportation Co.,[15] and the Mallory, Ward,[16] Clyde,[17] Plant, and Morgan Steam Ship lines.[18]

Monday, June 6.
Port Tampa

Five troopships with troops on board came in this morning from Mobile and anchored in the stream. They were added to the fleet and given numbers. The Captain sent me ashore to find out more about hawsers, the kind of troops to be taken on each ship, and, if possible, to when we were likely to sail. Could not find out anything. Went ashore again in the afternoon and got the following data which shows what each ship will carry in the way of men, horses, mules, etc.,

S.S. Line	
M. + M.T. Co.	"Berkshire," 474 men, and 174 horses.
M. + M.T. Co.	"D. H. Miller," 450 men, 50 horses, 249 mules
M. + M.T. Co.	"Alleghany," 450 men, and 190 horses
Ward	"Seneca," 900 men; "Seguranca"—
Morgan	"Gussie" 100 men, 50 horses, 300 mules.
Morgan	"Whitney" 100 men, 60 horses, 350 mules.
Ward	"Vigilancia" 1200 men; "Miami," 1200 men.
Ward	"Saratoga" 950 men; "Alamo," 900 men and engineers
Ward	"Yucatan" 950 men; "Olivette" 400 men, 13 horses.
	"Leona," 1250 men; "Rio Grande," 1100 men.
Clyde	"Iroquois," 950 men; "Cherokee," 1000 men
	"Concho," 1300 men; "Irizaba," 900 men, 125 mules
	"Comal," 952 men, 176 horses.
	"Breakwater" 502 men, "Morgan."
	"Matteawan," 766 men, 153 horses, 163 mules.
	"Stillwater" 72 men, 66 horses.
	"Arausus" 43 men, 6 horses, 114 mules.

This makes an army of 20,000 men with, 1000 horses, and 1300 mules.

---

15 The Merchants and Miners Transportation Company was founded in Baltimore in 1852. The company purchased the Baltimore & Savannah Steamship Company in 1876.

16 The Ward Line, also known as the New York & Cuba Mail Steamship Company, was established in 1841. In 1888, the owners purchased the Alexandre Line, its major competitor. During the Spanish-American War, its ships were requisitioned for use by the U.S. Army.

17 The Clyde Line operated five steamships in the West Indies during the latter part of the nineteenth century.

18 Charles Morgan founded the Morgan Line in 1835. During the 1880s, a large number of steamships was added to the fleet, averaging between 3,500 and 4,500 gross tons.

8 THREE SPLENDID LITTLE WARS

Army troops boarding transport

Transporters patiently awaiting word to leave Tampa

Tuesday, June 7
Port Tampa
Went ashore in order to get more information for the Captain in regard to the transports. It was very hot and unpleasant going around the ships, and I found it rather tiresome. Could not find out when we are to leave. Nobody seems to know anything about it. I have been reading again in the papers that the army has left. Even the Tampa paper says the fleet was an "imposing sight sailing down the Bay," and we have not moved an inch. They are getting the men, horses, and mules on board as fast as possible. The men are packed in very close, the bunks being built in 3 tiers one over the other and very little space between them. The horses are crowded in as close as possible, there not being any room for them to lie down, and as it is very hot and close below decks, I am afraid a great many of the animals will kick the bucket before Cuba is reached. The Officers are very comfortable in the passenger staterooms.

Wednesday, June 8.
Port Tampa
Was on watch today. After quarters drilled the first and second divisions at broadswords. Then went on shore to get more information for the Captain.

Everything was in readiness for the fleet to sail this evening. At one o'clock the *Helena*[19] got underway and started for the lower bay. All the ships were given orders to start as soon as possible. Five had left when a telegram was received from Washington with the message "Stop Expedition." I was sent in a steam-launch after one of the ships that was starting out, and the International signal "Don't sail until further orders" was hoisted. Nobody knows how long we are to stay here, or why the expedition was stopped. The Army is very much disappointed. The Naval Convoy hopes the expedition is over with. The *Castine*[20] was sent to the lower bay to send those ships back that had gone down. *Miami*[21] ran into *Florida*[22] making a large hole in side.

Thursday June, 9.
Port Tampa
The transport that had gone to the lower bay returned. It was rumored that several Spanish gunboats were sighted not far from here, and that was the reason the expedition was held over.

Went around to a number of the troopships to get information for the Captain. Several ladies and gentlemen came on board to look around. The transport went in

---

19 USS *Helena* (Gunboat No. 1) closed the port of Manzanillo and destroyed eight enemy vessels.

20 USS *Castine* (gunboat) blockaded Cuba in March 1898. It escorted Army transports to Cuba and remained in the area until the end of the war.

21 *Miami* transported the 6th U.S. Infantry Regiment and the 9th U.S. Calvary to Daiquirí.

22 USS *Florida* was at the battle of Tayacoba. A landing party from the ship was rescued by the men of the 10th Cavalry.

the canal and took the horses and mules off for an airing. The animals will not be put on board again until the ships are ready to sail. Took dinner on *Olivette*.[23]

Friday June, 10.
Port Tampa

Staid on board ship all day. Wrote a letter home. Transports are at anchor all around us. Many of them have bands, so we get lots of music. Almost too much when two or three of them are going at the same time. The troops on board appear to be comfortable and in good spirits. They cheer upon the least provocation.

Saturday June 11.
Port Tampa

Went on shore both in morning and afternoon. Loafed around the Inn a good deal. Went on board the "*Cumberland*"[24] "*Morgan*"[25] and "*Laura*"[26] for information. The "*Helena*" "*Castine*," "*Hornet*" and "*Morrie*" came back from the lower bay. The "*Newport*"[27] came in also. I saw Captain Tilley[28] on shore and had a little talk with him.

Sunday June 12
Port Tampa

Went on board the "*Clinton*"[29] and "*Knickerbocker*"[30] to get information for Captain Hunker. Found it very hot ashore. The Inn was crowded with people from Tampa. "*Gussie*"[31] ran aground and remained there all day. The transports have been taking on water all day. Had a severe thunderstorm in the evening. *Helena* went to lower bay.

Monday June 13.
Port Tampa

Went on board the *Olivette* for a list of signals concerning the sick. The *Olivette* is to go as a hospital ship. Also took instructions to the Captain of the "*Clinton*." The transports had orders to proceed to the lower bay as soon as possible. About twenty sailed this afternoon. I was sent to the *City of Washington*[32] to tell the Captain to

---

23 USS *Olivette* (steamship) made trips between Key West, Havana, and Tampa carrying messages between the U.S. consul and the Navy.

24 *Cumberland* was a steam lighter. It transported troops of the 1st Expeditionary Force from Tampa to Daiquirí.

25 *Morgan* transported Major Rafferty and Troop C, 2nd U.S. Cavalry, to Daiquirí.

26 *Laura* was a steam lighter and carried troops to Cuba.

27 *Newport* was a transport chartered from the Pacific Mail Steamship Company in 1898.

28 Benjamin F. Tilley (1848–1907) graduated from the U.S. Naval Academy in 1867 and from the Naval War College in 1897. He commanded the USS *Newport*, 1897–98, and was in charge of the naval station in Samoa. He was promoted to rear admiral in 1907.

29 *Clinton* carried Companies B and D of the 2nd U.S. Infantry to Cuba.

30 *Knickerbocker* transported two companies and the headquarters of the 2nd Massachusetts Volunteers to Cuba.

31 *Gussie* was a mule transport under command of Master Burney.

32 *City of Washington* was an Army transport ship.

leave immediately as she draws so much water (21 ft) she can only get over the bar at high tide. Had rain again this afternoon. Expect to leave tomorrow.

Tuesday June 14
Port Tampa

The rest of the transports left for the lower bay during the morning. The *Seguranca*[33] with General Shafter[34] and staff of the Fifth Army Corps left at 10 o'clock. The *Annapolis* followed at 11:30. On reaching the lower bay we found all the transports anchored in the order for sailing. At 4 o'clock the *Hornet* (dispatch boat and scout) was ordered to tell the vessels of the left column to get underway immediately. As soon as this column cleared the bar the *Annapolis* steamed by the vessels of the second column, ordering them to get under way. Then the right column received the same order, the entire fleet going in single file. The first column then slowed down and the second column took its position 800 yds on starboard beam of 2d column. The *Helena* leads the 1st Column, the *Annapolis* the 2d, and the *Castine* the 3d. The vessels showed the sidelights and red sternlights, no masthead lights being used. At 9 P.M. vessels appeared to be in proper places.

---

33 *Seguranca* was the headquarters ship of Gen. William Shafter.

34 William Shafter (1835–1906) was in charge of the Fifth Army Corps in Tampa, Florida. The corps fought at San Juan Hill and El Caney. It besieged Santiago but did not take the city, which fell after the naval battle. Shafter was ill during the war and unfit to lead.

II At Sea

1898

June 15, 1898
U.S.S. Annapolis *At Sea*
The Lucky Bag

Articles that are found lying about the decks are taken in custody by the Master at Arms and placed in what is known as the "Lucky Bag." Once monthly the Master-at-Arms distributes these articles that are marked to their owners who are reported to the Executive Officer. Those unmarked or unclaimed are sold at auction, the Master at Arms being the Auctioneer, and the crew the bidders. The men gather around the clothes piled on the deck and as the Master-at-Arms, holds up each piece the bidding is very lively, although it does not go very high, the articles being sold at about one fifth their value. The money made in this way is used to purchases books, etc. for the crew.

Wednesday June 15

At sea

The transports were somewhat scattered at daylight. The *Hornet* went the rounds telling them to close up, and they were soon in position again. Going about six knots all day. Passed a large four masted schooner. The *Hornet* was sent ahead to see if Captain Taylor's[1] fleet could be found. About eight o'clock she returned and reported the fleet at the southern end of the channel. Captain Taylor sent word to Captain Hunker to continue in the present formation during the night, that his fleet would take position on our starboard beam. Passed Rebecca Shoal Light about 9 P.M. A little later Captain Taylor's fleet was sighted on our starboard bow.

NOTES 1 Henry C. Taylor (1845–1904) commanded USS *Indiana* (BB 1) during the war. He was President of the Naval War College, 1894–1896. Taylor was promoted to rear admiral in 1901.

Thursday June 16

At sea

Had the mid-watch last night. The fleet under Captain Taylor was some distance off our starboard beam and got gradually closer during the watch. Fresh easterly wind with fairly rough seas and ship pitching considerably. At daylight fleet was in plain sight the *Indiana*[2] on our starboard beam. Our position was changed so that now we led the left column the *Castine* in the centre and the *Helena* the left. The *Detroit*,[3] *Osceola*,[4] *Hornet*, and several torpedo boats and converted yachts, acted as scouts. Moving along about eight knots. Took a meridian altitude to-day. Turned in at eight.

Friday June 17

At sea

Turned out at four for morning watch. The flagship hoisted several compass signals for changing course. The *Annapolis* ran into shoal water about six o'clock. Sent a man to the chains and got bottom at five fathoms. Hoisted danger flag and signal "I am running into shoal water." Ported our helm and ran across the bows of the *Castine* and *Helena*. Signaled the ships in our column to follow us. The *Helena*'s compass must be out at least a quarter of a point as we cannot steer the prescribed course and keep our distance at the same time. This fault in the *Helena*'s compass caused us to run in the shoal water. Having been steaming about eight knots with a moderate sea and fresh easterly wind against us. The transports have settled down to their proper distances in column. Sighted land at several different times during the day. In afternoon read a few short stories in old magazines, and played cribbage with Ensign Tompkins.[5] Crossed the Tropic of Cancer.

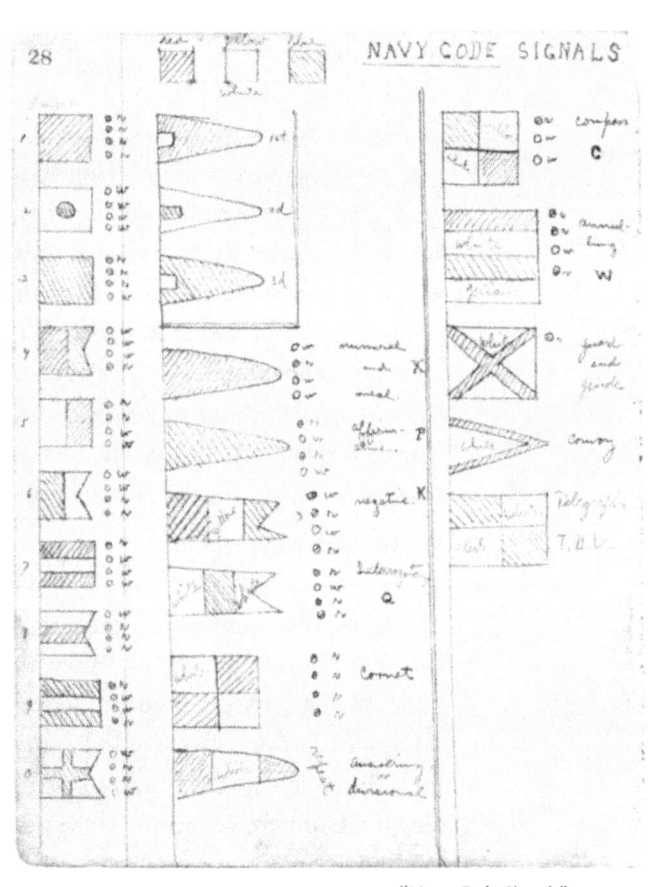

"Navy Code Signals"

---

2 USS *Indiana* (BB 1) was part of Adm. William Sampson's squadron. It bombarded San Juan, guarded Havana, and blockaded Santiago, where it destroyed two enemy destroyers.

3 USS *Detroit* (C 10) was based in Key West, Florida, during the war.

4 USS *Osceola* (AT 47) blockaded and captured the port of Manzanillo.

5 John T. Tompkins (1870–1927), U.S. Naval Academy, 1894.

"Wig-wag Signals"

tain Henry C. Taylor   Commander Richardson Clover

Saturday June 18
At sea

Had first watch last night. Nothing unusual happened until about 7 bells when the flagship started to signal a new compass course, but only got half through. Later the tug *Osceola* came within hail and said the signal had been annulled. This morning the flagship signalled the fleet to stop and all the vessels came to a halt. Then she signalled for several of the vessels to send boats for mail and dispatches. We waited about three hours before starting again. The *Annapolis* was made guide owing to the error in the *Helena*'s compass. High land in sight on our starboard beam during the afternoon. Played several games of cribbage with Ensign Tompkins. Took a meridian altitude. The convoy fleet is now composed of the battleship *Indiana*, the cruiser *Detroit*, the gunboats, *Annapolis*, *Bancroft*,[6] *Castine* and *Helena*; the converted gunboat *Manning*;[7] the converted yachts, *Eagle*,[8] *Hornet*, and *Wasp*,[9] the torpedo boats, *Rogers Erricson*[10] and *Foote*;[11] and the converted tugs *Osceloa* and *Wompatuck*.[12]

Sunday June 19
At sea

Had the mid-watch last night. Nothing happened out of the ordinary. The Executive Officer read the Articles of War at quarters this morning. Changed our course to South after sighting Great Inagua Island[13] about 10:40.

---

6 USS *Bancroft* (gunboat) carried troops to Cuba and did blockade duty at Havana and the Isle of Pines.

7 USS *Manning* (revenue cutter) patrolled and blockaded Cuba.

8 USS *Eagle* (patrol vessel, converted yacht) saw duty with the North Atlantic Squadron off Cuba. It captured the *Santo Domingo*, a Spanish merchant vessel.

9 USS *Wasp* (yacht) served on blockade duty off the Cuban coast.

10 USS *Rogers Ericsson* (TB 2), before the war, patrolled in Florida waters. Once the war began it was on blockade between Havana and Key West. It took part in the battle of Santiago Bay, firing on Spanish ships. It later rescued Spanish sailors from the *Vizcaya*.

11 USS *Foote* (TB 3) patrolled the coast near Havana Harbor and bombarded Morro Island.

12 USS *Wompatuck* (tug) operated with the North Atlantic Squadron. It cut the cable at Santiago and Guantanamo and destroyed eight enemy ships at Manzanillo.

13 Great Inagua Island, fifty-five miles off Cuba, is the third-largest island in the Bahamas.

Sighted the Cuban coast at about half past one. Passed Cape Maysi[14] and headed west.

Monday June 20
At sea and off Santiago de Cuba
Had the morning watch. High land was in sight at daylight. I thought we were off Guantanamo but found out that we were near Santiago. Stopped about twelve o'clock. The

Army troops being transported ashore at Santiago

Seguranca with General Shafter on board headed in for land. We marked time about fifteen miles from land until seven o'clock when we put out to sea again. It is evident that troops are to be landed here at Santiago.

Tuesday June 21
Off Santiago de Cuba
Had the first watch last night. It was very tiresome, the ship not being under way but rolling in the trough of the sea. Lieut. Kline and I passed the time talking about the Academy and we had a hard time keeping awake. About 11:30 sighted light at sea. The flagship signalled to *Manning* to find out what ship it was. Later the *Manning* came back with a newspaper boat. When I got up this morning we were heading in towards land. We stopped about 12 miles from shore. Could see the entrance to Santiago harbor and Morro castle distinctly. Could also see the *Brooklyn*,[15] *Texas*,[16] *New York*, *Iowa*,[17] *Oregon*,[18] *Massachusetts*,[19] and *New Orleans*;[20] a very powerful fleet. Could see a number of colliers. The Auxiliary cruiser *St. Louis*[21] headed towards us and stopped near the *Indiana*. She is a large ship the *Indiana* looking small beside her. The dispatch tug *Osceola* stopped on our port quarter and signalled

---

14 Cape Maysi, in Guantanamo Province, is the easternmost headland of Cuba.

15 USS *Brooklyn* (AC 3) was the flagship of Adm. Winfield S. Schley's Flying Squadron. It took part in the battle of Santiago Bay.

16 USS *Texas* (battleship) blockaded the Cuban coast and took part in the battle of Santiago Bay.

17 USS *Iowa* (BB 4) blockaded Santiago and took part in the battle there.

18 USS *Oregon* (BB 3) fought at the battle of Santiago Bay.

19 USS *Massachusetts* (BB 2) blockaded Cienfuegos, bombarded Santiago, and supported the occupation of Puerto Rico.

20 USS *New Orleans* (cruiser) bombarded the harbor of Santiago.

21 *St. Louis*, a merchant auxiliary, was leased by the Navy as a fast scout cruiser. The ship searched for Cervera's squadron.

"send a boat for dispatches." The Captain received orders concerning the landing of troops which is to take place to-morrow beginning at daylight. The ships of the fleet are to cover the landing and we are to send our steam launch in to help. Lieut. Mentz[22] told me to-night that I would have charge of the launch. I am tickled to death as we will probably have some excitement and good experience to see them land the troops.

my troops landing at Daiquirí

---

22 George W. Mentz (?–1906), U.S. Naval Academy, 1870.

III *Daiquirí, Siboney, and Santiago* 1898

Wednesday June 22.
At Daiquirí

I was turned out at four o'clock and told to get ready to go in the steam-launch. Put on my belt with sword and pistol and shoved off from the ship about five. We had a one pounder mounted on the bow of the launch, and carried besides six rifles and six revolvers, with plenty of ammunition for all. Besides the regular launch crew there were two gunner's mates to man the one pounder. Reported to Captain Goodrich[1] on board the *St. Louis*. Received orders from him in regard to landing. I was to take two boats in tow, go alongside the *Knickerbocker* (Transport No. 13) and load the boats with troops. Then take position astern of the *Wompatuck* in line with the other steam launches. At the signal from the *Wompatuck* we (the launches) were to advance in line abreast, clearing the beach with our one pounders and rifles. Then, when the *Wompatuck* hoisted a blue and red flag we were to land in a designated order. We were cautioned not to overload our boats and to keep the men seated. In steaming out to look for the *Knickerbocker* I noticed that a number of houses in the town (Daiquirí)[2] were on fire. I learned afterwards that the Spaniards had fired them to prevent their falling into our hands. Suddenly I heard the booming of guns and looking around saw the *Indiana, New Orleans, Detroit, Scorpion*,[3] and several of the Mosquito fleet bombarding in the vicinity of the town. We could see where every shell struck by the scattered dirt and smoke of the explosions. About five miles up the beach the *Annapolis, Helena,* and *Castine* discovered a battalion of Spanish infantry marching outside of Altares. A few shell from these ships soon caused them to do the disappearing act. In the meantime I was looking for the *Knickerbocker*, but she was not in sight. I reported the fact to Captain Goodrich and

---

NOTES 1 Caspar Goodrich (1847–1925) graduated from the U.S. Naval Academy in 1864. He served as President of the Naval War College, 1896–98. He was promoted to rear admiral in 1904. He received the surrender of Manzanillo during the Spanish-American War.

2 Daiquirí is east of Santiago de Cuba. Admiral Sampson's forces bombarded the village on 22 June 1898.

3 USS *Scorpion* (steamer) blockaded Santiago Harbor, attacked the Spanish at Manzanillo, and carried mail to Guantanamo.

he told me to take men from the *Seneca*. I took the last boat load from her and then went to the *Mateo* and took a load from her. In approaching the landing I noticed that a number of troops had already landed, as the bombardment had scattered all the Spaniards that were in the vicinity. From this time on I towed empty boats from the shore to the transports, and loaded ones back to the landing. The heavy swell and surf caused many of the boats to wash ashore, the soldiers scrambling to land through the water. At one time the whole beach was lined with boats, many of them having sprung a leak, or smashed. It was thought that only five transports could be unloaded the first day, and they were all that were provided for in the order. But the Spaniards gave so little trouble all the troops on these ships were landed by twelve o'clock. Captain Goodrich sent me to General Shafter for further orders. I found the General on board the *Seguranca*. He said he would like to have all the transports unloaded as quickly as possible. At one o'clock I stopped work for a while in order to give the men in the launch time to eat something. About half past one we went to work again. A little after this an American flag appeared on the tip-top of the hill at whose foot the town lies. Immediately every vessel in the harbor tooted its whistle, and for five minutes the noise continued. About half past six we needed coal and water for the launch. I reported to Lieut. Catlin[4] on the *Wompatuck* and he told me to get both from the *St. Louis*. We went along side, got the coal and water, and then received orders to go back to the *Annapolis* about 7:30. It was very dark and there were so many ships around we had a hard time finding the *Annapolis*. We had been out in the sun for fifteen hours and were very glad to get back.

I think about seven thousand troops were landed during the day. The soldiers were glad to get off the transports on to dry land again. We had a great deal of trouble in landing on account of the surf it being very difficult to go alongside the small wharf. Two soldiers were drowned, and several got their legs caught in between the boats and wharf. I carried one man to the *Olivette* who had his leg crushed and was helpless.

Untitled camp with huts, soldiers, mules, and a large hill in the background.

---

4 Albertus W. Catlin (1868–1933), U.S. Naval Academy, 1890.

Thursday June 23.
At Daquiri and off Siboney
I was glad I did not have to go in the steam launch to-day. Major was sent in my place. The landing of troops went on all day. The swell had gone down considerably, making it much easier to put the men ashore. About noon Captain Hunker got orders to go at once to Havana. I was sent with the mail to the *Seguranca*. General Shafter told me to tell Captain Hunker that a detachment of Spanish troops had been sent by rail from Santiago to Siboney as small town five miles to the westward of Daiquiri. He said a battalion of infantry had been sent against them, and that he would like to have a gunboat sent there. The *Bancroft* was sent, but as she found the American flag floating over the town, she came back.

Captain Hunker sent Major over to *St. Louis* to ask Captain Goodrich if he would take us until we could get to the *St. Louis*. Captain Goodrich said he would, so we put our effects in the steam launch and went on board the *St. Louis*. The *Annapolis* left for Havana as soon as the steam-launch returned. Major and I were given a big room and told to turn in right away as we would be wanted for night duty. The *St. Louis* left Daiquiri and went to Siboney ten five miles to the westward. The Navy had been landing troops here all day, and, although there is no wharf, it is a better place to land than at Daiquiri as there is a sandy beach and very little surf. A number of Cubans could be seen on shore, and seemed to have taken possession of the town.

Friday June 24
At Siboney
Right after supper last night I got in a steam launch and commenced towing troops ashore. The launching went on all night. Two whale boats were anchored just outside the surf. The loaded boats were towed to the whale boats and were dropped astern from them until they struck the beach, the soldiers jumping out without getting wet. The empty boats were then hauled out of the surf. At twelve o'clock my crew had something to eat, and we then went to work again. The *St. Louis*'s searchlight was kept on the beach all night, and the campfires of the troop were a great aid. I got pretty sleepy about three o'clock and came near falling asleep while standing up in the launch. About half past five I was relieved and immediately turned in. Slept all day. I understand that during the day the advance of our troops ran into an ambush of Spaniards. The fight lasted an hour, the Americans driving the Spaniards from the field. There were twenty-two Americans killed and about 80 wounded. The loss on the Spanish side was much greater, over a hundred dead men being found by our troops. Was told to stand by to do night duty, but it was decided later not to land troops during the night so I turned in and slept all night.

Saturday June 25
At Siboney
Had nothing to do all morning so read. In afternoon went to *Oregon*'s steam launch and landed troops, ammunition, and stores. Three transports loaded with General Garcia's[5] Cuban Army came in and we landed them. The Cubans were half naked and half starved. The U.S. soldiers gave them some old clothes and hard tack which they appeared to appreciate very much. I had to tow some of the men who were wounded in the engagement yesterday, from the shore to the hospital ship *Olivette*. I also had to tow drowned horses away from the vicinity of the landing. The horses were drowned in swimming from the ships to the beach. I was relieved in time for dinner, and told to stand by to go in the launch at one o'clock to-night. The *Vesuvius*[6] threw 3 shells into Morro.

Sunday June 26
At Siboney and off Santiago
Turned out at one o'clock last night and went ashore in the steam launch to relieve Hart as assistant beachmaster. When I got there I found that they were through work for the night so I went back to the ship and turned in again. Turned out at eight o'clock. Loafed all morning. In the afternoon we were told to get our traps together and stand by to be transferred to the *New York*. Buchanan, Fenner, Major, and I were then in the steam launch to the *Vixen*.[7] The *Vixen* carried us near the *New York*, where the steam launch was sent for us. On arriving on the *New York* we

The U.S. dynamite gun cruiser Vesuvius

---

5 Gen. Calixto García Íñiguez (1839–98) was an insurgent who provided the Americans with intelligence and maps that they needed for the invasion of Cuba. His army provided support at the battles of Caney and Santiago. García resigned when General Shafter refused to allow his army to participate in the surrender of Santiago.

6 USS *Vesuvius* (dynamite gun cruiser) was equipped with fifteen-inch pneumatic guns when it blockaded the Cuban coast. It served as a dispatch vessel between Cuba and Florida and later bombarded Santiago de Cuba.

7 USS *Vixen* (yacht) was built in 1896 and purchased by the Navy in 1898. It performed blockading, patrolling, and communication duties during the Spanish-American War. It bombarded Santiago, Cuba, and took part in the battle of Santiago Bay, where it sighted the first Spanish ship to sortie from the bay.

were immediately shown the steerage and sat down to diner. We found Lackey and Courtney here ahead of us. There are now twenty-nine in the *New York*'s steerage, 13 sleeping in swimming cots and hammocks. We received our mail as soon as we finished dinner. I received about eight letters, and a newspaper of June 4th.

Monday June 27
Off Santiago

Were not assigned to duty until this evening. Wrote letters, and helped Fenner, Lackey, and Buchanan, trace charts of Santiago Harbor and adjacent coast, all day. The *Yale*[8] came in this morning with about 1300 troops on board. They were landed at Siboney. Turned in early as I had the Gun Deck Watch from 12:30 AM to 5:00. Lieutenant Blue[9] returned from the interior with valuable information. It was learned that the water supply at Santiago has been cut off. It looks as if the Americans will have possession of the city in a few days.

Tuesday June 28,
Off Santiago

I had the gun deck watch from 12:30 to 5 last night. I had to inspect the twenty four guns every hour to see if the man stationed at each one was awake. There are thirty six men on lookout all the time during the night. The Captain came on deck while I was sitting down in a chair. He thought I had the quarterdeck watch and suspended me from duty for sitting down on watch. I saw the Executive Officer in the morning and told him I had the gun-deck watch so my suspension was removed immediately. I had the first dogwatch this afternoon. Nothing unusual happened. The Collier *Lebanon*[10] brought the mail and stores from Key West. I received two letters. The weather has been generally pleasant with a rain squall once in a while. There is generally a good breeze blowing.

Wednesday, June 29
Off Santiago

I had all night in last night, and was detailed for a boat duty to-day. This afternoon I went to a press dispatch boat for dispatches for the Admiral, then to the *Yale* to take the Admiral's steward, and then to the *Lebanon* to bring stores to the ship. Our picket boats near the entrance to Santiago harbor were fired on last night, but they were not hit. The Army is still moving towards Santiago. We are looking for an attack at any time. It is getting tiresome lying here doing nothing.

---

8 USS *Yale* (steamer) patrolled off Puerto Rico and blockaded Santiago.

9 Victor Blue (1865–1928), U.S. Naval Academy, 1887.

10 USS *Lebanon* (AG 2) delivered coal to U.S. ships in Cuba.

Thursday June 30.
Off Santiago
I had the first watch last night. Rained during the first two hours. Heard desultory firing on shore all during watch. In afternoon sighted a vessel to the southward. The *New York* and *Vixen* gave chase. The ship was very slow to show any colors. On reaching her found out she was the troopship *"Louisiana"* bound for Siboney. At 9 P.M. we made the signal to the other vessels to stand by to bombard the forts at the entrance of the harbor at six o'clock to-morrow, and that the army would advance on Santiago at the same time.

Friday July 1.
Off Santiago and Aguadores.
I had the midwatch last night. Nothing unusual happened. Turned in at four A.M. and out again at five. Had some toast and coffee. Went to general quarters at six and

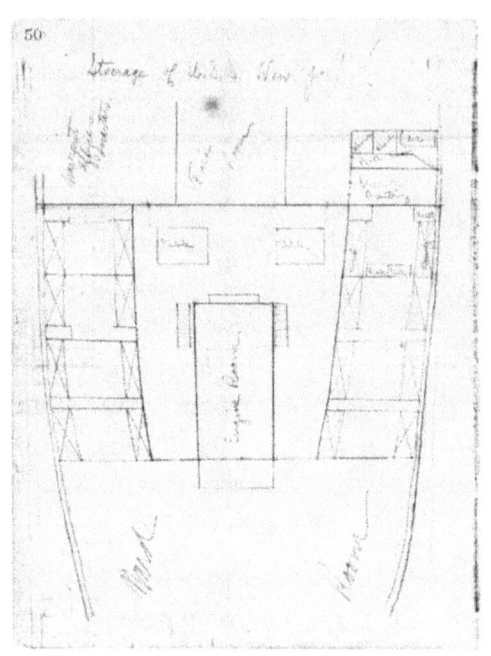

"Steerage of USS New York"

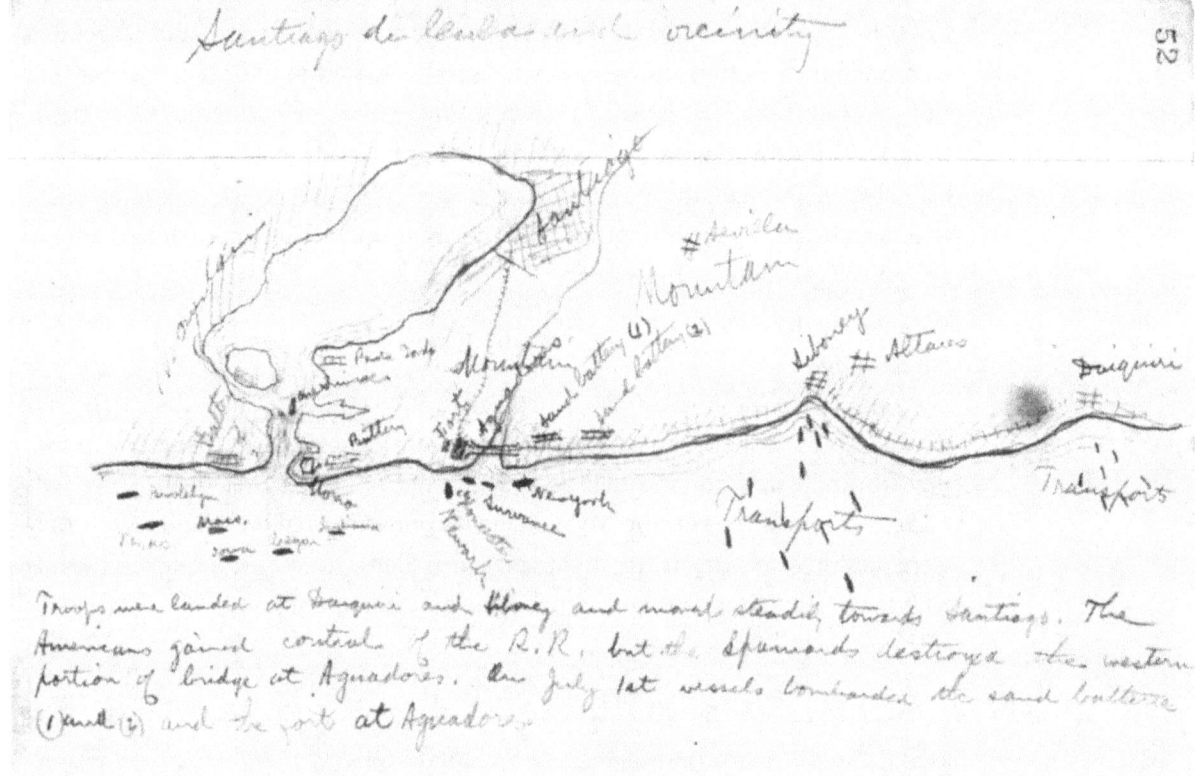

"Santiago de Cuba and vicinity"

approached Aguadores where there were two sand batteries and a fort where the Spanish flag was flying from the top of a high pole. At nine o'clock a detachment of troops came on a train from Siboney and we signalled to them with the wig-wag and asked them when we should commence firing. They answered when the second detachment of troops arrived. These arrived about ten o'clock, and the *New York, Suwanee*,[11] and *Gloucester*[12] commenced bombarding the fort and sand batteries (1) and (2). As soon as we got the range shell after shell fell in the fort and batteries leaving them all in ruins. I don't think the Spaniards fired a single shot at us, but left the fortifications and placed themselves in the railroad cut behind a hill. When the signal cease firing was given the flag was still flying. The *Suwanee* asked for permission to knock it down. The Admiral said they could take three shots at it. The first two shots struck right at the foot of the pole and at the third the pole fell over amid cheers of the crews. It was a fine piece of shooting. The Spaniards were heard firing from the R.R. cut behind the hill, upon our troops. The *Newark*[13] which has just come from the north asked for permission to shoot into the cut for target practice. The request was granted, and all the vessels dropped shell in the cut for an hour. The *New York* then trained her guns at the extreme elevation and fired in the direction Santiago was supposed to be. Of course we do not know whether any of the shells struck home or not. We ceased firing about half past twelve and went back to our positions before the entrance to Santiago harbor. I had the afternoon watch, and, as DuBose[14] was sent on boat duty, the second dog watch. I received letters from Mother and Charles from the *Newark*. We have heard that the Army advanced to the outskirts of Santiago, but with great loss as they had to take the enemy's intrenchments as they advanced. There were three men killed and several wounded of those troop that were at Aguadores.

---

11 USS *Suwanee* (armed yacht) blockaded Santiago, bombarded Guantanamo, and took part in the action at Manzanillo.

12 USS *Gloucester* (gunboat) took part in the battle of Santiago Bay.

13 USS *Newark* (C 1) blockaded Cuba and bombarded Manzanillo.

14 William G. DuBose (1876–1965) was an 1897 graduate of the U.S. Naval Academy. He served as Chief, Bureau of Construction and Repair, in 1938.

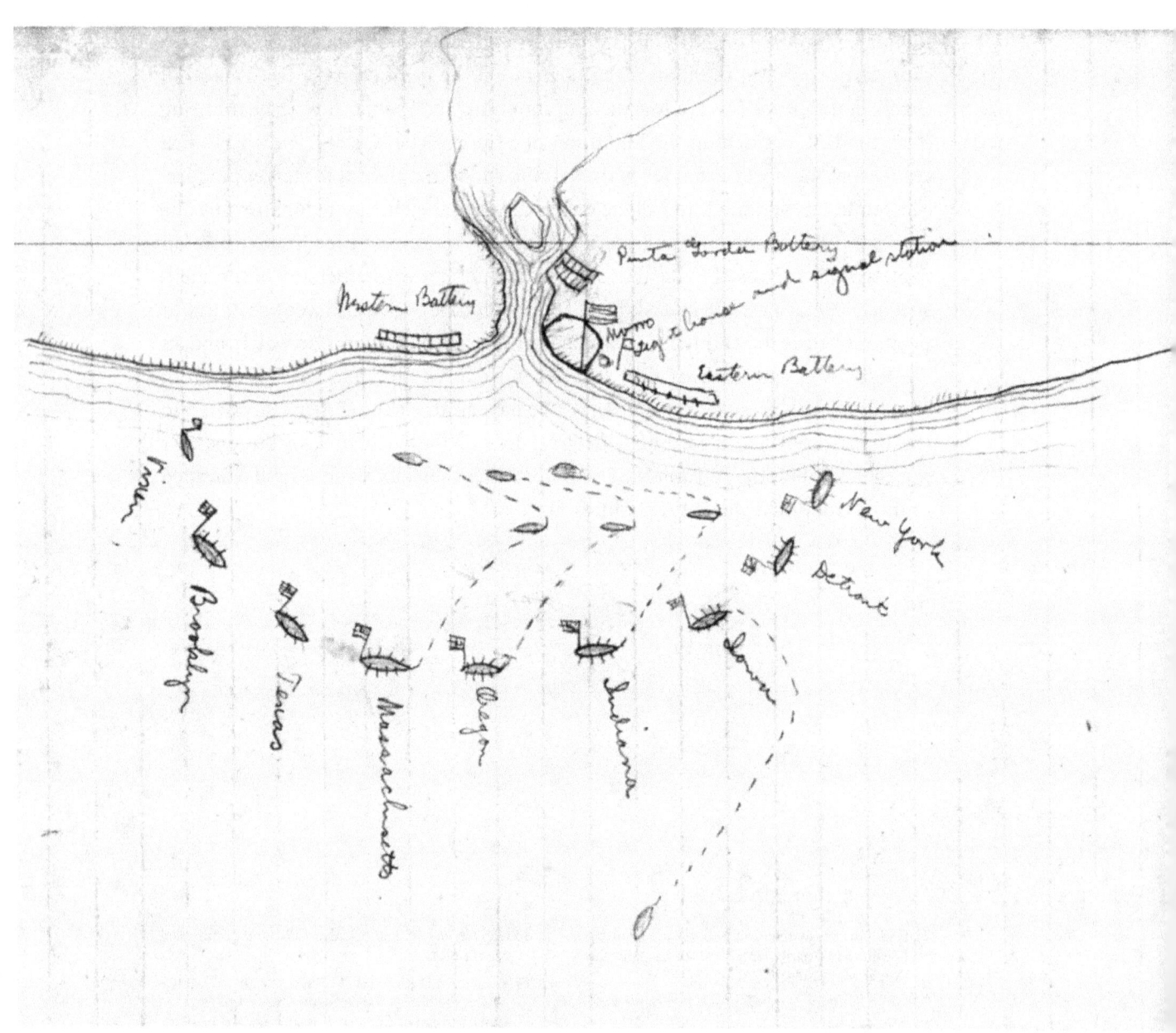

Sketch chart of ships off eastern batte

IV *Battle of Santiago Bay*

Saturday July 2.
Off Santiago—Bombarding

We were turned out at half past three and at five o'clock went to general quarters. The vessels took positions (shown on opposite page) and the bombardment commenced at once. The Western and Eastern batteries were soon silenced, and the *Massachusetts, Oregon,* and *Indiana* were ordered to move in closer and bombard the Morro. They filled this old fortification full of holes, and a shot from the *Oregon* carried away the flag. These three vessels then moored in front of the entrance and bombarded the Estrella and Punta Gorda batteries which are just inside the entrance. At eight o'clock we ceased firing. At times some shells struck very close to us and we could hear them go whistling over our heads. We believe that the ships from the inside of the harbor fired the shells that came nearest to us. Our men now take a bombardment as a huge joke, and show absolutely no signs of anxiety. It is believed that plans are being perfected to countermine the harbor so our ships can run in and get at the Spanish fleet. We hear that the army is steadily advancing ~~with~~ towards Santiago but with great losses, especially among the officers.

Sunday July 3.
Destruction of the Spanish Fleet

See pages 92 and 93 [in the original pagination—copy of official map, in chapter 6, after the July 24 entry]

The Spanish fleet was evidently watching its opportunity to come out of the harbor and make a bold dash to escape. The *Massachusetts* and *Newark* were at Guantanamo, and the *New York* had started for Siboney where Admiral Sampson[1] intended to land in order to confer with General Shafter. We had gotten about four

---

NOTES 1 William Sampson (1840–1902) was commander of the North Atlantic Squadron, which blockaded Cuba. His squadron defeated the Spanish at the battle of Santiago Bay. He was commander of the Naval Torpedo Station, Newport, Rhode Island, from 1884 to 1886. He served as commander of the North Atlantic Station, 1898–99 and was promoted to rear admiral in 1899.

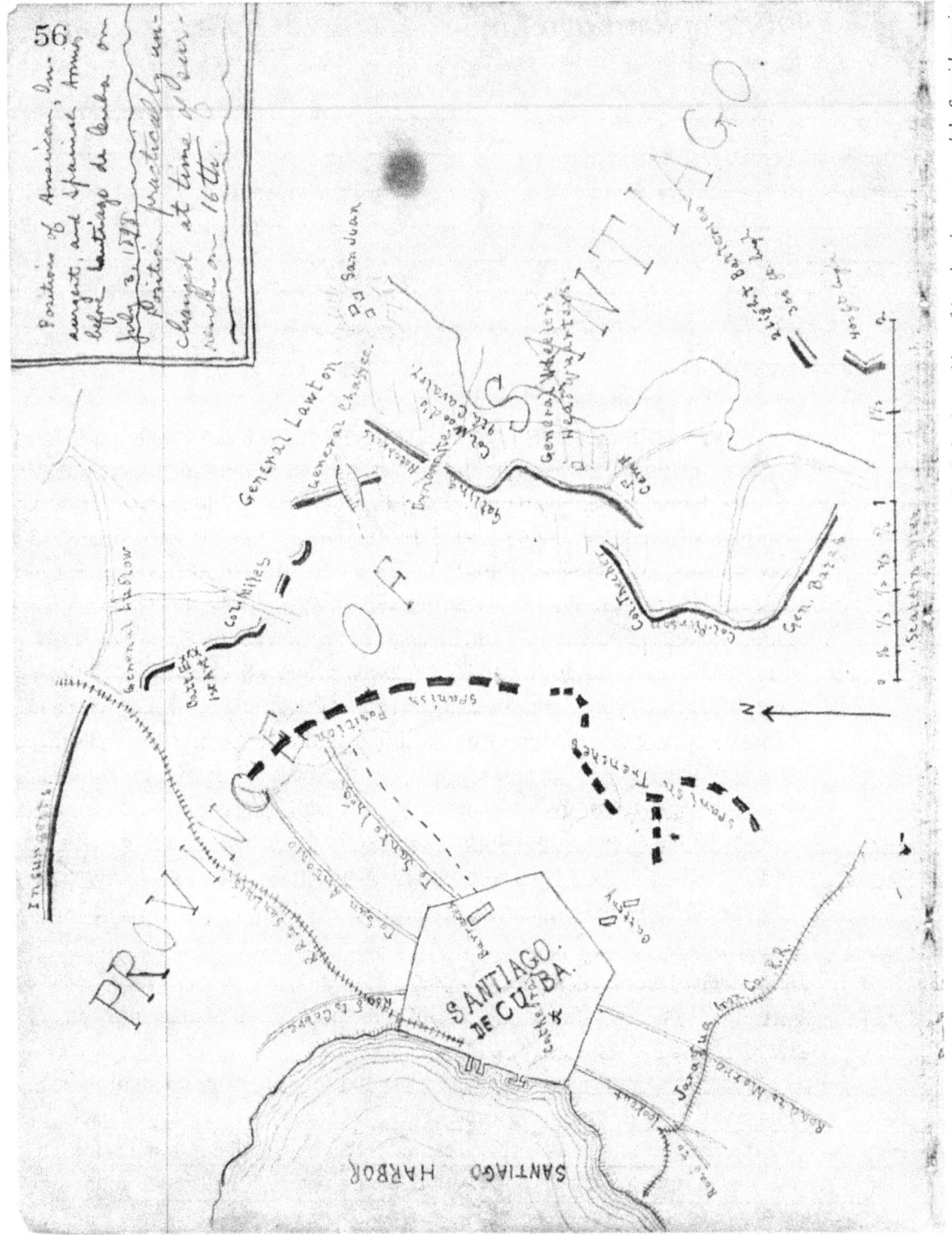

Sketch showing positions of American insurgents and the Spanish armies

miles away when the Spanish fleet was reported. This fleet consisted of the first class armored cruisers *Cristobal Colon*,[2] *Almirante Oquendo*,[3] *Maria Theresa*,[4] and *Viscaya*,[5] and the torpedo boat destroyers, *Furor*[6] and *Pluton*.[7] Our fleet consisted of the seagoing battleship *Iowa*, the coastline battleships *Oregon* and *Indiana*, the second class battleship *Texas*, and Armored cruisers *Brooklyn* and *New York*, and the converted yachts, *Vixen* and *Gloucester*. The Spaniards had the shore batteries to help them out, and as none of our ships fired on them, they kept up in a spirited canonading. The *New York* although within signal distance and long range, fired only four shots, one of them hitting one of the torpedo boat destroyers. So we had the five large vessels, and two yachts, against their four large vessels, two torpedo boats, and shore batteries. The advantage was considerably on our side, as our vessels had much larger batteries than theirs.

Captain Clark, Lieutenants Nicholson and Ackerman

Captain Clark and Naval Cadet Street

---

2 *Cristobal Colon* was built by the Spanish in 1896.

3 *Almirante Oquendo* was built in 1891.

4 *Infanta Maria Teresa* (as correctly spelled), a cruiser, was launched in 1890 and carried a complement of 497 men.

5 *Vizcaya* was built in 1891.

6 *Furor*, a destroyer, was built in 1896 and was a ship of Admiral Cervera's fleet. It was crippled and sunk during the battle of Santiago Bay.

7 *Plutón*, a torpedo boat, was commissioned in 1897 and was part of Admiral Cervera's fleet. It was attacked by USS *Gloucester* at Santiago Bay and crashed on the rocks, losing half of its crew.

The *New York* turned around immediately upon hearing the firing and started full speed towards the vessels. We could see the smoke from the vessels and shore batteries and hear the guns distinctly. The Spanish ships were running westward along the coast, in hopes of escaping in that direction. When we reached our old station before the entrance to the harbor the other vessels were about two to three miles ahead of us. All the shore batteries now directed their fire on us and the shells fell uncomfortably close. We did not return the fire but kept going full speed. We now saw the *Gloucester* a short distance ahead, engaging the two torpedo boat destroyers by her self, the other vessels having gone on after the cruisers. The *New York* now fired her only shots. One of the torpedo boats was all ablaze and the other was run high on the beach and deserted. Both had hauled down their colors, and Admiral Sampson signalled the *Gloucester* to take charge. Just ahead of us were the *Indiana, Iowa,* and *Texas* in the order named, and the Spanish ships *Viscaya, Maria Theresa,* and *Almirante Oquendo.* Farther on the *Brooklyn* and *Oregon* were after the *Cristobal Colon.* The *Maria Theresa* and *Almirante Oquendo* were riddled with shell from our ships, and the after part of each, burst out in flame they then headed in for the beach, hauled down their colors and showed white flags. A number of the crew had to

Members of the crew watching the fall of a sho

At the guns on the Broo

take to the water to save themselves from the flames. Several passed near the *New York* and cried out for help. We threw them life preservers. As we went on we saw explosion after explosion take place on the burning vessels which had been run ashore about three eights of a mile apart. The *Indiana* took possession of them in obedience to a signal from the flagship. The next ship disabled was the *Viscaya* which ran aground about two miles farther on. She was on fire like the others and was showing three white flags. Some Cubans either treacherously, or not knowing that the Spaniards had surrendered, fired on the men in the water. Admiral

Sampson ordered the *Iowa* to take charge of the *Viscaya* and to prevent the Cubans from molesting the Spaniards. The *Cristobal Colon,* the newest and finest of the ships, was some distance ahead.

USS Brooklyn

USS New York,
Admiral Sampson's flagship

In some way she had gotten past the *Brooklyn* early in the fight, and was now doing her best to get away. The *Oregon* and *Brooklyn* were nearest to her. Then came the *Texas* and *Vixen* and then *New York*. The *Brooklyn* and *Oregon* fired from time to time but they were hardly within range, the *Brooklyn*'s shells falling about three fourths of the way to her, while the *Oregon*'s fell much closer. At first the *Colon* held her own, but later her speed decreased markedly. The *Oregon*'s shells were now falling close to her. The chase had continued four hours (60 miles) when the *Colon* seeing escape was impossible headed in for the beach and hauled down her colors. She ran her bow over the bottom, although uninjured excepting ~~as to~~ a few holes where shells had struck her. She was a fine looking ship newly painted, and did not have the appearance of being cleared for action. A prize crew was placed on board, the Commodore (2d in command of fleet) the Captain, and Chief of Staff were brought on board the *New York*, and the Officers and crew were taken to the *Resolute*.[8] The *Oregon* towed her off the bottom, but she soon began to settle, and it was seen that the Spaniards had treacherously opened all the sea-valves. They also threw overboard many of the breech blocks from the guns, and ruined many of the interior fittings. The *New York* tried to push her back on the bottom, but she sank in water just deep enough for her port side to show out of the water after she went down and rolled over on her starboard side.

The Spanish loss was 600 killed, 1750 prisoners, 115 officers and the wounded being among them. Admiral Cervera[9] was taken on board the *Iowa*. The American loss was one killed and three wounded. The *Resolute* reported another Spanish man-of-war coming in from the eastward. The *Brooklyn* was sent after her and after overhauling her found she was the Austrian man-of-war battleship *Maria Theresa*.

USS Oregon
first-class battleship

8 USS *Resolute* (transport) was commissioned in May 1898. It aided the fleet in scouting for Cervera's squadron, was present at the battle of Santiago Bay, and bombarded Spanish shore batteries at Manzanillo. It convoyed U.S. troops home after the war ended.

9 Pascual Cervera y Topete (1839–1909) was in command of the Spanish Caribbean Squadron at Santiago Bay. Blockaded in the bay by the Americans during the battle, he tried unsuccessfully to run through the U.S. force, was captured, and then released after ten weeks' imprisonment in Portsmouth, New Hampshire. Upon his return to Spain, he was tried but defended himself and his men by pointing out that the fleet had received little support from the Cortes, or the government.

USS Texas
second-class battleship

USS Iowa
first-class battleship

USS Indiana

Monday July 4.

Off Santiago

Last night we went back to Santiago harbor. It was a relief not to have to look for the Spanish fleet. In the morning the British cruiser *Pallas*,[10] and Austrian ~~battleship~~ cruiser *Maria Theresa*, asked Admiral Sampson for permission to go in the harbor, as they wished to take away the British and Austrian refugees having heard that our Army was going to bombard the city. The Admiral gave them permission, but the Spanish authorities refused to allow them to enter. At twelve o'clock all the ships in the fleet fired a salute of twenty-one guns. An Armistice was granted the Spaniards so that the women and children could be gotten out of Santiago.

Tuesday, July 5.

In vicinity of Spanish wrecks.

Last night about half past eleven, the *Massachusetts* fired two red rockets signifying that the enemy was in sight. All hands were turned out and we went to general quarters. The *Massachusetts* then signalled: "The enemy is trying to sink a vessel in the entrance to the harbor." The *Massachusetts*, *Oregon*, and *Vesuvius* opened fire and succeeded in sinking the ship. This morning we could see her distinctly on the bottom in shoal water and nowhere near the channel. The *New York* went to take a look at the wrecks of the Spanish men-of-war this afternoon. The Captain, with several officers, were going on board what was left of the *Almirante Oquendo*, and Lackey and I got permission to go too. The *Oquendo* was a complete wreck. The heat of the fire (she was still smouldering) caused all her paint to fall off and leave her a dirty yellow color. Her decks are all burned away and only the beams and stanchions remain. Her protective deck, however, was intact. It was hard and dirty work climbing around her. We were looking for curios, and we found lots of burnt rifles, revolvers, swords, knives, forks, spoons, pieces of shells, etc. Around nearly all the guns were several dead bodies burned to ashes. The forward turret contained eleven dead sailors. She was simply riddled with shot, a number of twelve and thirteen inch shells hitting her near the waterline. If she had not run ashore when she did, she would have sunk in deep water. Just as we were about to leave I found a tin box containing money. Looking around for more I found more, some in

Admiral Sampson and Captain Chadwick aboard the USS New York

---

10 HMS *Pallas*, a second-class cruiser, was launched in 1890. It had a complement of 217 men and was 266 feet long.

boxes and more lying around loose. It was all more or less fused together, and just the thing for souvenirs. I reported that I had found more money than I could carry and some of the men came and got all they wanted. Lackey found the safe, intact, but with a few six pounders in it that had not exploded. We tried to get it open, but couldn't, so we brought it to the ship. On opening it found it full of copper pennies. In the evening we went back to our position before the entrance of the harbor.

The Oregon, *the* Texas, *and the* Indiana *firing*

USS Gloucester

Wednesday July 6.
Siboney
This afternoon the Admiral intended to go ashore at Siboney to confer with General Shafter, but not being well he sent Captain Chadwick[11] and Lieutenant Staunton.[12] Captain Paget R.N.[13] went also.

This evening I went ashore with telegrams. The prisoners from the *Merrimac*[14] had just been exchanged, and I brought them back to the ship in the steam launch. One of the men told me their experience: The *Merrimac* entered the channel and

Captain John W. Philip

Capatin Cook of the Brooklyn

Commander Bowman H. McCalla of the cruiser Marblehead

Lieutenant Commander Wainwright

Admiral William T. Sampson

Captain Robley D. Evans

---

11 French Chadwick (1844–1919) was a member of the U.S. Naval Academy class of 1865. He served as chief of staff of the North Atlantic Squadron (1898–1900) and president of the Naval War College (1900–1903). He was promoted to rear admiral in 1903.

12 Sidney A. Staunton (1850–1939) graduated from the U.S. Naval Academy in 1871. He was assistant chief of staff of the North Atlantic Fleet (1898–1899). He was promoted to rear admiral in 1910.

13 Alfred W. Paget (1852–?) was promoted to captain on 30 June 1896.

14 USS *Merrimac* (steamer) entered Santiago Harbor on June 3 and was hit by gunfire from a Spanish ship.

was immediately fired on by the batteries. One shell took away her rudder, and another carried away the key-board for setting off the torpedoes. She was uncontrollable, and she did not sink until a torpedo from the *Reina Mercedes*[15] struck her. This accounts for her not being across the channel as was intended. The men went down with her, and coming up climbed on the life raft. They drifted around until daylight (3 hours) and were then picked up by a boat from the *Reina Mercedes*. The Spaniards, in firing across the channel killed fourteen of their men. The crew of the *Merrimac* were placed in the Morro[16] until June 6th when they were taken to the city. Here they were placed in dirty and damp quarters, but the English Consul[17] demanded a better place for them and they got it.

The English Consul brought them things to eat and obtained hammocks and a pack of cards for them. Our men were fed better than the Spanish soldiers, but even then, they did not get nearly enough to eat. The Spanish soldiers are half starved, and ready to lay down their arms, so as to get bread and meat from the Americans. The men say they were treated well at all times, and became very much attached to the officer and doctor in charge of them. When the launch reached the ship the crew was assembled on the quarterdeck and poop and gave "three cheers and a tiger" for the men. Hobson[18] had returned before the men, and he was met with the same sort of reception.

---

15 *Reina Mercedes* (cruiser) was a harbor-defense ship at Santiago. It was scuttled in the harbor after extensive damage and was later salvaged by the U.S. Navy. It served as a receiving ship in Newport, Rhode Island, 1905–12.

16 Morro Castle is in Havana.

17 Sir Alexander Gollan (?–1902) held various posts in the British foreign office, including consul in Nicaragua (1876), Pernambuco (1883), and the Philippine Islands (1885), and consul-general in Cuba (1892–98), from which post he retired.

18 Richmond Hobson (1870–1937) graduated from the U.S. Naval Academy in 1889. He won the Medal of Honor is 1933 for his attempt to block the channel at Santiago with the sinking of the *Merrimac*. He resigned from the Navy in 1903 and was Democratic representative from Alabama, 1905–15. He received the rank of rear admiral in 1934.

V *Surrender at Santiago* 1898

Thursday July 7
Off Santiago

Did not do anything out of the ordinary all day. Some of the ships have gone to Guantanamo for stores and coal. The Army is doing nothing, awaiting the end of the armistice.

Friday July 8
Guantanamo

We left last night at two o'clock for Guantanamo and arrived about seven. The colliers *Niagara*[1] and *Lebanon* came alongside, and we coaled ship all day. The *Harvard*[2] is still here with some of the Spanish prisoners on board. This is a very good harbor, the anchorage being large enough for many ships. A number of Cadets from the *Oregon* came on board to pay us a visit. The Spaniards in the still control the *Marblehead*'s[3] steam launch which was doing patrol duty. Some mail came in on the *Wilmington*.[4] I received a letter from Mother.

Saturday July 9
Guantanamo

Coaled ship all day. I was on boat duty and kept busy, made trips to the *Harvard, Marblehead,* and machine ship *Vulcan*.[5] Was sent on board the prize steamer *Adula*, and brought the supposed Spanish agent, Señor Salice, on board the *New York* as the Admiral wished to see him. I took several dispatches ashore and brought others back. The cable and telegraph stations are those known as the Playa del Este, although there is not much of the village left it having been burned by the Marines after they captured it. The Cuban camp is there now. Camp McCalla is located on the

---

NOTES
1 USS *Niagara* (steamer) delivered coal to the fleet off Cuba, Puerto Rico, and Haiti.

2 USS *Harvard* (screw steamer) scouted the Spanish fleet, rescued survivors, and carried troops back to the United States.

3 USS *Marblehead* (cruiser) cut the cable at Cienfuegos and captured Guantanamo.

4 USS *Wilmington* (gunboat) was commissioned in 1897. It blockaded Cuba and took part in operations at Cardenas, Santa Cruz, and Manzanillo.

5 USS *Vulcan* (screw steamer), built in 1844, was purchased by the Navy in 1898 and converted to a repair ship. It performed salvage and repair work on U.S. ships during the war.

U. S. S. MASSACHUSETTS.

First-class battleship. Twin screw. Length on water-line, 348 feet; breadth, 69 feet, 3 inches; draft, 24 feet; displacement, 10,288 tons; speed, 16.2 knots. Main battery, four 13-inch, eight 8-inch, and four 6-inch guns. Secondary battery, twenty 6-pounder and four 1-pounder rapid-fire guns, and four gatlings. Armor, 17, 10, and 8 inches over barbette, and 17, 8½, and 6 inches over turret; other armor, 18, 14, and 5 inches near battery. 37 officers; 438 men. Cost, $3,020,000.

U. S. S. MARBLEHEAD.

Unarmored cruiser. Twin screw. Commissioned April 2, 1894. Length, 257 feet; breadth, 37 feet; draft, 14 feet, 7 inches; displacement, 2,089 tons. Speed, 19 knots. Main battery, nine 5-inch rapid-fire guns. Secondary battery, six 6-pounder and two 1-pounder rapid-fire guns, and two gatlings. 20 officers; 254 men. Cost, $674,000.

TORPEDO BOAT "ERICSSON."

top of a hill overlooking the harbor. The *New Orleans* came in with mail. I received a letter from Father. The *Oregon, Massachusetts, Newark,* and *Dixie*[6] of Commodore Watson's[7] Eastern Squadron, are here to be coaled. We have heard no news from the Army to-day.

Sunday July 10.
Guantanamo

The *Celtic*[8] came alongside this morning and we took on ice and stores from her. Had neither church nor quarters. Crew washed the decks nearly all day. About five o'clock left for Santiago. Passed the *Gloucester,* which reported that the *Brooklyn* and *Texas* kept up a slow fire in the direction of Santiago for two hours.

Monday July 11
Between Santiago and Siboney

A telephone has been established between the Army and the beach so the Army and Navy are now in touch. About eight o'clock General Shafter asked (through telephone and wig-wag) if we would throw shells into the city. The *New York, Brooklyn,* and *Indiana* moved in close to the beach, and each threw four 8-inch shells, every 5 minutes over the hills in the direction of Santiago. From the signal station on shore we were informed where our shells struck. They all fell in the city. This afternoon the *Yale* arrived from Norfolk. She had on board General Miles[9] and a large number of troops. Admiral Sampson went on board to confer with General Miles. The *Columbia*[10] came in this afternoon also. I received a letter from Mother, dated June 22, by the *Yale.*

Tuesday, July 12,
Same

I had the mid-watch last night, and it rained hard nearly all through. Rained nearly all day. Our army burned the towns of Siboney and Daiquiri on account of several cases of Yellow fever. The *St. Paul*[11] arrived with stores and ammunition.

Starboard bow close-up of the Vizcaya

---

6 USS *Dixie* (steam brig) convoyed troops to Cuba and blockaded Cuba. It captured Ponce, Puerto Rico and landed troops there.

7 John C. Watson (1842–1923) was an 1869 graduate of the U.S. Naval Academy. He was Commanding Officer, First Squadron, North Atlantic Fleet (June–September 1898). He was promoted to rear admiral in 1899.

8 USS *Celtic* (storeship) was commissioned in 1898 and supported U.S. troops during the Philippine Insurrection.

9 Nelson A. Miles (1839–1925) was commanding general of the U.S. Army during the war. He invaded Puerto Rico and served as head of the military government and occupation forces there.

10 USS *Columbia* (C 2) served in the war as a patrol ship. It convoyed troops to Puerto Rico.

11 *St. Paul,* leased to the Navy, scouted Cervera's fleet and attacked the Spanish destroyer *Terror,* disabling it.

Starboard bow view of the Vizcaya

Monday July 13.
Same

Everything was very quiet to-day. We stayed near the signal station between the entrance to the harbor and Siboney. The truce between the armies still continues. Mr. Hobson went ashore to represent the Navy in the negotiations for surrender. The *Massachusetts* and *Oregon* arrived from Guantanamo.

Tuesday July 14
Same

Everything quiet. Negotiations for surrender of Santiago still going on. The French cruiser *"Amiral Rignault de Genouilly"*[12] arrived in the morning. She fired a salute of 13 guns which was returned by us. I was sent on board to present Admiral Sampson's compliments to the Captain, who later came on board the *New York*. The *Massachusetts* and *Oregon* returned to Guantanamo as they could not bombard on account of the truce.

Friday July 15
Same

Staying here and waiting for something to be done is getting monotonous. This morning a signal came from the shore that Santiago had surrendered, and in the afternoon another signal came saying there was a hitch in the proceedings. The *Celtic* came from Guantanamo and we took on board from her, fresh provisions and small stores. We have not received a mail for a long time.

---

12 *Amiral Rigault de Genouilly* was a French ship built in 1876 of 1,700 tons, with a crew of two hundred and a length of 236 feet.

Starboard quarter view of the Almirante Oquendo

VI *War's End*

1898

Saturday July 16

General Miles came on board this morning and told Admiral Sampson that Santiago had surrendered. The whole province is turned over to the Americans who are to transport the Spanish Army of 24,000 men to Spain on Parole. The American flag is flying from the Morro at the entrance to the harbor. We anchored this morning close inshore at Aguadores. We can easily see the bridge from which the *Dolphin*[1] knocked a train load of Spanish troops. One end of the bridge was destroyed by the Spaniards some time ago to prevent the Americans from crossing. The ruins of the fort we bombarded on July 1st are very near. The beach is lined with men but I can't make out whether they are Spaniards or Cubans. The ~~French~~ German merchant steamer "*Staffa*" arrived. I do not know their mission. On account of the yellow fever on shore (now reported as 400 cases) Admiral Sampson has issued an order forbidding any unnecessary communication on shore except by signal.

Sunday July 17

Early this morning the *New York* anchored in the entrance of Santiago harbor. We got a fine view of the Morro, batteries, *Reina Mercedes* and *Merrimac*. The Morro and batteries showed the marks of our shells, the walls in many places being crumbled. The *Reina Mercedes* is lying on her port side, the starboard side and most of the main deck being out of the water. She has two smokestacks and three masts. Several of her guns are still mounted, but most of them are in the shore batteries. There are a number of holes in her made by the shells of our ships. The *Merrimac* is in the middle of the channel lying fore and aft. She rests on an even keel with only her top masts, ends of gaffs, and top of smokestack showing above water. The end of her main mast was shot away, and her smokestack and foremast are full of small holes made by rifle bullets. The steam launch was sent in the harbor and in about an hour came out and reported that there was a gunboat, five merchant steamers, and a number of sailing

---

NOTES 1 USS *Dolphin* (PG 24) had blockade duty off Havana during the war.

vessels in the harbor. Admiral Sampson sent prize crews from the *New York* and *Brooklyn* to take charge of the vessels. General Shafter objected to the Navy taking charge of any of the vessels, and the matter was referred to Washington, the result being in favor of the Navy. Lieutenant Marble[2] brought the gunboat "*Alvarado*"[3] out of the harbor. She is very small, being about 100 ft. long and 90 tons displacement. She has a 3-pounder Maxim-Nordenfeldt gun on the bow, and a machine gun of the same make on the poop. Lieutenant Capehart[4] was sent in the harbor to see about getting rid of the mines.

Monday July 18
I received permission to go ashore with a number of officers from the *NewYork*. The steam launch took us to a small landing just inside the entrance to the harbor. We landed and started up the road to the Morro. We ran across many boxes of rifle ammunition that had not been opened.

The road leading up the hill on which Morro stands is of solid rock. It is shut in by a stone wall. The hill is almost 300 ft. high, but it is a hard climb as the rocks are hard on the feet. That part of the Morro seen from the water is the a very little of it, as the rooms and dungeons extend down into the solid rock to the water's edge. The marks of our shells were evident, but we could have demolished the masonry completely, and there still would have been room for the troops in the castle, and in places where our shell could do no harm. All the rooms showed signs of having been occupied recently. They were void of furniture, only a few of them having a chair and a hammock, and there were half written letters and half cooked pots of rice lying around. When Santiago surrendered everything in the forts and batteries was left as it was. The rooms had solid rocks for the walls, floor, and ceiling, and as a rule were cool and damp. Many of them contained ammunition but most had been

View of the Vizcaya as she lay

Wreck of torpedo destroyer Furor

---

2 Frank Marble (?–1911), U.S. Naval Academy, 1888.
3 *Alvarado* (gunboat) was built in 1895 and captured by the U.S. Army.

4 Edward E. Capeheart (?–1917), U.S. Naval Academy, 1881.

used as quarters for the men. Extending to the eastward of Morro about 200 yds. on the brow of the hill and plainly visible from our ships, are the barracks. We could not see from the *New York* the damage that had been done these buildings. The roofs and walls of many of them had been knocked in by shells, and they were uninhabitable. I think these buildings had been occupied by the officers, as there were signs of more furniture than in the Morro. In one of the rooms a complete heliograph apparatus was found, and in another was a half starved horse which we let out. The light house is made of iron but only half of it stands as twelve shells went through it and some of them exploding inside blew out half of the house facing inland. We next went to the "Eastern Battery." This is a sand battery the protection being made by barrels and bags of sand covered over with dirt. The gun carriages are in ditches only the guns showing over the embankment. There are two old muzzle loading guns and two rifled howitzers here, the training gear of all of them looking as if it had not been touched for some time. Besides these there are two four inch breech-loading guns which had evidently been used lately. There was a great deal of ammunition near by consisting of time-fuse shells and schrapnel. The Estrella Battery is to the northward of the Morro, and on the water's edge. In this battery there were only two guns mounted, and about six others that were ready to mount. There was a great deal of ammunition here, mostly schrapnel. This battery had suffered from our fire considerably. Across from the Morro near the water's edge is a masked battery that we had not discovered before. This consisted of four Maxim-Nordenfelt machine guns, and one six-pounder.

The Cristobal Colon *lying on the beach*

Tuesday, July 19

I turned out at seven o'clock this morning to go in the boat with Lieut. Capehart and Gunner Morgan to get the remaining mines in the entrance to the harbor. We landed on the western side. The station from which the observation mines were exploded is a small thatched hut. In this is the keyboard and sight bars. A single cable leads from this house into the water. We picked this cable up in the boat, and underran it until we picked up the junction box in the middle of the channel. In this box the six parts of the cable separate into smaller cables leading in different directions. We underran one of these cables until we hauled up the chain sling attached to one of the mines. The *Suwanee* then came along and hoisted the mine. The mine was a Latimer Clark Muirhead mine,[5] and was a large iron box weighing about a ton. The bottom was broken out and about half the wet guncotton was still in it. We pulled this out and threw it overboard. We then unscrewed the cylinder containing the dry gun cotton and threw this away together with the fulminate of mercury. We then underran another cable and found it detached from the mine so did not bother with it. After lunch we dragged for a contact mine which had sunk in about ten fathoms of water. At four o'clock we were still at work, when we were sent for to come back to the *New York*. There were eleven observation and eight contact mines in the harbor, and it seems that none of them were in good condition. During lunch time I got permission to take some bread and meat to some people in a small village on an island called Cayo Smith. There were only a few families in the town the rest having moved out. We saw a number of places where our shells had struck they having come from outside over the hills on which the batteries stood. The people there were half starved Cubans. They said that on the 2d of July the Sailors from the Spanish fleet went through their houses, cutting up all the furniture and leaving them only the clothes they had on at the time. We went through the houses and saw that the Cubans had been telling the truth.

At seven o'clock I was sent in the steam launch with provisions and messages for the prize crews on the Spanish merchantmen at Santiago. It was beginning to get dark when I started so I did not see as much of the country as I should have liked to. The channel is very narrow for about three fourths of a mile and runs nearly due north, then the Harbor broadens out and lies about SW and NE. It is very much like a wide river, the scenery being very pretty. When I reached Santiago it was too dark to see anything of the city, and I had some trouble in finding the prize ships as there were about thirty U.S. Transports in the harbor. I got back to the *New York* about ten o'clock, and had just turned in when the Captain sent for me to take more messages to Santiago. There was one letter for General Shafter, and one for Lieut. Doyle,[6] who was in charge of the prize ships. I delivered the latter first, and then hunted around in the dark for a wharf to land. After landing I was stopped three times in going the length of the wharf by sentries with the challenge: "Halt! Who goes there?" I answered "Officer from the Flagship *New York*," and the sentries responded "Pass on." I delivered the letter to the Corporal of the Guard and then went back to the launch. I got back to the ship at two o'clock, and was pretty tired having been busy since seven in the morning.

This morning the *Hawk*[7] arrived with mail from Key West. I received two letters from Mother and Father besides a number of papers.

---

5 The Latimer Clark Muirhead Mine Company designed floating and submerged submarine mines for harbor security. The mines could be charged with guncotton, weights, cables, or wiring and then linked to a command center and detonated by remote control.

6 James Doyle (?–1909), U.S. Naval Academy, 1882.

7 USS *Hawk* (IX 14) was a ship of the North Atlantic Squadron.

General views of Santiago de Cuba

Wednesday July 20
Guantanamo

Started for Guantanamo during the night and arrived there this morning. A number of men-of-war and Merchant ships are in the harbor. Did nothing all day long.

Thursday July 21

Moved farther in the harbor and commenced coaling at 9 o'clock. Coaled ship all day long. The prizes from Santiago came in. They are the *Reina de los Angeles*,[8] *San Juan*,[9] *Mexico*,[10] *Martera*,[11] and [blank]. The *Yankee*[12] arrived from Norfolk with 200 tons of ammunition. She brought me letters from Father and Mother, and some newspapers. In the evening the *Southery*[13] came along side, and the *Terror*[14] came in and went on her other side. The *Terror* coaled ship all night. I had the watch from 10 to 12 P.M. A boat from the *Reina de los Angeles* came along side and said they wanted

---

8 *Reina de los Angeles* was a hospital ship captured at Santiago and used by the U.S. Army.

9 *San Juan* was a small passenger and cargo ship captured at Santiago.

10 *Mexico* was a transport with a capacity of one hundred people.

11 *Mortera*, a captured Spanish vessel, had a capacity of three hundred people.

12 USS *Yankee* (screw steamer) took part in the cable cutting at Guantanamo. It was on blockade duty at Santiago and patrol duty at Cienfuegos.

13 USS *Southery* (steamer) was purchased by the Navy from the British in 1898. During the war it served as a collier.

14 USS *Terror* (Monitor No. 4) captured and destroyed several Spanish ships off the Cuban coast. It took part in the bombardment of San Juan, Puerto Rico.

immediate assistance as there were some men on board they could not handle. I went in the steam launch with a sergeant of Marines and five privates. I reported on board to Lieutenant Doyle. He said there were four of the prize crew under the influence of liquor, and as he had no means of taking care of them, asked that I take them to the *New York*, which I did.

Friday July 22.
Playa del Este
Coaled ship all day. Admiral Sampson received orders to get the *New York* ready for a long cruise. It is rumored that we are to stay here for two weeks.

Saturday July 23
Playa del Este
Washed down the decks and ships side. This morning the *Fern*[15] arrived with letters and packages. I received two letters from her. This afternoon the *Cincinnati*[16] arrived with mail. I received three letters from her. There has been nothing of interest going on.

Sunday July 24
Same
Had quarters inspection by the Captain. The *Fern* left this morning and the *Cincinnati* this afternoon. Wrote letters during the afternoon. Wichart[17] from the *Marblehead*, and Helm[18] from the *Indiana* came on board to pay a visit.

Monday July 25
Same
The *Montgomery*[19] came this morning and left this afternoon. A Haytian fruit steamer arrived this morning from Port Antonio with a load of fruit on board which was distributed among the vessels of the fleet as a present from the Boston Fruit Co. A number of ladies and gentlemen came with her and paid us a visit during the afternoon. This evening the *Texas* left for the North. She is the first of the fleet to leave, and as she passed each vessel her crew cheered and the other crews cheered back. As she passed the *New York* the Officer of the Deck on the *Texas* shouted through the megaphone "Three cheers for Admiral Sampson," and the crew responded with a will. The Crew of the *New York* returned the cheer, and our band which had been assembled on the quarter deck played "The Girl I left Behind Me," the *Texas*'s crew applauding. Then through the megaphone came, "Captain

---

15 USS *Fern* (gunboat) served as a supply ship in Cuba.

16 USS *Cincinnati* (cruiser) blockaded Havana and bombarded Matanzas.

17 John W. Wichart was appointed ensign on 1 July 1898 and discharged on 8 September 1898.

18 Frank P. Helm (?–1954) was an 1899 graduate of the U.S. Naval Academy. He retired as a lieutenant commander, U.S. Naval Reserve, in 1940.

19 USS *Montgomery* (cruiser) blockaded Havana and took two prizes.

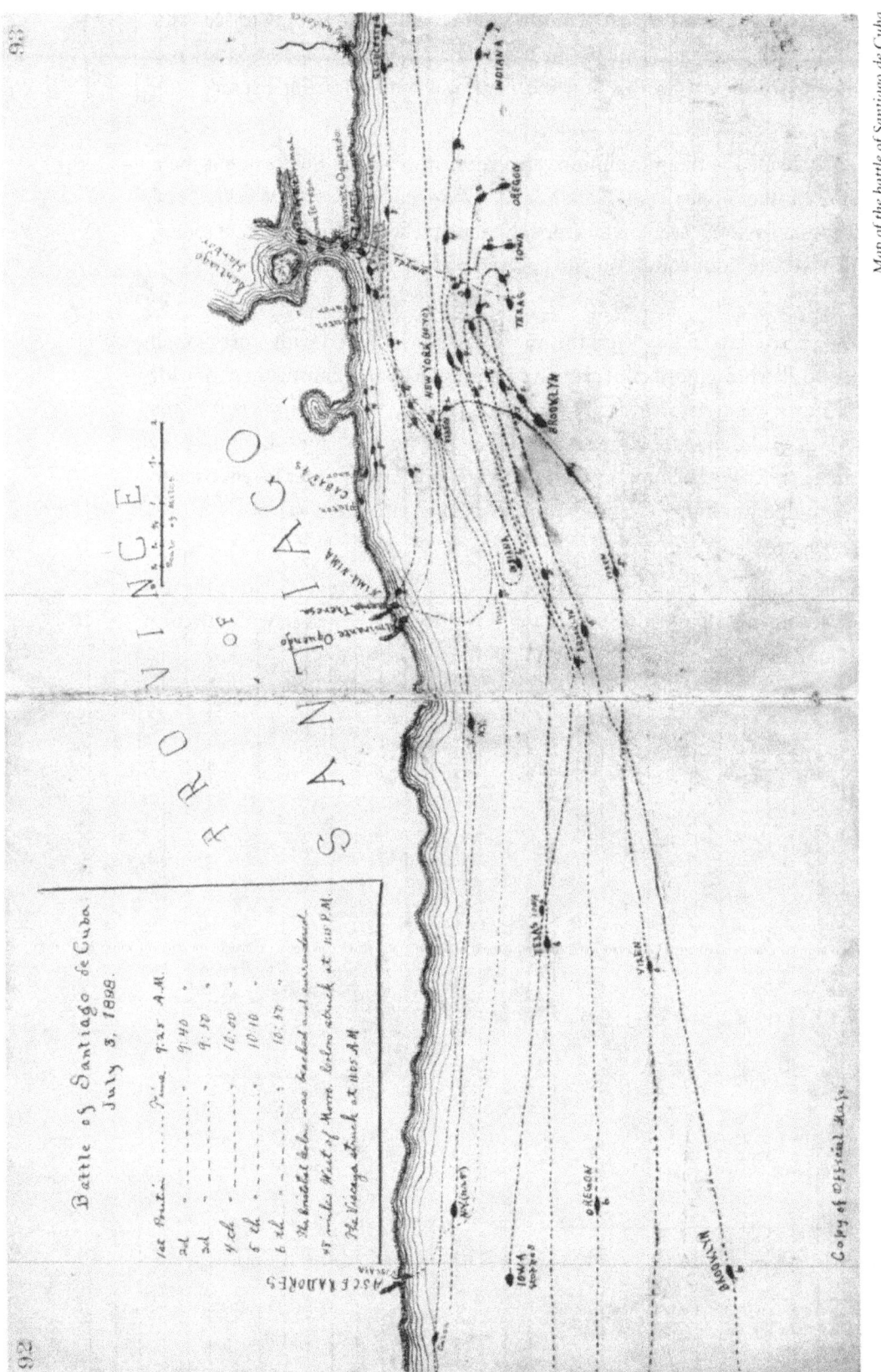

Map of the battle of Santiago de Cuba

Philip[20] says it is not the girl we left behind us but the girl we are going to see" and then the *New York*'s crew applauded. The band then played "Auld Lang Syne" and "Home Sweet Home," and by this time the *Texas* was out of hearing distance.

Tuesday July 26
The *America*, loaded with ammunition, arrived from Norfolk. She brought me a letter from Mother, one from Father, and a copy of Harper's Weekly. The *Marblehead* and *Samoset*[21] went in the upper bay and picked up three contact mines, all of which were in poor condition and covered with barnacles.

Wednesday July 27
The *Supply*[22] arrived from Key West this morning. She is loaded with stores for all the ships, and also has a number of express packages on board, among them one for me containing a white hat. It was my turn for boat duty to-day. First went to the *Iowa* and *Vulcan* and then took the caterers of the twenty-three messes on the *New York* to the *Supply*. Worked in the *Supply* all afternoon. After supper I went back to the *Supply* to find out if there was to be any work at night. There was not.

Thursday July 28
Went to the *Supply* this morning and brought off all the express packages for the *New York*. It took me all morning to find them as they were mixed in with the consignment stores. The *Niagara* was alongside the *New York* all day.

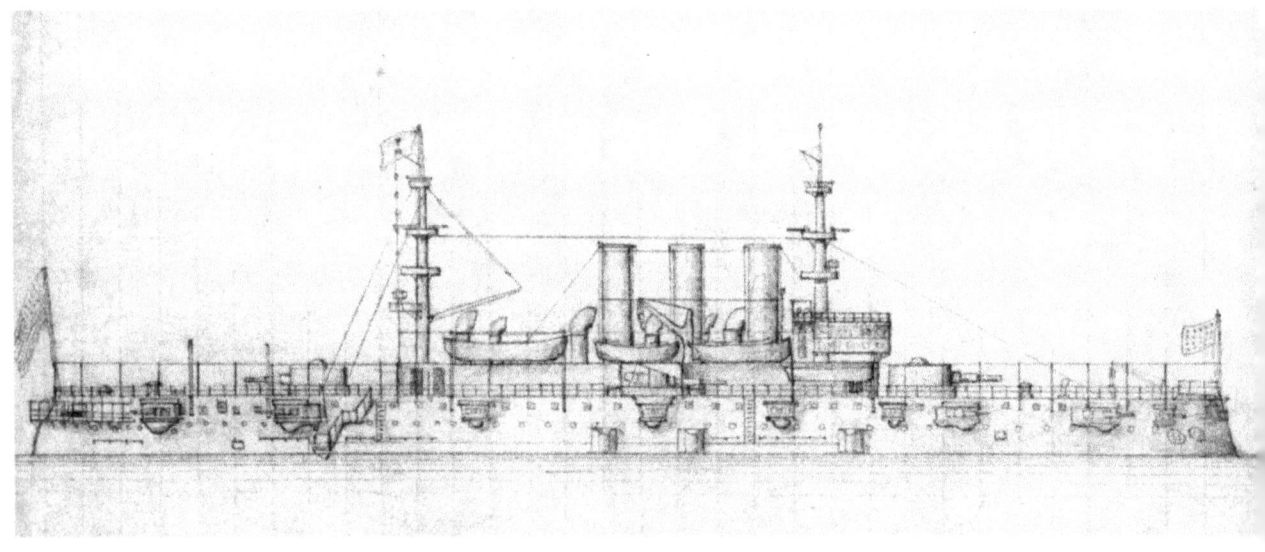

Untitled line drawing of warship, starboard side, three stacks and three flags.

---

20 John Woodward Philip (?–1900), U.S. Naval Academy, 1861.

21 *Samoset* (Harbor Tug No. 5) was launched in 1897. It was based at the Philadelphia Navy Yard and served on the Atlantic coast.

22 USS *Supply* (steamer) served as a supply ship.

Friday July 29

The *Niagara* was alongside until nine o'clock. When she left the *Ameria* took her place and we took ammunition on board. The Admiral went away on the *Yankee*,[23] and returned in the evening.

Saturday July 30

Nothing unusual happened. Two colliers arrived during the night. Some of the ships are taking on stores and coal. The *Celtic* left for the North carrying the mail.

Sunday July 31

The *San Juan*, one of the ships falling into our hands with the Surrender of Santiago, came in this morning, and after receiving permission from the Admiral proceeded up the bay to Caimanera. The *Mayflower*[24] arrived with mail from Key West.

Monday Aug. 1

Coaled ship all day from the collier *Leonidas*.[25] Was turned out at half past five to go to the *Supply* for vinegar and syrup. Got back about eight o'clock. The *Niagara* left for Puerto Rico.

Tuesday Aug. 2.

Everything in very quiet here. A few vessels came and went during the day. The Collier *Leonidas* was along side for a few hours this morning. Finished coaling ship.

Wednesday Aug 3.

I was on boat duty all day to day. Made a number of trips to the vessels in the harbor, and ashore with and for cablegrams. The signal was made this morning that the fleet would leave at 6 P.M. Friday. We expect to go to the Mediterranean. The *Dixie* arrived from Porto Rico accompanied as with a German steamer as a prize.

Thursday Aug. 4.

The *Massachusetts* arrived during the night and immediately commenced coaling from both sides. As the squadron expects to sail tomorrow evening I suppose the *Mass.* will coal all night. The Marines here broke camp and are on board the *Resolute*.

Friday Aug. 5.

The signal was made to the fleet last night that we would not sail for Europe on account of peace negotiations. We do not know how much longer we will be here, but it is probable that we will go North before long. The *Frolic*[26] arrived with the mail. I did not get any.

---

23 USS *Yankee* (screw steamer) was commissioned in April 1898. The ship was on blockade duty in Santiago, patrolled off Cienfuegos, delivered ammunition to Guantanamo, and then returned to blockade duty.

24 USS *Mayflower* (patrol vessel) blockaded Havana and guarded the ports of Santiago and Cienfuegos.

25 USS *Leonidas* (destroyer tender) was converted to a collier in 1898 and supported the fleet during the war.

26 USS *Frolic* (patrol vessel) delivered mail to ships in Cuba and Puerto Rico.

Saturday Aug 6.

Sunday Aug 7

Monday Aug 8.
During these three days nothing of importance has happened. Every day has been the same. Several men-of-war and colliers have come in and gone out. The Marines at Camp McCalla have broken camp and are back on the ships. *St. Louis* arrived.

Tuesday Aug 9
The *St. Louis* went out, and the *St. Paul* came in, also the *Badger*.[27] I received mail from both the latter.

Wednesday Aug 10
Captain Clark[28] of the *Oregon* has been detached on account of illness, and Captain Barker[29] of the *Newark* ordered to command the *Oregon*. Captain Goodrich of the *St. Louis* was detached from the and ordered to command the *Newark*.

Thursday Aug. 11
We got up anchor at 3 A.M. and started for the wreck of the *Infanta Maria Theresa*. Arrived there at 8 A.M. The *Theresa* is still on the bottom and has a great deal of water in her. She has steam up in one boiler, and is pumping the water out as fast as possible. This afternoon I went on board her with a number of officers and a large working party. We got up both lower and both sheet anchor chains. The *Merritt* tug is to take the cables off so as to lighten the *Theresa*. In looking at the vessel is seems as if it would be impossible to make use of her. All her interior is burned out, many of the beams bent and broken, and the superstructure entirely gone. Most of the shot holes have been stopped up. The *Almirante Oquendo* looks more of a wreck than she appeared the last time I saw her.

Friday Aug. 12.
At ten o'clock last night the *Scorpion* arrived from Guantanamo with dispatches for the Admiral. We immediately started out on a course SE by W 1/2 W and steamed at 16-knots all night. We were under the impression when we started that we were going to Manzanillo, Cienfuegos, and the Isle of Pines[30] to notify the vessels there to stop hostilities; but it soon became apparent that we were after some vessel, or rather trying to cut her off. It was rumored that Blanco[31] had escaped from Havana,

---

27 USS *Badger* (side-wheel steamer) was on blockade duty off Cuba.

28 Charles E. Clark (1843–1922) graduated from the U.S. Naval Academy in 1864. He was Chief of Staff, Eastern Squadron, from July to August 1898. Clark served as governor of the Naval Home from 1901 to 1904. He was promoted to rear admiral in 1902.

29 Albert S. Barker (?–1916) graduated from the U.S. Naval Academy in 1863. He retired in 1905.

30 The Isle of Pines is thirty miles southwest of Cuba.

31 Ramón Blanco y Erenas (1833–1906), captain general of Cuba, was not able to pacify the island. With Admiral Cervera under his command, he ordered the sortie out of Santiago, notwithstanding the loss of ships and lives. To Blanco, it was a matter of honor.

and we were trying to cut him off. I had the morning watch from 4 to 8 A.M., and at daylight could see the coast of Cuba on our starboard quarter. Before long Jamaica hove in sight on our port bow. We headed in close to the shore and at ten o'clock sighted a steamer, which, on seeing us after her, immediately ran within the three mile limit, so there was no use keeping after her. We then ran along the Jamaican coast. The island is beautiful, is well cultivated, and appears civilized. The villages and villas looked well kept and prosperous, being in marked contrast with those in Cuba.

About noon we sighted a steamer and immediately started after her. When we were about two miles from her we fired a blank charge, and she hove to immediately. She soon hoisted the signal: "Unless your business is very important I would like to proceed," and she started ahead, but another blank charge brought her to a stop. She was the British steamer *"Acme"* bound for Mobile from the Cape Verde Islands. A boat was lowered, sent to her, and brought her Captain on board the *New York*. After a careful examination of his paper, the *Acme* was allowed to proceed. We then headed for Guantanamo, evidently having failed to catch what we were after.

Towards evening we struck a heavy blow, the sea getting high enough to make it necessary to close the berth deck ports, and consequently making it very uncomfortable below decks.

Saturday Aug. 13.

I got on deck this morning about seven o'clock and found us lying near off the Cuban coast near Guantanamo. Close to us was a large ocean liner flying the Spanish colors. She turned out to be one of the Spanish ships chartered to take the surrendered army back to Spain, and she was allowed to proceed. We anchored in Guantanamo Bay at half past eight. The *Brooklyn, Iowa, Indiana, Massachusetts* and *Oregon,* we and a number of smaller vessels were in the harbor. The Admiral received a telegram from Secretary Long[32] saying to cease all hostilities and for the fleet to come to New York. We made the signal "Be ready to sail at 10 A.M. tomorrow." So I suppose our work in these waters is over.

Sunday Aug. 14.

This morning about half past eight the British Consul and a number of French ladies and gentlemen from Guantanamo paid us a visit. We showed them around the ship. At 9:45 the signal was made to the fleet to get up anchor, and promptly at 10 o'clock we were under way. The crew of the *Badger* cheered each vessel as it passed them, the cheers being returned. The *New York*'s band played the patriotic airs and "A hot time in the old town to-night." The six vessels formed in line in the following order: *New York, Iowa, Indiana, Brooklyn, Massachusetts, Oregon.* We kept along the

---

32 John D. Long (1838–1915) served as Secretary of the Navy from 1897 to 1902. He was responsible for organizing the navy for the Spanish-American War and for planning the naval expansion that followed.

coast during the afternoon, passing several steamers probably bound for Santiago. We passed Cape Maysi and headed North about seven o'clock. Expect to reach New York on Saturday.

Monday Aug. 15
Some of the Bahamas were in sight nearly all day. Passed several steamers. The squadron is a fine sight there being a marked contrast between the way the men-of-war keep their position in line and the way the transports kept their places. At sundown San Salvador was on our port beam. It is not a very prepossessing island as viewed from a distance. Our speed has been about nine knots.

Tuesday Aug 16.
Steamed at 9 knots nearly all day. The *Indiana* broke down once and we had to slow down until she could be repaired. If it was not for the *Indiana* we could steam much faster. The wind and sea are moderate. While playing whist in my room this morning a wave came in the port and flooded the room besides soaking us.

Monday Aug. 17
Formed double column this morning. *Indiana* broke down again, but Admiral Sampson signalled her we would not slow down. Later she caught up to us.

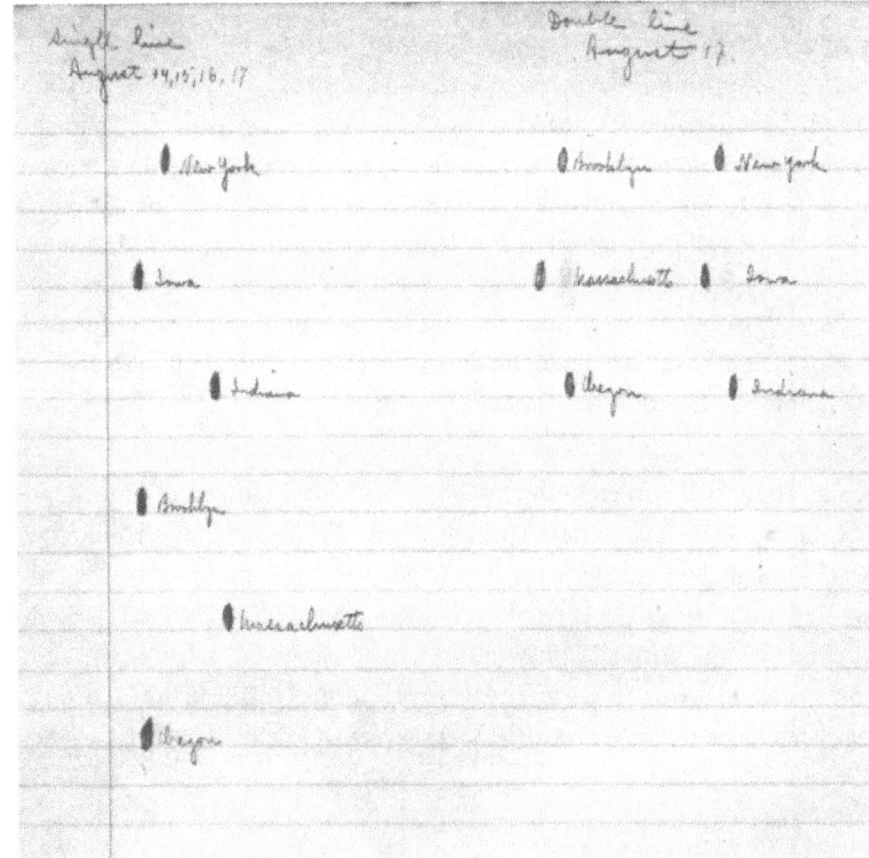

Single- and double-line formations

USS Yorktown

USS San Francisco

Stiletto *firing Howell torpedo*

USS Detroit

USS Dupont

Torpedo boat Cushing

USS Newport

USS Porter

USS Miantonomoh

VII   *Letter to Charles Taussig*   *1898*

Charles Taussig (1881–1949) graduated from Cornell University, where he was a football star. He graduated from Harvard Law School in 1905 and practiced law in New York City.

U.S.S. "New York."
Off Santiago de Cuba,
July 2, 1898

My Dear Charles:

I was very glad to get your letter of June 2nd, which was brought me yesterday by the *Newark,* and delivered just before we bombarded the fort and batteries at a small place called Aguadores just five miles from the entrance to Santiago harbor. The Army advanced towards Santiago, sent a few troops around by Aguadores just to attract attention, and we covered their "Fake" advance.

The Attack on Aguadores.

We were ready to bombard at five o'clock but had to wait five hours for the Army which came from Siboney by train. At ten o'clock the *New York,* the converted yacht *Gloucester,* and the lighthouse tender *Suwanee,* opened fire on the fort and batteries. As soon as we got the range we landed shell after shell into the fortifications. I do not think the Spaniards returned the fire at all but did the disappearing act behind a hill and placed themselves in a railroad gap. The firing from our ships was beautiful, and it was a fine sight to see each shell explode as it struck, the dirt, rocks, etc., being thrown way up in the air. The fort and batteries were completely demolished. The fort, especially, fared badly, parts of it falling down the hill side. When the signal to cease firing was given the flag was still flying but the pole was standing at an angle of sixty degrees, a shell having exploded near its base. The *Suwanee* asked for permission to knock down the flag. The Admiral granted the request provided that they could do it in three shots. The first shot struck at the base of the pole, but it stood still. The second shot apparently struck in the same place and every one expected to see the flag go, but she stood. The third shot went, struck at the base of the pole, and over it went. All the crews cheered, and the officers on board said they never saw three finer shots. The *Suwanee* then reported that the Spaniards had taken position in a railroad cut behind a hill from us. The *Newark,* just arrived from the north a few hours before, asked for permission to fire in the gap for target practice. It was granted and for an hour the four vessels dropped shells into the gap. The *New York* then trained her 8-inch guns at extreme elevation and fired in the direction Santiago was known to be. About fifteen shells were thrown in this way, but, of course, we have no idea where they landed. We stopped firing about half past twelve and went back to our positions before entrance to Santiago.

This morning we were turned out at half past three and at five all the ships started in to bombard the Morro and forts at the entrance to the harbor. We took our position and commenced on the batteries. It was the finest sight I ever saw. From my gun port I could see nearly all the vessels firing and the shells continually falling into the batteries. The Spaniards, as usual, left their batteries and got behind the hills. I don't blame them, though, because if any of them had remained they would certainly have been killed.

Bombardment of Morro and Forts and Santiago Harbor

The enemy left their flag flying and continued firing from some battery behind the hill. This battery could not be seen. I saw several shells drop pretty near us. Lackey, who was stationed in the top, said he counted twenty five shells that dropped in the neighborhood of the ships. I could hear some of them whistle as they went over us and, although, I was below decks I dodged involuntarily every time. Every body does it, although when the whistling sound is heard, the danger is all over. We ceased firing at eight A.M., and I thought it was after twelve. This is the longest day I ever spent. We did not stop firing on the Morro until after her flag was knocked down. The *Oregon* has the honor of doing this. She, together with the *Indiana*, and *Massachusetts* were ordered to go in nearer and after they had filled the Morro full of holes they went in front of the entrance to the harbor and bombarded the inner forts and battery. Tomorrow we expect to countermine the harbor so we can get in. We hear that the Army has advanced to the outskirts of Santiago with great loss.

Sunday, July 3rd, 1898

Sunday seems to be the day for the United States Navy, and we have had a day of it today. We were not turned out early because we did not intend to do anything. At nine o'clock we started for Siboney where the Admiral intended to go on shore and confer with General Shafter. At a quarter to ten we were about ten miles away when we heard firing in the rear. From the bridge came the word: "The Spanish ships are coming out of the harbor!" The call to general quarters was sounded and we were ready for action in a few minutes. But we were ten miles to the eastward and were afraid we would not get in the fight. As we moved along at full speed we could see our ships blazing away and the Spanish vessels returning fire. All the forts and batteries on shore were firing at our ships. The *Gloucester* was in nearest the entrance to the harbor, when the ships started out, and she ran right along with the Spanish Cruisers keeping up her fire for all she was worth. It was evident that the four Spanish Cruisers and two torpedo boat destroyers were trying to escape our fleet by running to the westward. We were now off the entrance to the harbor again. My how slow the *New York* seemed to go! All the forts at the entrance directed their fire at us. *Whir-r-r-r* went the shells over our head every body ducking mechanically. Some of them landed uncomfortably close and many burst in the air very near us. We could now see the torpedo boat destroyers ahead of us, the *Gloucester* tending to them alone, as the other vessels were after the Cruisers. We fired two eight inch shells at them and both hit the mark. One of the destroyers was on fire, the other was run on the beach and deserted. The flags on both were hauled down and the *Gloucester* sent a boat to take possession. The *Gloucester* did more than any other ship in the fleet and deserves a great deal of credit. The *New York* kept going at full speed and soon came along where the *Viscaya* and *Almirante Oquendo* were on the beach, both burning fiercely with white flags flying from their masts. The *Indiana* was ordered to take charge of them and we kept on going. Several men from the Spanish ships were swimming and called out to us. We did not have time to stop for them, but threw life preservers overboard, and had the satisfaction of seeing them get them. The *Ericson*, which was some distance astern, was ordered to pick them up. We could see the *Maria Theresa* a short distance ahead. She was going for all she was worth with several of our ships firing at her. Suddenly she was headed for the beach, flames burst out on her quarter deck, and she showed three white flags. Many of the crew tried to save themselves from the flames by jumping overboard and swimming ashore. Some Cubans on the hills nearby commenced firing on the poor men in the water. This outrage, (for they had surrendered), made the Admiral angry, and he sent a torpedo boat back to tell the Cubans if they did not cease firing at the helpless Spaniards he would have one of our vessels open fire on them (The Cubans).

    The last of the four cruisers, the *Cristobal Colon*, was some distance ahead, with the *Oregon* and *Brooklyn* at her heels, firing at long range. The *Texas* and *New York* were in the chase also, the *New York* gaining rapidly. We were afraid the *Colon* might get away, as she is a fine cruiser, while our ships are all in poor condition, not having been in dry dock for a long time. We saw a 13-inch shell from the *Oregon* drop near her, and the next minute she was headed in for the beach, her colors having been hauled down. In a few minutes we were very near her. She is a beautiful ship, new and neat, was apparently uninjured, we being able to find where only about ten shells struck her. Her bow was high on the beach. The Spaniards now did some of their honorable work. After they surrendered they deliberately ran their ship aground, opened all the sea valves, and threw most of the breech plugs overboard besides destroying many of the effects on the ship. A prize crew from the *New York* and *Oregon* was sent aboard, and the prisoners were taken to the *Resolute*. The

Oregon towed the *Colon* off the beach but she settled rapidly and sank, only her main deck being about two feet out of the water. I hope the vessel can be saved as she is a fine ship. Thus ended Spain's second fleet. They put up a poor fight, acted cowardly after they surrendered, and do not deserve much credit. However, what credit they do deserve is for the bold dash they made out of the harbor. It is supposed it was the only thing left for them to do, and they hoped to escape by running, evidently having little hope of doing much damage in the fighting line. If they had stayed near the forts, they would have done much better. But just think, they had four first class armored cruisers and two torpedo boat destroyers against our four battle ships, the *Iowa, Indiana, Oregon,* and *Texas,* and the cruiser *Brooklyn* together with the Yacht *Gloucester.* Of course we had, by far, the superior force but the *Gloucester* alone handled the two torpedo boat destroyers although she was not armed as heavily as either of them. Then their three cruisers were destroyed in less than half an hour, while the fourth, which escaped under cover of smoke, was captured as soon as we got in striking distance. We simply riddled the first three cruisers with shells, but it is a question whether our shells set them on fire or whether they fired themselves so as not to fall in our hands. And we only had one man killed and two wounded, all on the *Brooklyn*. It seems strange that while we put shot after shot into them, they could only hit our ships a few times. It was a great victory and easily won.

The *New York,* altho' under heavy fire only fired two shots, but we were right there and could see it all. We were not needed. Just think what the *Massachusetts* missed! At half past five this morning she left for Guantanamo for coal. I do not know where the *Newark* was. We have fifteen hundred prisoners on the *Harvard* and *Resolute.* The Commodore, the Captain of the *Cristobal Colon*, and a staff officer are aboard her. Admiral Cervera is on the *Iowa*.

July 4, 1898

We left the *Cristobal Colon* about half past eleven last night. I had the mid-watch, and as we steamed towards Santiago, I could see the remains of the Spanish Fleet still burning. Once in a while there was an explosion and wreckage was thrown way up in the air. This morning the British Cruiser *Blake*,[1] and the Austrian Battle Ship, *Maria Theresa,* arrive here.

The Army has given the city of Santiago twenty four hours to surrender. If they do not lay down their arms then the city will have to be bombarded. We are all well, and feel that the Navy has done her work well, and with an incredible small loss. I would not be surprised but that we were north before long.

With much love to all.
JOE.

NOTES 1 HMS *Blake*, built in 1891, was 375 feet long and carried two nine-inch and ten six-inch guns, sixteen three-pounders, and four torpedo tubes. It had a complement of 590 men.

Part 2: The Philippine Insurrection and the Boxer Rebellion, 1899–1901

VIII   *At Sea in the Caribbean*   1899

March 23, 1899
New York & Tompkinsville

At 10:30 A.M. cast off moorings from the Cobb dock Navy Yard, New York, and were towed out in the stream by the yard tug. Steamed to Tompkinsville where we anchored to await the navy yard tug with the mail for the fleet. After receiving the mail got up anchor and started for Guantanamo Bay where we were to join Admiral Sampson's fleet. During the passage to Guantanamo, Courtney and Tomb[1] stood engine room watches; Johnson,[2] Forman,[3] and I stood the forecastle watches.

March 29, 1899
Guantanamo

Sighted Cape Maysi early in the morning after a pleasant six day trip of fine weather and easy steaming. Coasted along the southern coast of Cuba, and entered Guantanamo Bay about three o'clock in the afternoon. The scene was very different from that of nearly a year before. The converted yacht *Eagle*[4] was the only vessel in the harbor, being there as a station ship. The only signs of life on the shore was the erecting of a light house on the east side of the harbor entrance. We did not drop our anchor, simply giving mail and papers to the Captain of the *Eagle* who came alongside on his dingy. We then turned around and started for Kingston, Jamaica, where we expected to join the fleet.

NOTES
1 William Tomb (1877–1941), U.S. Naval Academy, 1900.
2 Alfred W. Johnson (1876–1963), U.S. Naval Academy, 1899.
3 Charles W. Forman (1876–1939), U.S. Naval Academy, 1899.
4 USS *Eagle* (patrol vessel, converted yacht) was built in 1890 and purchased by the U.S. Navy in 1898. It was assigned to the North Atlantic Blockading Squadron in Cuban waters, where it captured the Spanish merchant ship *Santo Domingo*. It operated as a surveying ship in the Caribbean until decommissioned in 1919.

March 30, 1899

Kingston

Sighted lights at entrance to Kingston Harbor early in the morning. At daylight took a pilot, a negro, on board. We could see the fleet on the other side of the reef so made our number "272." It was answered by the *New York*. Then entering the harbor we were directed by wig-wag signal from the Flagship to anchor ahead of her in the line. A number of signals were exchanged to the effect that we had mail for the fleet, and regarding salutes. We were boarded by a British Warrant Officer who asked the usual boarding questions. Captain Goodrich boarded the *New York* to pay his respects to Admiral Sampson. On the Captain's return we got up anchor and stood out fifteen miles to sea for target practice, it being the next to last day of the quarter. We were very much disappointed as we hoped to see something of the city. The target practice lasted all day, being delayed somewhat by the breaking of the target by a 6-pounder. In the evening we anchored outside the harbor. Johnson, Forman and I were ordered to do signal duty during our cruise with the fleet.

March 31, 1899

En route to La Guayra

As soon as the fleet got under way, we got up our anchor and stood by to take our place. The fleet made a fine appearance a it stood out of the harbor in column. The *New York*, flying Admiral Sampson's flag, led, then the *Brooklyn, Indiana, Texas, Marblehead* and *Detroit* followed in the order named. We were signaled to take position in column astern of the *Texas*, and I think we did it in very good style. The speed of the fleet was nine knots. We are heading for La Guayra, Venezuela.

April 3, 1899

Curacao

Maneuvering nearly all day which meant lots of work for the signal officers. Sighted Curacao in morning and passed close enough to the city of St.—— to distinctly see the people on shore. The city looked very attractive with its yellow houses and red tile roofs. We were very sorry our itinerary did not call for a stop here as Admiral Cervera's fleet coaled here before going to Santiago. I understand that the Dutch government requested that we not stop as the treaty of peace had not been signed.

April 4, 1899

La Guayra & Caracas

We arrived at La Guayra early in the morning and anchored in line well outside, the *Marblehead* and *Detroit* going inside the breakwater. There is no harbor here whatever, the vessels being exposed to northerly winds. Although we were the nearest to the beach we were farthest from the landing, and, as no steam launch was lowered and there was a fresh breeze it was a hard pull to the shore.

La Guayra is an unattractive place of about 10,000 inhabitants. Back of it is La Silla, a mountain 8,600 feet high, and one of the Venezuelan range of Andes. The streets, or rather the street, is crooked, narrow, dirty, and lined with unattractive residents, and poorly furnished stores. Indian and Spanish blood, mixed, predominates. Above the city on the rocks are several old forts which are said to have seen exciting times. It is very hot in spite of the strong easterly breeze. Recently a very serviceable breakwater has been built which affords good protection to average sized vessels. The *Philadelphia*[5] of the Red D line was in port during our stay. The anchorage is bad not only on account of lack of protection, but the water is deep and the bottom is a poor holding ground. The Venezuelan Navy consisting of several small and dirty gunboats, was assembled inside the breakwater.

A narrow gauge railway connects La Guayra with Caracas, a distance of about 30 miles, although there is a trail over the mountain only 9 miles long. The railroad was built and is owned by English capital.

As soon as *pratique* was granted, a signal from the flagship said that communication with the shore was in order. I received permission to go ashore and went with a number of officers in the first available boat. On shore we met many officers from the other vessels of the fleet and all boarded the train for Caracas as there was nothing of interest at La Guayra. The trip up the mountains is said to be one of the most beautiful in the world. The train passes through groves of palms through which a stream runs from the mountains to the sea. Along the banks of the stream are hundreds of women washing clothes. When the assent begins the train winds around in a most marvelous manner, there being few straight stretches 300 yards long in the whole thirty miles. At times, at first, a fine view of the ocean is seen far below; and then the valleys with their luxurious vegetation and little goat farms form the chief attraction. There are places where three and four tiers of the track can be seen at once. The train passes though a number of short tunnels. The average ascent is 197 feet to the mile, and the highest altitude is about 3,000 feet. The trip took about two and a half hours. My impressions on arriving at the station in Caracas were not favorable, on account of the poor condition of the people and of their houses in the neighborhood. However, like most of our cities at home, the poorest part was near the station. We got into a carriage and drove to the Gran Hotel de Venezuela, where several of us occupied a room on the fourth floor. The Hotel had a large central court around which, for each floor, was a balcony upon which the rooms opened. Several of us took a walk around the city which appeared clean and well kept. There are several nice parks, or rather plazas, as they are called. The Administration

---

5 *Philadelphia* was a ship of the Atlantic and Caribbean Steam Navigation Company, known as the "Red D Line." Founded in 1881, it operated passenger service between New York and Venezuela. The two-thousand-ton *Philadelphia* was built in 1885 and scrapped in 1925.

building, opera house, theatre, and medical university are imposing but rather cheap looking buildings. The narrow gauge trains are pulled by two small horses. In the evening several of us went to the "Teatro Caracas" where comic opera was in session. I could not understand enough Spanish to see the funny part of it and fell asleep in the second act, so left at the end of it. There is a law at Caracas (due to the revolutionary spirit of the inhabitants) that all stores, houses, etc. must be closed at 11 P.M. Even the street cars and carriages are not allowed to run after this hour. The residences are built with the central court, are low, and cover a great deal of ground.

April 5, 1899
At La Guayra

Turned out early to catch the train for La Guayra. The descent took about the same time as the ascent it being necessary to go slow on account of the curves. At the half way station we passed the up going train which was occupied nearly entirely by officers from the fleet. On arriving on board ship I took the boat duty and made several trips to the landing. The first trip, I made sail and attempted to beat in against a fresh breeze, but had to give it up at the end of half an hour. It was quick work sailing back. In the evening a signal was made to the effect that President Andrade[6] would give a ball to the Officers of the fleet the next evening, and that Admiral Sampson desired as many officers as possible to attend. So I received orders to go to Caracas the next morning.

April 6, 1899
Ball at Caracas

Left for Caracas in the morning, carrying my dress suit case with Evening dress uniform. As I wasn't favorably impressed with the Gran Hotel de Venezuela, went to the Hotel Klindt instead and found it much more satisfactory. In the evening Courtney, Johnson and I walked to the Union Club where the ball was given. We were received by President Andrade and Admiral Sampson. The ball was a grand affair, all the elite of Caracas being there. The gay dresses of the women and the uniforms of the officers made an attractive appearance. I only danced once and had a pretty hard time of it as the girls dance very differently from those at home. They hop instead of glide. Johnson, being able to speak Spanish well, had a fine time. In the enclosed garden adjoining, supper was served. I left at 2 A.M. and returned to the hotel.

April 7, 1899
La Guayra

Two trains left for La Guayra in the morning—the first being the regular one, and the second a special one with President Andrade and Admiral Sampson. The

---

6 Ignacio Andrade was president of Venezuela, 1898–99.

President was on his way to visit the fleet. Along the railroad at intervals of from three to five miles squads of soldiers were drawn up, and as the Presidential train passed they were brought to "present arms." All the shipping at La Guayra was decorated with flags. When President Andrade boarded the *New York,* every vessel in the fleet saluted him with 21 guns.

In the evening the fleet weighed anchor and headed to the eastward, bound for Trinidad. Tomb was detached from the *Newark* and ordered to the *Alliance*[7] which was expected any time.

April 8, 1899
En route to Trinidad
Passed the *Alliance* about 11 P.M. She exchanged signals with the flagship. Maneuvered most of the day changing from line to column and vice-versa, and forming double column from single, etc. At times the maneuvers were very fine, but the position pennant was hoisted under every ships distinguishing pennant at times.

April 9, 1899
Port of Spain, Trinidad
Passed through the *Boca* ———[8] shortly before sun-set, and about dusk anchored off Port of Spain about 3 1/2 miles from the landing. The *Marietta*[9] was at anchor close in to the shore.

April 10, 1899
Port of Spain
I went ashore to take a look around the city and found it a very attractive place. The streets are wide and scrupulously clean—a class of birds resembling the buzzard, but smaller, being used as scavengers. I drove around and saw the Queen's Park, and stopped for a while at the Queen's Park Hotel. I then drove out to the Coolie Village which is a few miles from the city. The Coolies appear very comfortable in their native costumes. They were generally engaged in making rings and bracelets of silver which they sold to visitors. I bought a ring of four silver links which could be put together to make a fancy design. I took it apart and haven't been able to put it together again. The people here are very anxious to see a game of base-ball as it has never been played on the island. A team from the *Newark* is going to play a picked team from the rest of the fleet, at the cricket grounds.

---

7 USS *Alliance* (screw gunboat) was an apprentice training ship, 1895–1903.

8 *La Boca,* known as "the serpent's mouth," was the body of water between Trinidad and Venezuela.

9 USS *Marietta* (patrol gunboat) served with the Asiatic Squadron supporting American forces during the Philippine Insurrection, 1899–1901.

April 11, 1899
The Fleet plays base-ball at Port of Spain, Trinidad

Went ashore in the morning and took a carriage to the cricket grounds. Here two men were placed at my disposal and we set to work to mark out a base ball field. About noon everything was ready for the game. The teams came ashore early in the afternoon and started in for preliminary practice while the crowd gathered. A brass band was in attendance and this enlivened things very much. As the game was being played I explained the different points to a couple of newspaper men. They said base ball "is not so good as cricket." However they were very much impressed with it. The audience was particularly pleased when a fielder caught a fly, when a long hit was made or when a man stole a base.

April 11
Port of Spain, Trinidad—Ball Given to Officers of the Fleet

The accounts of the base ball game in the papers were very amusing. One paper said it appeared to be a "combination of rounders and prisoners' base." The people of Port of Spain invited Admiral Sampson and his Officers to a ball. So I was ordered to attend. The ball was very fine but not on such a grand scale as at Caracas. The people did not know how to dance the *deux*-tempo at all, and could not dance the waltz according to the American idea of how it should be done. I danced just once. A very elaborate supper was served about mid night. The Officers from the *Newark* left shortly before one o'clock as we expected a boat at that hour. When we reach the wharf the boat had just left with the Navigator who had been out for a bicycle ride. We had to wait nearly an hour before it returned.

April 12, 1899
Port of Spain, Trinidad—Ball given by Fleet to City

In the afternoon the Officers of the fleet gave a ball on the *New York*, to the people of Port of Spain. Every steam launch in the fleet, each towing a cutter, was sent into the wharf to bring the people off. I was in charge of one of our steam launches, and took a load of people to the Flagship, which was handsomely decorated with bunting, and crowded with people. The dance was very successful and I think all the people went home with a good impression of the American Navy shortly after the last visitor left the *New York*, the signal "up anchor" was made and in a few minutes we were on our way to Barbados.

April 13, 1899
Barbados

The fleet arrived at Bridgetown after dark and had some difficulty in getting anchored owing to the various depths of the water. I was kept busy at the signals. We anchored in a good berth about two hundred yards from the *New York*.

April 14, 1899
Bridgetown

Barbados is a fertile looking island and appeared more cultivated than the other places we had been. The harbor is open and affords a good anchorage for many ships. The Britannic Majesty's ship *"Pallas"* and *"Indefatigable"*[10] were at anchor close to the shore. In the morning Courtney and I went ashore. Here, as at Trinidad, the good results of British colonization were evident. The people appeared happy; the city was clean and well taken care of. The roads were very smooth and hard. We hired a couple of bicycles and rode outside the town into the country. In passing a school house we dismounted and looked into the window. The room was full of young colored boys and girls all very busy with their lessons. The teacher was a negro also. We explained that we were from the American fleet and would like to see the school so he invited us in. On entering every child stood up, saluted, and said in unison, "Good morning, Sirs." We examined their writing, problems, etc., and they were really very good showing a proper stage of advancement. When we left, the same courtesy was shown us as when we entered. The riding was very enjoyable, and we had an exciting time coasting down a hill with a sharp turn in it almost running down several pedestrians and vehicles on the way. Naval Cadet Boone '98[11] reported on board for duty. He came from the *Marblehead*.

April 15, 1899
Bridgetown, Barbados

H.M.S. *Proserpine*[12] came in during the morning. We all admired the seamanlike way in which she anchored in her berth. The Governor, Lord Hay, and his wife sent out cards for a lawn fete to be given in the afternoon. I was on duty so could not go.

April 16, 1899
En route to Port Castries, Saint Lucia

The *Newark* had orders to proceed to Valparaiso, Chile, so the Admiral ordered us to go to Port Castries, St. Lucia, in company with the *Texas* and *Marblehead*, for coal. We left late in the afternoon getting under way, and forming column according to signals from the *Texas*, Capt. Sigsbee.[13] The *Newark*'s station was between the other two ships. The rest of the fleet was expected to leave for St. Lucia the next day.

---

10 HMS *Indefatigable*, a second-class cruiser, was launched in 1891.

11 Charles Boone (?–1955), U.S. Naval Academy, 1898.

12 HMS *Prosperine* was a *Pelorus*-class light cruiser.

13 Charles D. Sigsbee (1845–1923) graduated from the U.S. Naval Academy in 1864. He was hydrographer in the Bureau of Navigation, 1893–97. He was commanding officer of the USS *Maine* in 1898. Promoted to rear admiral in 1903, he served as Commander, South Atlantic Squadron, from 1904 to 1905.

April 17, 1899
Port Castries, Saint Lucia

We arrived off the little harbor of Port Castries at day break, were given *pratique* immediately, and ran in, the *Texas* and *Marblehead* waiting at the entrance to the bay. We passed the Dutch Cruiser *Leeland*[14] anchored in the bay. Her band played "The Star Spangled Banner" as we passed. Captain Goodrich took the *Newark* alongside the wharf as if she were a launch. In a few minutes we were ready to receive coal on board. The wharf held several large piles of coal amounting in all to something over 30,000 tons. The coaling was done by hundreds of colored women who carried the baskets on their heads and deposited the contents into the chutes. They were paid by the number of baskets they deposited, receiving a chip for each one. The women appeared almost savage. Their clothes were very dirty, the dress being held up as high as the knee by a cord around the hips. They were all very muscular as might be expected. We were overrun with wash women who were a marked contrast to the coaling women. The former were very neat and clean looking in their freshly washed dresses.

The *Marblehead* went along side also and commenced coaling. The *Texas* moored to buoys in the stream.

In the evening the *Massachusetts* anchored at the harbor entrance. The last time I saw her she was in dry dock at the Brooklyn Navy Yard. She came direct from New York.

April 18, 1899
Port Castries

Coaled and took on water during the morning. The *New York*, *Brooklyn*, and *Indiana* arrived, anchoring in the bay. We had to stop coaling before our bunkers were full in order to make room for the *New York*. Hauled out in the stream. Cleaned ship in order to be ready for Admiral's inspection in the morning.

April 19, 1899
Port Castries—Admiral's Inspection

The Admiral's inspection commenced in the fore room. Admiral Sampson, Captain Chadwick, Lieut. Staunton, and Naval Cadet Perrill[15] came onboard and inspected the ship and crew. Divisional drills were held, and afterwards, fire, collision, and abandon ship drills. The Admiral said he was very much pleased.

---

14 *Zeeland* was a 3,900-ton ship with a length of 294 feet, a beam of forty-eight feet, and a draft nearly eighteen feet.

15 Harlan P. Perrill (1874–1962), U.S. Naval Academy, 1897.

April 20, 1899
Port Castries—Admiral's Inspection

Cleared ship for action during the early morning. Admiral and staff came on board about nine. Went to general quarters and had great gun drill. In afternoon armed and called away boats which were inspected. Naval Cadet Elson '98[16] was detached from the *Massachusetts* and ordered to the *Newark* without any warning. We had orders to sail for Valparaiso. About 9 P.M. asked permission by signals to get under way and carry out orders. Steamed out of the harbor and stopped near the *Massachusetts* until Naval Cadet Elson and his effects were brought on board. Headed south east expecting to make Montevideo with coaling.

April 21, 1899
En route to Rio Janeiro

Passed within a few miles of Barbados in the morning. Could see Bridgetown distinctly. Boone, Johnson and I were ordered to stand the regular deck watch from 8 A.M. to 6 P.M. In addition we were to work the regular day's work in Navigation every day, and keep up our journals. Elson, Courtney, and Forman were to stand the engine room watches.

April 27, 1899
En route to Rio Janeiro

Have had very pleasant weather during the past week. Nothing out of the ordinary has happened. We expect to cross the Equator tomorrow A.M. This afternoon I was subpoenaed to appear before the Court of Neptune in order to be made one of his loyal subjects. Every body on the ship who had not crossed the line were ordered to appear also.

April 28, 1899
Crossed the Equator—Neptune's Court

We crossed the equator about 8 A.M. The official time of crossing was 1 P.M. The crew was called to quarters and shortly afterwards from under the forecastle came the cry: "Ship Ahoy! What Ship is that?" Mr. Cutler answered: "This is the U.S.S. *Newark*," where upon Neptune, Amphitrite, and Triton seated on a chariot drawn by six dolphins appeared. Following was Neptune's court comprising nymphs, mermaids, etc, and a gang of policemen who were to round up those called before the court. Neptune had beautiful flaxen curls and a silver trident. All the costumes were very ludicrous, paint of all colors having been freely used. Neptune returned each division's salute with pompous dignity. When the quarterdeck was reached the contingent halted, and Neptune descended from his chariot and addressed the Captain in a little speech. The Captain then said a few words of welcome, after

---

16 Herman J. Elson (?–1953), U.S. Naval Academy, 1898.

which his boy appeared with three glasses of champagne on a waiter. The Captain proposed the health of Neptune and his beautiful spouse, Amphitrite. Neptune and Amphitrite each took a glass, and Triton grabbed for the third, but was prevented from taking it by the Captain saying: "No more for the child." So the Captain took the third glass, and the toast was drunk. Triton watched it with a very long face.

Neptune and his court then went forward on the forecastle where the court was held. Under the break of the forecastle a large sail was rigged as a tank. This was filled and kept full by a steady stream of salt water. The court having met, "Tarpot," the Secretary called the name of the first culprit, whom the police brought forward immediately. He was placed in a chair and his face smeared with a mixture of lamp black and grease. He was then placed in the barber's chair, where the lather, comprising a mixture of molasses, oil, flour, slush and salt water, was roughly applied with a large paint brush. The culprit was asked a question and when he opened his mouth to answer, the paint brush was shoved in. He was then carefully shaved with a large wooden razor about two feet long. Four nymphs picked him up and threw him bodily into the tank below where he was pounced upon by the dolphins who ducked him until they considered him a loyal son of Neptune. This process was followed with each "land lubber," the more they objected the worse they were treated. After the court finished with the crew the officers were ordered to appear. We told Neptune that we did not desire to be shaved, but were willing to pay a fine instead. He said we could buy ourselves free with six bottles of beer apiece. We all agreed.

IX South America

1899

April 29, 1899

Passed Cape St. Roque in the morning. Have been in sight of land all day.

May 5, 1899

Rio Janeiro, Brazil, Brazilian Men of War, Coaling

Passed Cape Frio early in the morning. Skirted along the coast until early in afternoon when we entered the fine Harbor of Rio Janeiro. The "Sugar Loaf" at the entrance to the harbor is a magnificent rock. As we passed the fort in mid channel we fired a salute of 21 guns with the Brazilian flag at the main. We dropped anchor in the midst of the Brazilian fleet, and saluted the Brazilian Vice Admiral with 15 guns. There were two other flag officers in the fleet which comprised the *Aquidiban,*[1] *Riecluslo,*[2] *Borazas,*[3] and *Tupy.*[4] The two former played conspicuous parts in the Brazilian war of the Revolution, the *Aquidiban* having been sunk by a torpedo. The *Riecluslo* resembles the old *Maine.* The *Borazas* is a sister ship to our *New Orleans.*[5] The *Tupy* is a torpedo boat destroyer. Fearing contagion from the fevers ashore, the Captain decided that we should hold no communication with the city whatever. Orders were given to disinfect everything that touched the harbor water, as it was though by doing this we should not be placed in quarantine when we reached Montevideo. I was very sorry not to go ashore as the city from the harbor is the most picturesque place I ever saw. We started coaling from lighters alongside within an hour after we anchored. The coal was passed in through the coal ports by the natives and taken on the inside by our men.

NOTES 1 *Aquidaban,* a two-turret battleship, was built in Stettin. It was 241 feet long, had a displacement of 3,566 tons, and a crew of 440 men.

2 *Riachuelo,* a two-turret battleship, was launched in 1883. It had a displacement of 5,900 tons and a crew of 390 men.

3 *Barrozo,* a cruiser, built in 1896 at Elswick, had a displacement of 3,450 tons and carried a crew of three hundred men.

4 *Tupy,* a torpedo cruiser, was built in Kiel in 1896. It was 259 feet long.

5 *New Orleans* was originally built for the Brazilian navy as the *Amazonas.* It was purchased by the U.S. Navy in March 1898.

May 6, 1899
Coaling

Coaled all night and all the day until about five P.M. A fresh breeze was blowing causing the coal dust to scatter over everything and make the ship very dirty. For a short time during the afternoon the Organ Mountains were in plain sight. At 6. P.M. we got up anchor and left the harbor for Montevideo. The anchor chain, and anchor were disinfected with a bichloride solution.

May 10, 1899
Montevideo, Uruguay

Our run has been uneventful. This morning we entered the Rio de la Plata. Passed a number of sailing vessels and steamers en route to and from Buenos Ayres and Montevideo. On account of the shallow water near Montevideo we anchored several miles from the landing, after sunset.

May 11, 1899
Flores Island—Quarantine

Saluted the fort at 8 A.M. afterwards saluted the British Commodore on the *Flora*.[6] The health authorities refused us *practique* in spite of our precautions at Rio de Janiero. We had to go to the quarantine station on Flores Island, about 18 miles from the city. I went in the steam launch arriving shortly in advance of the ship. There were several merchant steamers ahead of us so we had to wait our turn.

May 12, 1899
Flores Island—Disinfection of Ship

This morning all the officers' soiled clothes and the men's hammocks were sent ashore to be disinfected. The clothes and hammocks were towed ashore in cutters, thrown on the landing, placed in hand cars, and shoved to the disinfecting room. Here they were placed in large vats and steamed for about half an hour. The process was very slow taking nearly all day. In the evening we returned to Montevideo.

May 13, 1899
Montevideo

We lay at anchor in the stream waiting for *practique* which was granted in the evening. Mr. Battini has been supplying us with fresh provisions since we have been in quarantine.

May 14, 1899
Montevideo—Sunday

I went ashore with several officers in the morning. Walked around the city for a while and was impressed with the broad, well paved streets, and good sidewalks. This is the best city we have been in since we left the United States. In the afternoon

---

6 HMS *Flora*, an *Astraea*-class light cruiser.

Courtney and I took a drive around the city. We stopped for a while to watch the football (association) game between the local athletic club and the sailors from the British man-of-war in the harbor. The latter won the game. We then went to the Prada, the large park of the city. Here the band was playing, and refreshments cold be obtained. There were a great many fashionable turnouts, with fine horses and stylish liveries, around the city. The people, in fact, put on a great deal of style. I did not think much of the beauty of the women. They are too stout and use too much paint and powder. The great number of lottery tickets on the market was very noticeable.

May 15, 1899

Official Calls at Montevideo

This afternoon I went ashore with the Captain as his aide. At the wharf a fine carriage was awaiting us. We called on the American Minister, Mr. Buchanan,[7] of Iowa, the American Consul Colonel Schawburn, the Minister of Marine and the Captain of the Port. While at the Minister of Marine's office we saw a regiment of Uruguayan troops pass. They looked and marched very well. Coaling ship from lighters alongside.

May 16, 1899

Coaled ship all day.

May 17, 1899

Coaled ship during night and this morning. Cleaned ship's side when through coaling. Late in the afternoon we left for Valparaiso.

May 21, 1899

En route to Valparaiso

Expect to enter the Straits of Magellan tomorrow morning. The weather has been very pleasant since leaving Montevideo. In addition to the day's work in Navigation we had to take sights of stars for Lat. and Long. every evening. The intersection of the two lines was plotted on a mercator's chart.

May 22, 1899

Straights of Magellan—Possession Bay, Patagonia

Sighted Cape Virgins early in the morning. A Chilean man-of-war was lying at anchor near the light house. We did not pass close enough to recognize it. Anchored in Possession Bay about four miles from the beach. The Captain and several officers, I among them, were rowed ashore in a cutter. It was a long pull taking something over an hour. Those who had shot guns carried them, the rest carried revolvers. We

---

7 William I. Buchanan (1853–1909) was envoy extraordinary and minister plenipotentiary to the Argentine Republic, 1894–1900, where he was an arbiter in the boundary dispute between Chile and Argentina at Puna de Atacama. He served as director of the Pan American Exposition in Buffalo, New York, in 1900 and was the first minister to the Republic of Panama.

passed a number of ducks-divers on the way in, but did not shoot at any of them. We landed on a wide, gently sloping beach on which was a corrugated tin house, evidently a stone house belonging to the large ranch on which we were. The land is apparently used as a pasture, but the grass is dry now, it being the fall of the year. A narrow strip along the coast to the top of a ridge of low hills about 400 yards inland belongs to Chile. On the other side of the hill (and we walked over) is Patagonia. We saw a herd of horses belonging to the ranch. Boone saw a fox, but did not get a chance to shoot at it. The Captain shot the only bird—a flicker, I think. In the pull back to the ship the Officers took a hand at the oars.

May 23, 1899

The Narrows—Mt. Sarmiento—Cape Froward—Fortesque Bay

We got under way early in order to get the benefit of the tide. The Captain gave orders to make all the speed possible without using force draught. Our speed at the fastest was fifteen knots, but we covered 22 knots one hour with the aid of the current when passing through the Second Narrows. We were very fortunate in having a clear day—a rare occasion in the straits—so that when we entered the long reach stretching to the southward we could see the snow covered peaks of the mountains at the southern extremity, 100 miles away. At noon we passed Sandy Point (Punta Arenas), the southernmost point in South America. As it promised to be a clear, moonlight night the Captain decided not to stop but to make Fortesque Bay if possible. We had a fine view of Mt. Sarmiento shortly before sunset. We rounded Cape Froward at dusk, our southernmost latitude being 53 [degrees] 53' and about 53". With the moon shining it was sufficiently light for safe navigation so we steamed until 9 P.M. when we anchored in Fortesque Bay.

May 24, 1899

Snow—Cape Crosstide—Glaciers—Port Cherucca

Got underway early. It rained and snowed at intervals during the morning, but cleared during the afternoon. In rounding Cape Crosstide—the dividing line between the Atlantic and Pacific Oceans—noticed a great many seals and birds.

We passed Field's anchorage and had a fine view of the glacier there. Saw several other glaciers during the day. About two o'clock we steamed in the narrow entrance to Port Cherucca and anchored in the Bay. This is the most remarkable anchorage I ever saw. The entrance appears to be impassable from a short distance and it looked as if we were going to run into the side of a mountain. The mountains rise nearly perpendicularly from the waters edge from 2000 to 3000 feet high. They completely surround the bay. The bases of the mountains are covered with thick moss and plants of stunted growth; above this is a wide zone of bare rock, and above this the snow covered peaks. On one of the mountains is a fine glacier. It looked from the ship as if we would not have room to swing without touching the shore, but when we landed, which all hands did, we saw that there was room for twenty ships, the *Newark* appearing very small in the center of the bay. There were a great many ducks and geese flying about, so we amused ourselves shooting *at* them with revolvers. We left a sign here with: "U.S.S. *Newark*, May 24, 1899" painted on it. There were a number of signs about, left by other vessels.

May 25, 1899
Smyth's Channel—Isthmus Bay
We left Port Cherucca about sunrise and steamed across the western entrance to the straights to Smyth Channel. The wind blew half a gale and it rained very hard all morning. The clouds hung low shutting off many of the finest views. It partially cleared in the afternoon. At 3:00 we anchored in Isthmus Bay and all hands were allowed to go ashore. The U.S.S. *Newark* sign board was nailed to a tree. I had the watch so did not go ashore.

May 26, 1899
Smyth Channel—Puerto Bueno
We got under way early, as usual. During the day we passed through some very narrow channels. It rained and blew hard all day. At 5:30 we anchored at Puerto Bueno. It was too dark to see what the place was like. We have not seen any natives yet.

May 27, 1899
Cockle Cove, Pilot Island
We made Cockle Cove, Pilot Island in the evening. The Captain intends to leave the straits tomorrow morning via the Gulf of Trinidad. It is blowing and raining hard.

May 28, 1899
Bad weather
The weather was too stormy for us to leave the anchorage in the morning. It quieted down some what in the afternoon so we got up anchor and headed out to sea about three o'clock. We ran into a long, low, swell that caused us to roll considerably.

May 29, 1899
Shortage of coal—Albatross, Pigeons, etc.
It was discovered today that instead of having 293 tons of coal on board, as was thought, there was a deficiency of 220 tons, leaving only 73 tons. This was not nearly enough to take us to Talquanho, so the Captain decided to make for Ancud, on the northern end of Chiloe Island. It has been blowing about 7 during the day and night, making a rough head sea for us. We are being followed by hundreds of cape pigeons, albatross, and molly hawks. They fly very close to the ship and seem very inquisitive.

May 30, 1899

We had over a knot current against us during the last 24 hours, so we will not be able to make Ancud. The Captain has decided to go to Port Low where the sailing directions say is a good anchorage. The strong wind from the northward continues.

May 31, 1899

Port Low, Guaicanec Island

Anchored in Port Low during the morning. This is a good harbor, shut off in all direction from the wind. The shores are thickly wooded. A few Indians live ashore in a thatched hut. There are no other people here. The Captain intends to start the crew to work chopping wood tomorrow morning. We should be able to leave here in about a week.

June 1, 1899

Port Low, Chile

All the deck force went ashore this morning to chop wood. Three of the watch officers went along, the fourth taking the day's duty. The cadets doing deck duty are to take turns as boat officer in the steam launch to tow the wood to the ship. The other two are to have charge of the unloading and stowing on the berth deck. We are to stand a heel and toe watch at night. The dynamos are shut down as we have no fires except in the galley. The ship is very cold, so we make stoves with candles, but they make so much smoke it is disagreeable. The lamps do not burn properly as it is too cold for the oil to run easily. As the wood is cut ashore, it is piled up by the cord on the beach. We brought more of it onboard to-day.

June 9, 1899

Chopping Wood—Preparations for Boat Expedition to Ancud—Natives

The wood chopping has continued during the past week. As fast as it was cut it was loaded in the ship's boats and towed alongside where it was discharged and stowed in the bunkers. The whole ship's force has worked very hard, a great deal of it being done in the rain. The ship has been very cold at night. We have given up using lamps and use candles all together. We got all the wood—122 cords—on board yesterday, and lit fires. Up to now we have not been able to get enough steam to start the auxiliaries. Yesterday, when it was found doubtful if the wood would burn, a boat expedition was planned to go to Ancud and Quellón for coal and provisions. Both steam launches, one cutter and the wherry were to be taken. Lieut. Cutler[8] and Ensign Day[9] were to go to Ancud; Lieut. Bryan[10] and Boatswain

---

8 William G. Cutler (?–1920), U.S. Naval Academy, 1875, retired with the rank of captain.

9 George C. Day (1871–1935), U.S. Naval Academy, 1892, retired with the rank of rear admiral.

10 Henry Bryan (1865–1919), U.S. Naval Academy, 1887, was promoted to rear admiral in retirement.

Moncrief[11] were to accompany them across the open stretch (about 30 miles) between Guaicanec and Chiloe. Both launches were taken in case of a break down to either one. The cutter carried extra coal, and sea stores to trade at Quellón with the natives for fresh provisions. The distance to Ancud is about 140 miles; to Quellón about 60 miles. The intention was to telegraph from Ancud for coal to be sent us in a collier. The bad weather during the last two days has prevented the expedition from starting. The natives in the vicinity have learned of our whereabouts and have been bringing us fish, potatoes, and ducks.

June 11, 1899
Bad weather

The weather yesterday again prevented the expedition from starting. However, to-day they got off, the steam launches in tandem towing the cutter with the wherry in it.

June 18, 1899
Target Practice—Fresh Water

During the past week we have been having small arm target practice. Today we had great guns practice using some rocks for a target. We have had several hunting and clamming parties the results always being good. There is fresh water on the island near the beach so we bring a sailing launch full to the ship every day. Mr. Bryan and Boatswain Moncrief returned in the 2d steam launch with the cutter in tow. The abundance of fresh provisions at Quellón according to the sailing directions was not to be found, so that part of the expedition was not very successful.

June 19, 1899
Collier—Pisagua Arrives—coaling

This afternoon the Chilean Collier *Pisagua* arrived from Ancud. Mr. Cutler and Mr. Day returned on her, having left the steam launch at Ancud. Mr. Cutler tried to get coal by telegraphing to Lota and Conception but he received no answer to his messages, so he had to accept the offer made by the Chilean government and take the coal on the *Pisagua*. The *Pisagua* came alongside and we commenced coaling immediately. The coal was bagged so we hoisted it on board with whips and tackles.

June 20, 1899
Coaling at Port Low

Coaled all night and until 3 P.M. today. On Observation Island, a small rock near where we were anchored, we erected a large sign board with U.S.S. *Newark* and the dates of our stay, painted on it. At 3:30 we got underway for Ancud.

---

11 George B. Moncrief was acting boatswain in USS *Newark* in 1898. He was appointed from the state of Virginia and had seven months' sea service in May 1898.

June 21, 1899
Ancud, Chile
At 8:30 A.M. we anchored in Ancud Bay and commenced coaling from lighters immediately. We did not get a chance to see any thing of Ancud. The old Chilean ship *Pilcomayo*[12] was at anchor in the Bay. About four o'clock we left for Valparaiso.

June 24, 1899
En route to Valparaiso—Mooring in Valparaiso Harbor—Rain
We have had a rough passage. Last night it was almost impossible to remain in our bunks on account of the rolling of the ship. We rounded Reef-topsail Point about half past nine. The French Gunboat *Papin* entered the harbor the same time we did. A heavy swell was running due to the recent heavy winds. We made fast temporarily to one of the numerous mooring buoys. The Captain of the Port came on board and assigned us a berth nearer the shore. We moored according to the harbor regulations. When about 30 yards from the buoy we dropped our port anchor passing the buoy on our port hand. We swung around with port helm veering chain to 90 fathoms. A hawser was taken to the buoy and a second hawser was taken to the buoy and a second hawser to a buoy astern. The ship was then warped ahead until the bow touched the buoy when the chain cable was shackled on. A small chain was made fast to the buoy astern. During the afternoon and evening it rained very hard. The heavy swell—to which the mole was exposed—made landing in a boat very uncomfortable.

June 26, 1899
Tallying Coal—Coaling
I went ashore to tally coal as it was put into lighters. My orders were to see the coal weighed. Mr. Lyon, the agent took me to Viña del Mar where the coal was stored. I found that they had no scales, simply shoveling the coal in cars that were supposed to hold four tons each. I returned to the ship. The lighters commenced coming alongside during the afternoon. The natives coaled, but worked very slow. The stevedores appeared to have no control over the men under them.

    A great many of Johnson's relatives live here, so they and their friends have been visiting the ship. Nearly every body here speaks English, more or less. There is a large English colony, but comparatively few Americans.

June 27, 1899
Valparaiso, Chile
I went ashore this afternoon and walked around the lower part of the city as best I could—not succeeding very well on account of the muddy conditions of the streets. The recent hard rains have caused the mud from the upper part of the city to wash

---

12 *Pilcomayo* was a six-hundred-ton ship built in 1864.

down the hills making the streets below impassable. The doors in the houses at the foot of the hills were all barricaded to keep out the mud and waster. However, gangs of men were clearing the streets as much as possible. I returned to the ship before dark.

July 3, 1899
Valparaiso, Chile

During the past week we have been trying to get our coal on board, but feast days, rain, and laziness on the part of the men coaling, have prevented us from getting on more than 50 tons a day. To day, I went to the French Gunboat to take the Captain's Compliments and invite them to dress ship, and fire a salute at noon tomorrow. The Capt. of the *Papin* said he would dress ship, but not having any saluting guns was sorry he could not fire a salute. It has been raining a great deal, but until to day the wind has been very moderate.

July 4, 1899
Dressed Ship

At sun rise we dressed ship rainbow fashion. The *Papin* and a British ship dressed also. At noon we and the batteries onshore fired a salute of 21 guns. The wind has been blowing fresh all day making the harbor very rough. The nasty weather since we have been here has not made our stay very pleasant, and has prevented our seeing the good parts of the city.

July 6, 1899
En route to Coquimbo, Chile

We left at 11 A.M. for Coquimbo. Our orders are to go to Callao, stopping at intermediate ports if desired. I think the captain intends topping at several places before reaching Callao.

July 7, 1899
Coquimbo, Chile

We anchored in Coquimbo harbor at one o'clock. The Chilian reserve squadron comprising the cruiser *Blanca Enclada*,[13] the second class battleship *Almirante Cochrane*,[14] the torpedo boat destroyer *Almirante Simpson*,[15] and two small torpedo boats, are here. This is the best harbor in Chile, so that Coquimbo bids fair to be a large city some day, i.e., as soon as the railroad connecting it with Santiago is finished. The city is built on the side of an immense rock that forms one side of the harbor. There is no vegetation whatever on the rock, giving the city a very desolate

---

13 *Blanca Enclada*, a cruiser, was built in 1893, displaced 4,400 tons, and was 370 feet long.

14 *Almirante Cochrane*, a battleship, fought in the War of the Pacific against Peru and Bolivia, where it captured the Peruvian ironclad *Huascar*.

15 *Almirante Simpson*, a destroyer, was built in 1896 at Birkenhead. An eight-hundred-ton ship, it was 240 feet long.

appearance. There is a good boat landing. As yet there are no piers for vessels to load and unload from, but one is in contemplation.

The houses are mostly small and low. Mr. Kerr, the American Consul, has the best house and store in the city. It is three stories high and very nicely finished and furnished. There is an English Club, to which the few Americans here belong. There is the usual plaza in the center of the city. The people appear, in general, to be poor, but contented. Our exchange here, as at Valparaiso is about 3 for 1, but prices are more than correspondingly high. The Chile line and P.M.S. line vessels stop here regularly. Also, the merchant steamers of the Kosmos line, and W. R. Grace & Co's steamers. The chief export is copper. The *Newark* is the first American man-of-war that has stopped here for many years.

July 9, 1899
La Serena, Chile

To day Gunner Sheldon[16] and I went ashore and hired a couple of horses for a ride. We were told that the best place to go was La Serena, a city 9 miles from here. The road there is simply the beach which is hard and at low tide very wide. It is used altogether for the traffic between the two cities. Along the beach we passed a few old guns that have undoubtedly been out of commission for many years. The ride was very pleasant and interesting owing to the people we passed on the way. La Serena is slightly larger than Coquimbo, but being about a mile from the beach has not the advantages of the latter place. Nor is it so clean or the people so prosperous. The land in the vicinity is very fertile. We ate dinner (not a good one) at the only hotel which is managed by a German.

July 15, 1899
Painting—Coquimbo, Chile

During the week the ship and boats have undergone a thorough cleaning and received two coats of paint, so now we look better than at any time since we left New York. As the Junior Officers have not had very much to do here (this makes up for the very much we did have to do at Valparaiso), I have had a number of opportunities to go ashore, and meet some of the people—The American Consul, his two daughters, Mrs. and Miss Cowan, Mr. and Mrs. Parker, son and daughter. The latter family is related to relatives of Johnsons. We spent several pleasant afternoons playing tennis with the young ladies on the Parkers' court. One evening we called on the Consul and daughters and had a very pleasant time and some exceedingly good tea.

One afternoon Forman and I hired a carriage and drove to Guayacan where we visited the copper smelting works. We were shown around, everything explained to us, and given some samples of the copper ore in the different stages of purifying it.

---

16 Clifford H. Sheldon was a gunner in USS *Newark*.

On the drive back the horses commenced to balk and soon broke all the harness by kicking. Forman and I walked the rest of the way to the boat landing.

This morning at 7:30 A.M. we regretfully left for Iquique, or next stopping place. I enjoyed my stay at Coquimbo more than at any other place we had visited.

July 17, 1899

Iquique, Chile—Shipping—Pelicans

We have not seen the sun or stars since leaving Coquimbo so we made the run by D.R. entirely and made land 20 miles to the southward of the city. Iquique has no harbor, a small island lying close to the shore forming a partial break water for the generally predominating southern swell. We moored low and stern to buoys in the anchorage north of the island. There are about 40 sailing ships moored in several rows in the harbor. All the great nations are represented and some of the ships are very fine ones. They bring coal, lumber and stores, and take away nitrate, this being the largest nitrate port in the world. The loading is very slow, it being done entirely be heavy lighters which are handled by two men. The boat landing is good but the channel leading to it is spotted with rocks and shoals, making it particularly dangerous at night. The rocks are the homes of thousands of pelicans that fly about in very fantastic formations.

It very seldom rains here, and as there is no stream to start an irrigation system, the city and surrounding country are absolutely devoid of vegetation. The streets of the city are wide and clean, the houses made of wood but not particularly well built. There is a plaza and theatre. A street car line surrounds the city and goes to Limanche, the summer resort of the city. A mile back of the city the pampas rise to about 1000 feet. A rail road runs along a ledge to the top and thence to the nitrate fields.

Iquique was formerly a Peruvian city but was conquered by Chile in the late war.

July 18, 1899

Iquique — Limanche, Chile

Dr. Huntington,[17] Elson and I went ashore this afternoon, and walked to Limanche. There is a concrete walk along the beach all the way, making it very pleasant, although very warm. At Limanche we found shooting galleries and bowling alleys. The bath houses were not occupied, it being the wrong time of day. We took breakfast in the restaurant—an open pavilion built over the breakers. We were surrounded by plants and cages containing many varieties of birds. The meal was the best we have had since leaving New York. We rode back to Iquique in the street cars, and transferred to a double-decker with a woman street car conductor. Although

---

17 Elon O. Huntington was an assistant surgeon aboard the *Newark*. He had three months' sea service at this time.

the upper deck was second class we preferred to ride there so as to see the sights. A lottery ticket is given every time one rides in a car.

July 19, 1899

We left Iquique at 3 P.M. for Mollendo Peru.

July 20

Mollendo, Peru—Boat Landing—R.R. to Arequipa, Peru—The "Misti"

We arrived at Mollendo about 10 A.M. on the 20th. The Peruvian Cruiser Liner was anchored off the port. As at Iquique there was no vegetation except a few trees in the plaza. There is no harbor here whatever, the town being built on a point. A worse site for a settlement could not have been chosen. The Engineer Meigs[18] selected the location for the ocean terminal of the railroad which he built to Arequipa, Cusco and Pimo, as he wished it to run via the Tambo Valley, a few miles to the southward and eastward.

The ships boats were not lowered as the approach to the boat landing is very dangerous unless the channel is thoroughly known. Shortly after mooring to a buoy, a large surf boat rowed by four natives came alongside, and the Captain, and a party of officers, I among them, got in and were rowed to the landing. The channel is very narrow, the surf running high and beating against projecting rocks on either side. The wharf is built over the rocks on which the surf beats continually.

We disembarked with difficulty. Climbing up a steep, but low, hill we came to the rail road station—the best building in Mollendo. We got in the train immediately and were soon under way. The road is owned by an English company, but all the local officials are Americans. For ten miles the road runs along the beach and then begins the ascent via the Tambo Valley. This valley is checkered with an irrigation system, that causes it to produce all fruits and vegetables. It is spotted with large ranches which appear to be gardens from the heights overlooking the valley. At Tambo, 1000 feet above the sea level we bought sugar cane from the Indians, and ate it during the day. The track is laid out very much like the Caracas road, and although it climbs higher than the latter the scenery is not so fine owing to the lack of vegetation. A few cacti were all we saw during the first ascent. Our reaching the pampa, about 4,000 feet high we had a fine view of the sea of mountains stretching to the south and east. At La Joya, 4,141 feet, we stopped for breakfast. The proprietor of the hotel an Indian was very much worked up because the Consul at Mollendo had telegraphed that we would want lunch, and we asked for breakfast. We had lunch which consisted of about ten courses that were fairly well served considering the circumstances. The Peruvian Minister to Bolivia was traveling in a

---

18 Henry Meiggs (1811–77), speculator and builder of railroads in Peru and Chile, had left San Francisco, where he had been involved in a fraudulent scheme, to seek his fortune in South America.

special car of our train. He took lunch with us and insisted on paying for it all on the old plea of the "custom of the country."

The pampa is a desert waste on which nothing grows. It slopes gradually from 4,000 feet at the summit of the first ridge of mountains, to 6,000 feet at the foot of the second ridge about 50 miles away. The hot air causes a peculiar mirage effect, the bases of the mountains in the distance appearing elevated above the plain. One of the peculiarities of the pampa is the thousand upon thousand of sand hills stretching as far as the eye can reach. These hills are in the shape of crescents with the points stretching to the northward. They are built up by the prevailing southerly winds which carry the very find sand on the surface of the pampa depositing it in these peculiar hills. They average almost six feet high and 30 feet across the points.

The road after reaching the foot of the second ridge winds about on the edge of a precipice overlooking the Chile River which runs through a cañon of varying width. Every available piece of land in the cañon is cultivated, the open places being occupied by farms and small towns.

Arequipa is situated in a fine valley, 8000 feet above the sea level. It is at the foot of the volcano Misti 19,200 feet high and over 11,000 feet above the city. It is a fine mountain, symmetrical and snow capped. On the summit is the Harvard meteorological station.[19] The Superintendent and Chief Engineer of the rail-road met us at the station and took us to their bungalow known as the Casa Grande, where refreshments were served. We then took the street car for the Gran Hotel. After going a block we had to get out and put the car back on the track. We were given nice rooms at the hotel which is built on the interior court system. Mr Clymer, a Harvard graduate connected with the Harvard Observatory here showed Elson, Sheldon and myself around the city. The population is about 30,000 comprising a great many Indians. There is a large plaza with an immense and imposing two-towered Cathedral on one side, the Government House on another and the best stores in the city occupying the other two sides. The number of cathedrals, most of them of the last century, is marvelous.

July 21, 1899

The Harvard Observatory at Arequipa—To Tingo on horse back

Our nights rest was not very restful, as about two o'clock in the morning all the church bells began to ring making a very loud and discordant sound. This ringing (celebrating some feast day) was kept up during the night keeping us awake. About six o'clock we heard what we thought was rapid musketry fire and Sheldon came

---

19 The Boyden Observatory was located in Arequipa from 1889 to 1927. Uriah Boyden, a mechanical engineer in Boston, bequeathed $238,000 to Harvard University to further astronomical research. Harvard astronomers who studied stellar spectra encouraged the establishment of a station in Peru, where conditions for viewing were considered excellent. The site proved less advantageous than originally thought, and the station was moved to Maselspoort, South Africa, in 1927.

running through my room saying he thought a revolution was on as we heard that one was likely to occur here at any time. We were all rather disappointed when we found the people were simply exploding fire-crackers, as another form of celebration.

In the morning we met Mr. Brown one of the officials of the rail road. We hired four horses and he acted as our guide to show us the surrounding country. We first went to the Harvard Observatory where we met Prof. Bailey[20] who is in charge. We spent a pleasant hour there on the porch of his house, the chief topic of conversation being the Spanish-American war. We then started out for Tingo, a famous Peruvian summer resort, noted for its fine spring water baths. We lost the road and soon found ourselves riding through yards and fields. Elson's horse ran away and he only succeeded in stopping him by running him into the front door of a house where he nearly ran over six or seven Indian children. He appeased the anger of the father and mother by presenting them with a *sol*. For ten minutes we were mixed up with a flock of sheep, a precipice on one side and a wall on the other preventing us from getting by. We next encountered a drove of pigs that insisted on keeping in front of us until they were driven into their sty on the side of the road. Our next enemy was train of loaded jackasses which we were unfortunate enough to meet in a part of the road barely wide enough for two horses to pass. Before we reached Tingo we encountered horses, mules and cows, and were disappointed at not meeting a llama train. As it was we only saw one of these, but he was a very dignified animal. We rode over stone fences, up a steep rocky hill and down a steeper incline, almost a precipice, and finally by riding through a church yard found a road that took us to the baths. This is not the right season for bathing, but we were very warm and the water (in tanks about 60 feet square) looked very tempting, so we had a very small and dirty indian boy bring us some bathing suits which we donned in a hurry. The water was cold and had a peculiar effect on my ears due to the atmospheric pressure which only shows 22 inches here. Nevertheless we enjoyed the bath very much, a crowd of small boys and girls standing around watching us.

After riding up a flight of ten steps at the railroad station we struck the main road to Arequipa, and did not leave it, all of us being very tired. Needless to say we turned in early. Our slumbers were again disturbed in the morning by the ringing of the bells.

---

20 Simon I. Bailey (1854–1931) was a professor of astronomy at Harvard University. He was selected to find the site for the observatory in Peru and remained there until 1923, when he returned to Cambridge, Massachusetts. Bailey wrote a history of the Harvard Observatory.

July 22, 1899
Embarking Under Difficulties
After breakfast we settled our hotel bill which was 23 *soles* or $10 for the three of us. We had stayed at the hotel two nights, parts of three days and had wine with all our meals.

Our return trip in the cars was devoid of interest, excepting the two large condors that we saw. Our reaching Mollendo, the Captain and several of the officers went to the Consuls, the rest of went to the wharf. When we reached the landing the sea was very smooth, but in a half hour a heavy swell was running, making it impossible for our boat to come alongside.

When the Captain arrived it looked as if we would not be able to get out to the ship that night. However the Captain was offered the use of the cargo derrick, and he accepted. Steam was got up as quickly as possible and a trapeze hung on the hook of the tackle. Several of us stood on the bar of the trapeze, and were swung over the water. Then at a favorable movement the boat, which was magnificently handled by four natives, was run in on a wave until directly under the trapeze. We were quickly lowered, all hands letting go and falling in the bottom of the boat the instant we touched. The next moment we ran twenty yards away on the out going wave. The second lot was lowered in this manner, and we then were rowed to the ship. We had some difficulty in getting on board owing to the heavy sell and the rolling of the ship. Steam was up and everything ready to slip moorings so we left immediately for Callao.

July 25, 1899
Callao, Peru
Arrived at Callao this morning after a pleasant and uneventful run. Passed close to the island of San Lorenzo in entering the harbor. Anchored about half a mile from the shore. One of the Chili line of Steamers arrived from the North. I was sent to her for the mail. Found Paymaster Mohun[21] and his clerk Porter on board. They are to relieve Paymaster Simpson[22] and Pay Clerk Gaffney. I took them to the *Newark*. The Peruvian Cruiser *Constitution* is at anchor in the harbor. She was formerly one of the WR Grace Co. steamers. English and American Cable steamers here also.

August 9, 1899
Callao, Peru—Coaling—Horse Races—Lima, Peru
Our stay at Callao has been devoid of special interest. The crew has had small arm target practice at the butts on San Lorenzo Island. We coaled from lighters alongside during the last few days of our stay. The *Marblehead* arrived and anchored near us.

---

21 Philip V. Mohun was appointed from Washington, D.C.

22 George W. Simpson was appointed from New York and assigned to USS *Newark* in 1898.

I have been ashore several times. The first time, Sunday, I went to the races at the course halfway between Callao and Lima. The races were not very good, only one of them being very exciting. All the fashionables of Lima were present, and every body bet on the horses. So did I and lost 3 *soles*. The President of Peru[23] came attended by his body guard. When he passed the grand stand everybody stood up and applauded. The President of Peru, in Peru, appears to be a "bigger man" than the President of the U.S. in the U.S., judging from the attention he receives.

Lima is a nice city, but not particularly interesting. The big cathedral on the plaza contains what are said to be the remains of Pizarro. I had the satisfaction of seeing what is left of them. La Libertad was celebrated by fire works and processions. The President held a big reception at the Government House. The streets along which he passed when driving were lined with soldiers who presented arms as he passed. The Peruvian soldiers drill entirely by bugle call enabling all orders—manual of arms included—to be heard a great distance.

I took dinner one evening with Mrs. and Miss Johnson at the Hotel Maury. They are on their way to Chile, and have been waiting here a month for the *Newark*.

We gave an afternoon tea and dance on the *Newark*. A number of young ladies were present. The British Cruiser *Leander*[24] arrived.

All the cadets visited the American Cable Steamer "*Relay*" for instructions in Submarine Cables.

The *Marblehead* and *Newark* have orders to proceed to San Francisco; the former via Panama, the latter in via San José de Guatemala. Both vessels are to be there by September 1st, but I do not think the *Marblehead* will be able to make it. Both ships left Callao this afternoon, the *Marblehead* about an hour ahead of us. We passed her about sundown. We should beat her to San Francisco by a week.

August 12, 1899
Crossed the equator about 3 P.M.

August 18, 1899
San José de Guatemala—R.R. to Guatemala City—Banquet at American Club.
The evening of the 15th (10 P.M.) a heavy squall struck us without warning the wind increasing from a calm to a gale in a few minutes, and the rain coming down in torrents. All our awnings were spread, and there was some excitement in getting them housed. The next morning at four we anchored off San José de Guatemala. There is no harbor, the coast stretching for miles in a straight East and West line. Ships at anchor are exposed to a continual heavy swell. A long pier extends out into the ocean. In very smooth weather ships can run alongside this, but usually they discharge their cargoes in lighters. About eight o'clock I went ashore with the Capt. and a

---

23 Nicolás de Piérola was president of Peru from 1895 to 1899.

24 *Leander* was a 4,300-ton ship with a complement of 309 men.

party of Officers. The Captain intended to call officially on the President of Guatemala,[25] the rest of us went along to see the sights. We had a special car on the regular train and were not allowed to pay any fare as the President intended that we should be guests of the Republic. The Captain had to decline the invitation as none of us had come prepared for this courtesy.

The track is narrow gauge (3 feet) but the engines and cars are broad gauge with narrow gauge trucks. The road runs through a country covered with luxurious vegetation, passing several Indian villages. At these stations the Indians would gather around with fruit to sell. The women are small and much prettier than the South American Indian women. They dress in very gay colors, their costume consisting of a breast covering, a blanket wrapped tightly around the hips, and silver ornaments. They are very picturesque. At Esquintha we were met by a Guatemalan Colonel and his staff. They came to present the President's compliments to Captain Goodrich. We had breakfast here but were not allowed to pay for it. The latter half of the journey is something of a climb there being many steep places in the ascent. We reached Guatemala City late in the afternoon. We went to the club—the first American one we struck since leaving New York—and looked over the late papers.

Here I a met a Mr. McNiter who knew my brother, Hawley, at Cornell, and a brother of whom was a classmate of Dr. Huntington at P. and S. He invited us to lunch the next day. There was a large ball in the evening, but as none of us were prepared for it we could not go. Instead, most of us ran across a roulette game. I had never seen it before so I thought I'd take a hand. It was very fascinating, so I managed to lose £2 before I stopped. Dr. Huntington and Elson won.

The exchange here is 8 for 1 and the prices nearly correspondingly as cheap. I bought several souvenirs made out of silver money which appears to have been coined for this purpose.

The city has a population of something over 100,000. A census has never been taken as it is feared that such a thing would cause the people to think that was being taken for a revolution and thereby start one.

At the hotel three of us slept in a room. The next morning Dr. Huntington and I ate lunch with the McNiter family. Afterwards we walked around the city to see the sights. The streets are roughly paved with gutters in the middle. The pavements are new-made of concrete, but narrow. Carriage line is cheap but the streets are too rough to make it enjoyable. Food and clothing can be bought in the large market for almost nothing.

In the evening we were tended a banquet by the American Club. This was very enjoyable there being toasts and songs. We also had native *"musica."* In the morning we left for San José and on arrival went on board ship, getting up anchor

---

25 Manuel José Estrada Cabrera was president of Guatemala from 1898 to 1920.

immediately, and leaving for Acapulco, where we will coal. On returning to the ship found Johnson in his bunk sick of typhoid fever.

August 21, 1899
Acapulco, Mexico—Coaling

Arrived at Acapulco early in the morning, and I was sent ashore immediately to inform the American Counsel of our arrival, and look out for the tallying of coal. I was too early to get the coal, in spite of the fact that we had telegraphed to have it ready for us. We could not commence coaling until eight o'clock. The coal was conveniently bagged, the average weighing about 125 pounds. I was on the wharf to take the tally for the ship. A large number of men were employed each man carrying a bag of coal on his Shoulder. As they passed through the scale house a man counted—"*uno, dos, tres, cuatro*"—etc. up to *dies*, each tenth bag being regularly placed on the scales. This method proved very satisfactory both to the merchant and to us as we tallied together and there was no question as to the amount of coal bundled. The bags were placed in lighters, which, when full, were towed alongside by our steam launch, and immediately discharged by passing the bags through our coaling ports. This proved a rapid method of coaling, we taking on board 300 tons in ten hours.

The harbor here is a fine one, being land locked. However it is a very hot place and consequently disagreeable. I did not see much of the city, and was not favorably impressed with the part I did. The streets are narrow and dirty, the houses small and unattractive, the people not pleasing to look upon.

About sunset we left for San Francisco. I do not think the Captain has decided whether to stop at San Diego or not, his indecision being due to Johnson's illness.

August 29, 1899
Accident to Engines—San Francisco, Cal.

We arrived at San Francisco this afternoon after a pleasant and uneventful run. As we steamed to the anchorage we passed the *Boston*[26]—on her way to Mare Island—and exchanged numbers. Shortly after this there was a sudden and loud thumping in the port engine room which caused the whole ship to vibrate, I feeling it distinctly on the fore castle. The port engine was immediately stopped, and it was found that the P.L.P [probably "port low-pressure"] piston rod had broken close to the piston, and had come up against it several times before the engine could be stopped.

The *Iowa* was at anchor off Folsom street: we anchored near her. I was sent to the Pay Office for mail, and got eight bags. The city is gaily decorated with flags in honor of the return from Manila of California volunteers. In the evening the Press

---

26 USS *Boston* (cruiser), of the Asiatic Squadron, took part in the battle of Manila Bay and remained there until 1899.

Club entertained us with a vaudeville performance given on board an excursion steamer alongside.

August 30, 1899

The crews of the *Boston* and *Newark*, and some of the recently returned troops from Manila were entertained at the different theaters of the city.

September 1, 1899

Change of Captains

This morning Captain Bowman H. McCalla[27] relieved Captain Caspar F. Goodrich of command of the *Newark*. The latter assumed command of the *Iowa*. Johnson was moved to the Nutt's Hospital.

September 4, 1899—Mare Island

We came to Mare Island this morning and moored to a buoy in the stream. The *Philadelphia*[28] is here undergoing extensive repairs, one of the most important being the installation of new electrical ammunition hoists. The *Ranger*[29] is lying in the stream ready to go in commission. Admiral Farragut's flag ship the *Hartford*[30] is undergoing a thorough overhauling and refitting. She is to be used as a training ship for landsmen. The *Boston* is being dismantled preparatory to being placed out of commission.

September 30, 1899

Navy Yard, Mare Island—Repairs—Drills—Landing Party—Base-ball, Dancing, Golf

The ship has been undergoing the usually navy yard repairs, the chief of which are being done in the engine room. The P.L.P. piston, piston rod, connecting rod and cross head have been sent to the Navy Yard shops where a new piston rod is being made and the piston repaired. A new S.L.P. [probably "starboard low-pressure"] piston rod is being made also, the older one being found bent. Both fire and bilge pumps were sent to the shops for a general overhauling. The uninjured cylinder cover is being repaired on board by the Navy Yard workmen. This is being done by routing the metal on the inside of the cover in the wake of the crack; caulking it and

---

27 Bowman McCalla (1844–1910) graduated from the U.S. Naval Academy in 1865. He served in the Spanish-American War as commanding officer of the USS *Marblehead* and took Guantanamo. He led a landing party during the Boxer Rebellion to relieve the legations at Peking. He was promoted to rear admiral in 1903.

28 USS *Philadelphia* (cruiser) was commissioned in 1890 and recommissioned in 1898 as flagship of the Pacific Station (1898–1902). It was present at the ceremony transferring sovereignty of the Hawaiian Islands to the United States. In 1899, the ship anchored in Samoa to settle problems encountered by the Samoan commissioners.

29 USS *Ranger* (screw steamer). Recommissioned in 1899, it served as survey ship off Mexico and Baja California.

30 USS *Hartford* (screw sloop). The ship was launched in 1858 and commissioned in 1859. During the Civil War, it served as the flagship of Admiral David Farragut and was in the battles of New Orleans, Vicksburg, and Mobile Bay. In 1882, it was the flagship of the North Atlantic Squadron. Recommissioned in 1899 as a training ship on the Atlantic coast, it was finally decommissioned in 1926.

filling with soft copper. A patch is being placed over the cracked portion and the whole cylinder head strengthened by shrinking on a 2" wrought iron band around the circumference. The other repairs in the engine room consist in cleaning boilers, testing condensers, adjusting bearings and overhauling auxiliaries.

Two days in each week the *Newark*'s crew has occupied the rifle and pistol ranges. The improvement in the scores the past month has been very noticeable.

The battalion has been instructed in camp and outpost duties. The 1st and 3rd divisions, Lieutenant Pratt[31] in charge, and I as assistant, received orders to camp on the south west side of the island. We started at 8 A.M. and after reaching the marine barracks, advanced and rear guards were established and the force proper being kept together as a marching column. In this case, single men represented squads of various sizes. Among the trees above the light house a camp was established and sentries immediately posted. A detour of the camp was made by a squad to see if the enemy were in the vicinity. The sentries were regularly relieved every two hours, and inspections made by the officers to see if they were alert and understood their instructions. We remained here all day returning at sun set. On the march back to

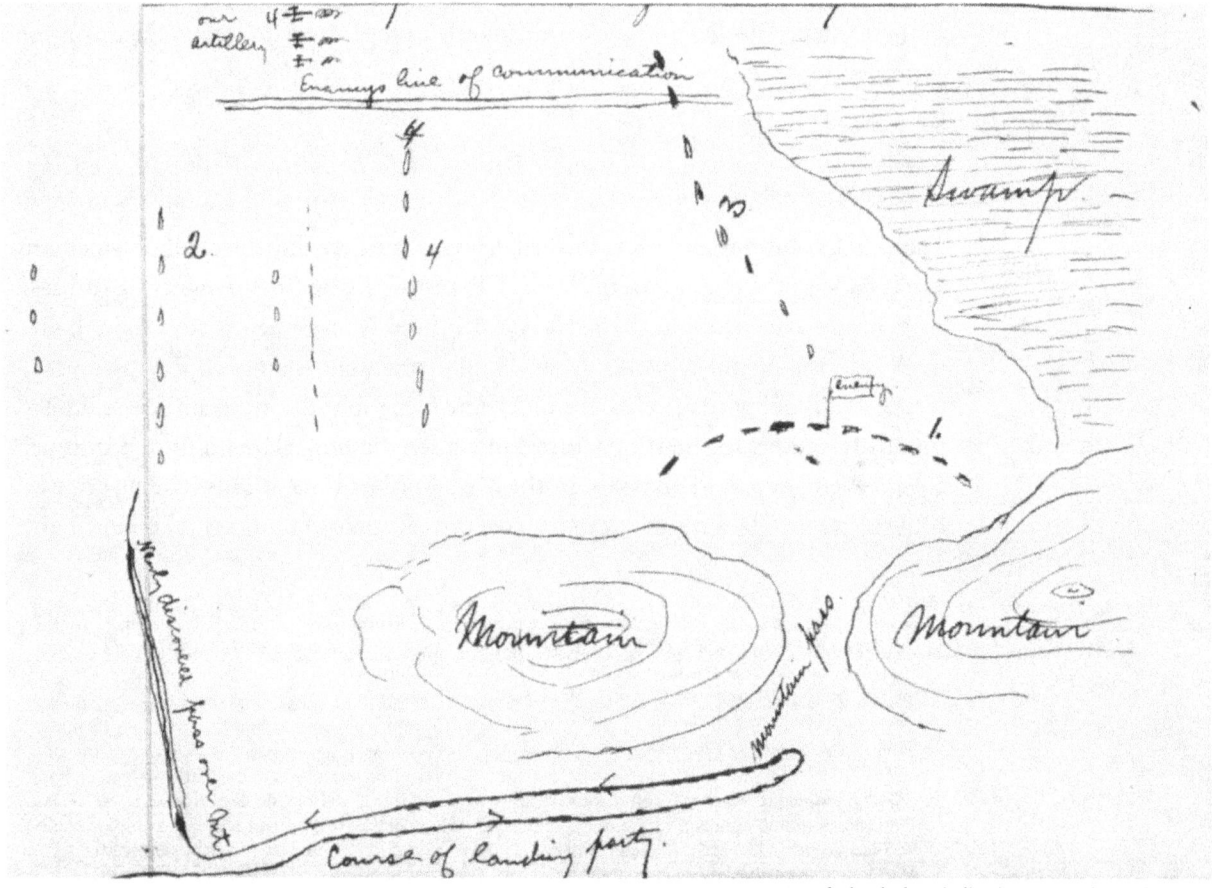

Rough sketch chart indicating mountains and swamp

---

31 Alfred A. Pratt (?–1911), U.S. Naval Academy, 1893.

the ship, the rear guard was strengthened, as we were supposed to be leaving the enemy's country.

A landing party was made—the problem being to attack an enemy holding a mountain pass, the enemy supposing this pass to be the only way for our troops to reach them. However, we were to find a pass leading over the mountain, and thus threaten the enemy's line of communication. The force, being divided into outposts, advanced guard, main body, support, reserve and rear guard, advanced slowly toward the mountain pass. The outposts sent written reports to the commanding officer, relating to the condition of the ground and position of the enemy (which was represented by flags). It being seen that the enemy held a position (1. in fig. 1) [page 94] in front of the pass from which it would be impossible to dislodge them by a direct attack from the front, as soon as we were seen by them, a small force was left at the entrance of the pass to hold it, and make a demonstration while the main body doubled on its line of march and proceeded over the newly discovered mountain road. They deployed in position marked 2. A field hospital and ammunition base of supplies was now established and the attack began. On discovering us the enemy withdrew a part of its main body from in front of the pass and threw their line out fronting ours. As we advanced the artillery was thrown out on our left flank and bombarded some houses held by the enemy. They also threatened the enemy's line of communications forcing them to extend their line so as to cover it. Before the final assault was made the enemy were posted as at 3, while our troops held the position 4. The enemy gradually fell back towards the swamp in their rear. Our charge was delayed by the failure of the artillery to come up soon enough. The reserve being brought on the line, bayonets were fired, rapid fire, kneeling, commenced, and at the order our party charged forward shouting, forcing the enemy into the swamp. After the battle the force was drawn up in a hollow square and the battle reviewed as seen from the enemy's position by Captain McCalla. Our chief faults had been in not always seeking proper cover, and in the failure of the artillery to come up as soon as expected. All the communications between the officers of the landing party were read. Some of these did not have the time they were sent and received or the location from which they were sent.

While at the yard the *Newark*'s base ball team has played several games winning all of them except one to the *Hartford* Crew.

A very pleasant afternoon dance and tea was given on board the *Newark* by Capt. McCalla. The ship was decorated with bunting, and the *Independence* band officiated. The deck was covered with French chalk which made it a very agreeable dancing floor. The afternoon was very successful.

Recreation while at the yard consists of playing golf and tennis, with a run to San Francisco now and then on the *Unadilla*,[32] generally known as the "Charity Boat." Lt Cmdr. Low[33] was detached.

October 10, 1899
Orders to Manila—Change in Duty
We have received orders to go to Manila as soon as we can get ready. Consequently work is being resched so that we can get away in a week if possible. Six ships, including the *Brooklyn* have been ordered to Manila also.

A second landing party was sent ashore during the past week. It attacked the enemy in an open field.

On the 2nd I was transferred from deck duty, where I had been doing the duties of watch and division officer, to duty in the engine room.

The *Marblehead* and *Badger* are at the yard. The *Solace*[34] has arrived from Manila via Yokahama.

October 17, 1899
Mare Island Dry Dock—Preparations for sailing
We have been in dry dock, our bottom being scraped and painted, and sea valves overhauled. Have been taking on coal, ammunition and stores during the past few days. This morning we left the Navy Yard for San Francisco. Here we received over 400 bags of mail for the fleet and army in the Philippines. From the Yerba Buena training station, 50 boys were sent us as passengers to Manila. Previous to leaving Mare Island, Ensign Leahy[35] and Naval Cadets Pettengill[36] and Bloch[37] were ordered to this ship for passage.

October 18, 1899
Left San Francisco early in the morning, weather fine, and the sea, smooth. We are steaming under three boilers.

October 25, 1899
Honolulu, Hawaii
We sighted land early this morning and anchored off the harbor shortly after eight o'clock. We have had a rough passage, but in spite of this we averaged nearly 13

---

32 USS *Unadilla* (harbor tug) was built at Mare Island Navy Yard and launched in 1895.

33 William L. Low (?–1921), U.S. Naval Academy, 1869.

34 USS *Solace* (hospital ship) was in service during the Spanish-American War and carried provisions, passengers, and mail to the Philippine Islands, Japan, and China in 1899.

35 William D. Leahy (1875–1959) graduated from the U.S. Naval Academy in 1897. He served as Chief of Naval Operations (1937–39). Before World War II, he was governor of Puerto Rico (1939–40). During the war he was ambassador to France (1941–42), then Chief of Staff to Commander in Chief, U.S. Army and Navy (i.e., to the president). Promoted to fleet admiral in 1944, he retired in 1949.

36 George T. Pettengill (1877–1959), U.S. Naval Academy, 1898.

37 Claude C. Bloch (1878–1967), graduated from the U.S. Naval Academy in 1899. He served as Commander in Chief, U.S. Fleet, 1938–1940. He retired in 1945.

knots. The mail steamer *Australia*,[38] which left San Francisco on the afternoon of the 18th only beat us in by three hours. We received mail from her. The tug *Iroquois*[39] is the station ship here. This afternoon I went ashore and walked around the city for a while. The residence port is very attractive. The rain prevented us from walking long. We had dinner at the Hawaii Hotel. Here we met two Army Officers who are on their way home from Manila, on the transport *Ohio*[40] which arrived here this afternoon. We drove around the city with them in the evening.

October 26, 1899
Waikiki, Honolulu

This afternoon Boone,[41] Courtney and I rode to Waikiki in the cars. We went in surf bathing. There is a fairly good beach here, it being spoiled somewhat by the coral. The people here use surf boards on which they lie and ride in with the surf. Some of the natives become very expert in the use of these boards being able to stand up on them while riding shoreward rapidly on the crests of the waves.

November 1, 1899

We have been coaling from lighters alongside and finished this morning. The crew has been having target practice. Courtney and I called on President and Mrs. Dole.[42] They were not at home. This afternoon they left for Guam. We are going to make the run on two boilers.

November 16, 1899
San Louis d'Apra, Guam

We slowed down during the night so as to arrive at the harbor of San Louis d'Apra at day light. The *Yosemite*[43] and *Brutus*[44] are in the harbor, the latter no longer in commission. The *Zafiro*[45] arrived during the day from Manila. She reports no material change in the situation there. We ran alongside the *Brutus* and commenced coaling from her.

The harbor is well protected from the heavy seas outside by a reef which extends part of the way from Cabras Is. to Guam. It is necessary for vessels to lie out some distance from the shore owing to the innumerable coral reefs.

---

38 *Australia* was chartered from the Oceanic Steamship Company in 1898 and 1899. The vessel displaced 27,555 tons.

39 USS *Iroquois* (steam tug) was commissioned in 1898. It was stationed at Mare Island, then served as a tug, mail boat, and surveying ship in Hawaii.

40 *Ohio* was chartered from the Empire Transportation Company in 1898 and 1899.

41 Charles Boone (?–1955) was an 1898 graduate of the U.S. Naval Academy. He retired in 1949.

42 Sanford Dole (1844–1926) was first president of the Republic of Hawaii (1894–1900), and first governor of the territory (1900–1903). A son of missionaries, he served in the legislature and the Supreme Court. He worked for annexation of Hawaii to the United States.

43 USS *Yosemite* (auxiliary cruiser) took part in the Spanish-American War and in 1899 was a station ship in Guam.

44 USS *Brutus* (AC 15) was assigned to Guam as a station ship from 1899 to 1901.

45 USS *Zafiro* served as a collier during the battle of Manila Bay. It delivered supplies, troops, and messages during the Philippine Insurrection.

November 17, 1899

Coaling

Coaled ship until 5 P.M. In evening the crew of the *Newark* gave a minstrel show that was very good. Governor Leary[46] and the Captain and Officers of the *Yosemite*, *Brutus* and *Zafiro* were on board.

November 18, 1899

Road to Agaña, Guam

This afternoon Dr. Huntington, Courtney and I went ashore in the *Yosemite*'s boat. The steam launch towed us as far as the first reef, and then dropped us. The channel at low water is very crooked and narrow in some places being just wide enough for the whale boat to pass through. It poured down rain so we got soaking wet. We landed at Piti, a village of a few huts, and not finding any cabs started to walk to Agaña five miles distant. The road was very good considering the way it is raining. It is made of macadamized corral gravel. Palm trees grow along the sides of the road, and several single street villages are scattered along. We also saw a number of rice fields. The road follows the beach the entire distance. We crossed many little bridges varying from ten to thirty feet long, each one leaving a sign on which is painted a name, as "Puente de Asin," "Puente de Anigua," etc,—the names of villages near them. They span small streams running from the interior to the sea. The villages are all alike, the houses being built at equal distances apart. They are made of white boards with thatched roofs. The floor is raised about two feet from the ground. The pigs, of which there are a great many occupy the space thus formed. We passed several native men and women none of whom appeared to mind the rain in the least. They all carry a crude knife used in cutting the cocoa-nut.

When about halfway to Agaña we were overtaken by a small boy driving a cow hauling a two wheel cart. We all got in seating ourselves on the one seat, and drove in state to the city. Agaña has a population of about 10,000. The houses are placed in rows in equal intervals apart, a street running between each row of houses, with cross streets about every hundred yards. Most of the houses are made of wood but several (probably those of the richer people) are made of adobe with tile roofs. Pigs and chickens run around the streets.

There are two marine companies stationed in the town. They do no drilling, but a great deal of work making the Governor's palace, barracks, hospital and other buildings habitable. The Governor's palace is a large two story building rectangular in shape. It is being thoroughly overhauled and refitted. Its front is upon the plaza which is to be the marines drill ground. Around the plaza are the barracks, hospital, cathedral and prison. In the latter are the quarters of the Guardia Civil—the native

---

46 Richard P. Leary (1842–1902) was an 1864 graduate of the U.S. Naval Academy. He saw action in the Civil War and the Spanish-American War, in which he commanded the USS *San Francisco*. He served as naval governor of Guam from 1899 to 1900.

police. There is one prisoner—a Filipino—sentenced to 15 years for murder. A distilling plant has been recently completed. This furnishes all the water used by the marines, that in the wells not being wholesome on account of the poor sewage system in the city. As it is there is an epidemic of typhoid fever among the marines, two having died yesterday. There is only one doctor in the village. He has to attend the 10,000 natives besides the marines. Consequently he is kept very busy. The natives have a great aversion to work as they have only done what the Spaniards forced them to do, and received no pay for it. Now, however, when they are persuaded to do anything of course they are paid—that is usually in canned beef and hardtack which they prefer to money as it can't be spent. The generally opinion of the natives who can speak English in regard to money is general expressed, "What good money?—No can spend." Which statement is practically true, there not being a store in the city.

Four of us drove back to Piti in a small cab hauled by a smaller horse. There was too much weight in rear of the axel, the driver having to stand on the shafts to keep us from lifting the horse off the ground whenever we went over a slight rising in the road. It being high tide when we reach Piti we were enabled to sail in a direct line to the ship.

The coaling today was greatly hindered by the hard rain that fell during the afternoon.

November 19, 1899
Although this is Sunday we have been coaling ship all day. Completed necessary repairs in Engine room and are ready to leave.

November 20, 1899
Left about 7:30 this morning. After getting well clear of the land swung ship for compass compensation. Started steaming under two boilers.

November 23, 1899
At 1 A.M. last night connected up a third boiler as the Captain wishes to reach the entrance to San Bernadino Straits before dark on the 24th.

November 24, 1899
Passed San Bernadino light at 1 P.M. Have been making about 16 knots over the ground since then, due to the aid of the current.

X The Philippine Islands and China
1899–1900

November 25, 1899
Cavite, P.I.

Entered Manila Bay by the south channel and anchored off Cavite near the *Baltimore*[1] at 11:20 A.M. We have been just 37 days and 10 hours San Francisco. Seven days were spent at Honolulu, and 4 days at Guam making just 26 steaming days. Below is a table showing the runs:

Run from	Distance	Number of Boilers	Time	Average run 24 hrs.	Average speed per hr.
San Francisco to Honolulu	2100	3	7^d 3^h	295	12.28
Honolulu to Guam	3300	2	13^d 18^h	240	10.0
Guam to Manila	1500	2 / 3	2^d 17^h / 2^d 10^h	293	12.2
San Francisco to Manila	6900		26^d 0^h	265.4	11.0

The *Baltimore*, *Monterey*, *Helena*, and *Glacier* are at anchor here. The *Baltimore* has just returned from the north coast of Luzon where she went to look for the *Charleston* which ran upon an

Engineering log entries

NOTES 1 USS *Baltimore* (Cruiser No. 3) took part in the battle of Manila Bay and remained on the Asiatic Station until 1900.

104 THREE SPLENDID LITTLE WARS

The *Baltimore, Monterey,*[2] *Helena,* and *Glacier*[3] are at anchor here. The *Baltimore* has just returned from the north coast of Luzon where she went to look for the *Charleston*[4] which ran upon an uncharted reef. She was abandoned, and it is supposed has been broken to pieces as nothing could be seen of her. No lives were lost, the officers and crew reaching land 18 miles distant.

The fleet under Admiral Watson's command now comprises the following vessels: *Oregon, Concord,*[5] *Monadnock,*[6] *Callao,*[7] *Baltimore, Helena, Bennington,*[8] *Manila,*[9] *Castine, Princeton,*[10] *Petrel, Newark, Monterey, Monocacy,*[11] *Yorktown,*[12] *Wheeling;*[13] the supply ship and coalers *Culgoa,*[14] *Iris,*[15] *Glacier, Naushan, Nero,*[16] *Zafiro, Celtic;* the gunboats: *Pampanga,*[17] *Zostous, Paragua,*[18] 201 tons, *Samar,*[19] 201 tons, *Albay,*[20] 151 tons, *Calamianes,*[21] *Panay,*[22] 142 tons, *Manileno,*[23] 142 tons,

---

2 USS *Monterey* (Monitor No. 6) provided gun support against the Spanish in 1898–99. It served as a station ship in China (1900–1903).

3 USS *Glacier* (Supply Ship No. 4) supplied stores to the Asiatic Fleet at Manila and China, 1899–1902.

4 USS *Charleston* (Protected Cruiser No. 2) took Guam from the Spanish and witnessed the surrender of the Spanish after the battle of Manila Bay. It remained in the Philippines through 1899, where it supported the U.S. Army.

5 USS *Concord* (patrol gunboat) was launched in 1890. It joined Dewey's squadron that fought at Manila Bay and remained in the Philippines until 1901 as a patrol craft.

6 USS *Monadnock* (screw steamer) was commissioned in 1896. In August 1898, it joined Dewey's fleet in Manila, where it blockaded the coast. In 1899, it was in China protecting American interests and guarding Shanghai.

7 USS *Callao* was a Spanish gunboat captured at the battle of Manila Bay. It was a tender to Admiral Dewey's flagship *Olympia.* It supported U.S. Army operations during the Philippine Insurrection.

8 USS *Bennington* (patrol gunboat) was commissioned in 1891. It took possession of Wake Island in 1899 and cruised in the Philippine Islands until 1901.

9 USS *Manila* (schooner) was taken by the U.S. Navy from the Spanish in 1898, in the Philippines. It served there from 1899 to 1903, patrolling, cruising, carrying troops, and bombarding San Fabian and Zamboanga.

10 USS *Princeton* (gunboat) was commissioned in 1898. It patrolled off Central America during the Spanish-American War and joined the Asiatic Fleet in Manila, where it blockaded ports and patrolled off Luzon. It briefly cruised in Chinese waters, then returned to the Philippines, where it remained until 1903.

11 USS *Monocacy* (screw gunboat) was launched in 1894. It was on the Asiatic Station (1867–1900) and supported the allied forces in the Boxer Rebellion.

12 USS *Yorktown* (Gunboat No.1) was launched in 1888. It was stationed in the Philippines in 1899, patrolling and convoying troops. In 1900 it was stationed in Taku, China, and then returned to the Philippines for two years.

13 USS *Wheeling* (Gunboat No. 14) was launched in 1896. It was stationed in the Philippines, where it was on blockade duty and convoyed troops. During the Boxer Rebellion, it patrolled the north coast of China.

14 USS *Culgoa* (storeship) was a refrigerator and supply ship for the Asiatic Squadron.

15 USS *Iris* served in the Philippine Islands as a general utility ship for the Asiatic Squadron in 1899.

16 USS *Nero* (supply ship) was commissioned in 1898. It supported U.S. forces during the Philippine Insurrection, 1900.

17 USS *Pampanga* (Patrol Gunboat No. 39) bombed and blockaded the insurgents during the Philippine Insurrection.

18 USS *Paragua* (patrol gunboat) was a prize of the Spanish-American War. It served as a patrol vessel in the Philippines, interdicting arms shipments and policing trade.

19 USS *Samar* (gunboat) was captured by the U.S. Navy during the Spanish-American War. It served in the Philippines during the insurrection.

20 USS *Albay* (gunboat) was built for the Spanish navy in 1886 and was captured in the Philippines in 1898. It served in patrol and survey duty from 1899 to 1904, in the islands.

21 USS *Calamianes* (patrol gunboat) was built in 1888. It was captured by the Americans in 1898. It patrolled the Philippine Islands, blocking supplies to the insurgents and fought two engagements in 1901.

22 *Panay* was a gunboat used by the U.S. Army in the Philippines.

23 USS *Manileno* (gunboat) was built in Hong Kong and acquired by the Navy in 1899. It patrolled the coast in the Philippines and convoyed troops and supplies.

Mareveles,[24] 142 tons, *Mindoro,*[25] 142 tons, *Basco,* 42 tons, *Gardoqui,*[26] 42 tons, *Urdaneta.*[27]

December 5, 1899

Vigan is the second city in size on the Island of Luzon. It is situated in the NW part of the island about four miles from the sea, on a small and unnavigable river called the Abra, which is also the name of the province. The seaport city is named Cavayan and is inhabited entirely by natives. About two weeks ago the battalion from the U.S.S. *Oregon* landed at Cavayan and marched to Vigan. Upon approaching the city a band met the battalion and escorted it to the plaza, the natives welcoming the *"Americanos"* with open arms. The *Oregon*'s sailors and marines occupied the place until relieved by a battalion of 33d U.S. Volunteer Infantry composed of about 250 men. The troops policed the city, and General Young,[28] the Senior Army Officer, in this neighborhood, decided to make Vigan a base of supplies; so stores and provisions were brought there and stowed in one of the buildings facing on the plaza.

That part of the Insurgent Army in the province of Abra are in need of food and supplies, so hearing of those held by the army, decided to make a bold attack on the city and capture them. The night of the *Newark*'s arrival (December 4th), the attack was made. The Insurgents succeeded in occupying the Government building at the west end of the plaza, but after a sharp engagement were forced to leave it, several of their number being killed and wounded. They all crossed the river before day light.

December 5, 1899

On the Beach Near Vigan

Captain McCalla, on learning the situation, immediately landed a battalion consisting of 40 marines and officers and 6 men from the *Newark* and 50 marines and men from the *Princeton,* which was at anchor when we arrived. The men were equipped in heavy marching order, each being supplied with 180 rounds of rifle ammunition. The three inch field piece with 138 rounds of schrapnel was taken along. The paymaster provided three day's rations. The boats were towed to the beach by one of the steam launches. The men had to wade ashore owing to the shallowness of the water. On account of lack of transportation facilities, the 3" ammunition and some of the rations were sent back to the ship.

---

24 USS *Mareveles* (gunboat) was built in Hong Kong and commissioned in 1899. It patrolled the Philippine Islands (1900–1902).

25 USS *Mindoro* (gunboat) was built in Hong Kong in 1886. A prize of the Spanish-American War, it took part in operations against insurgents in the Philippines.

26 USS *Gardoqui,* originally a Spanish gunboat, was captured during the Spanish-American War.

27 USS *Urdaneta,* originally a Spanish gunboat, was captured during the Spanish-American War. It served in the Philippines during the insurrection and ran aground in 1899. It was recaptured by the Americans and continued in service.

28 Samuel B. M. Young (1840–1924) was born in Pittsburgh, Pennsylvania, and was educated at Washington College. He served in the Civil War with the Pennsylvania infantry, with the U.S. infantry on the western frontier, and commanded a division in the Spanish-American War. From 1899 to 1901 he saw action in the Philippine Insurrection. From 1902 to 1904, he served as the first Chief of Staff of the U.S. Army. Retiring in 1904, he was governor of the Soldiers Home, 1910–20.

December 6, 1899
The Palacio at Vigan

The next morning at 6:30 I was sent ashore with the field piece ammunition and two barrels of water. I had with me an escort of five men equipped in heavy marching order. In spite of a small surf the ammunition and water was landed without difficulty. Some of the natives came to the beach to meet us and I explained to them that I wanted carts to carry the boxes to Vigan. In an hour I succeeded in getting two small carts, each hauled by a bull. These carts are about 6' by 3', the body is built entirely of bamboo. The wheels are solid and very narrow. The axles are made of iron wood about 6" in diameter. There were six boxes of ammunition, each weighing 315 pounds. I placed these boxes in each cart, but the wheels sank so deep in the sand the bulls could not move them. So I motioned the Filipinos who were standing around to catch hold and shove, which they did with a will. However, we made slow progress, and I was on the point of taking one box out of each cart and coming back for them when we reached the hard road (about 200 yards away), when a third cart came along. We placed two boxes in it and soon with the aid of about twenty Filipinos succeeded in reaching the good road. I was unable to take the water with me on account of lack of transportation facilities.

The road to Vigan is good. It is crossed by two streams over which are foot bridges built entirely of bamboo. The carts were hauled across through the water. Passing through a cut between the hills, I noticed trenches on one of them. They were unoccupied there being no insurgents between the coast and Vigan. We arrived at Vigan without any noteworthy incidents.

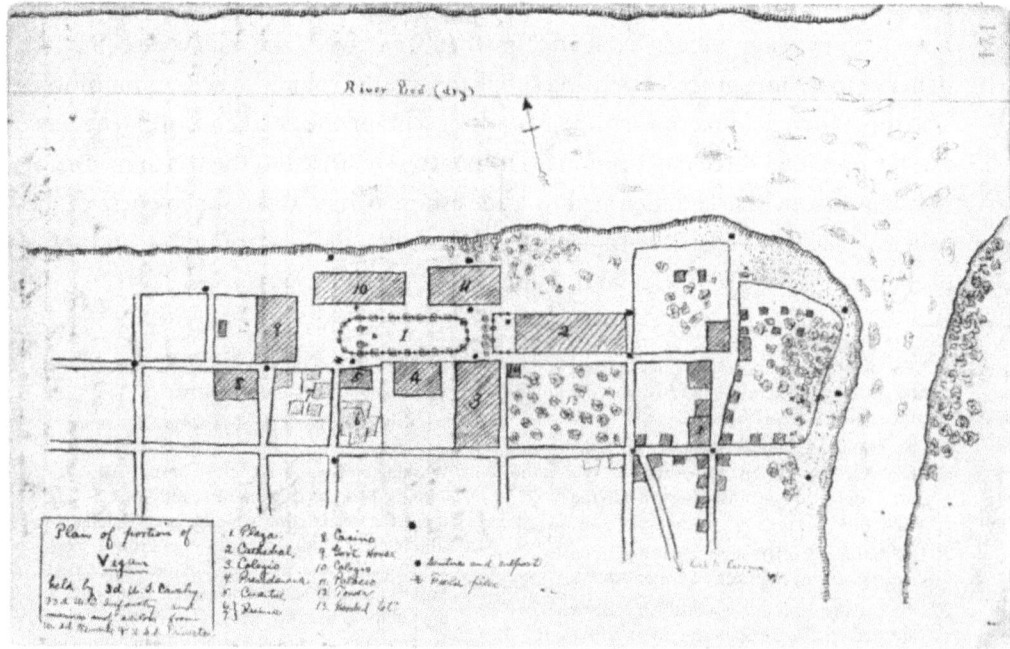

"Plan of portion of Vigan"

As in other Spanish Colonial cities the principal buildings in Vigan are built around a plaza. This plaza was originally fenced off but only the large stone posts are now standing. In it are two band stands and a monument. The Cathedral is built of stone, the rest of the important buildings are built of brick covered with adobe. The cathedral and building marked P. was occupied by the *Princeton*'s men. The *Newark*'s men occupied the *Colegio* (3), the *cuartel*, and camps marked N [page 104]. The Army occupied buildings 10 and 11, and No. 9 was used as a hospital. Outposts were placed as shown.

The river bed has very little water in it and is easily fordable at the north east corner of the city. There are a number of sand dunes covered with long grass in this part of the river that could afford excellent protection for an attacking army. In fact the insurgents tried to enter the city that way as is shown by the fact that several dead ones were found behind the dunes.

December 7, 1899

The day after my arrival the cavalry made a reconnaissance in the surrounding country and found no signs of any hostile people. I think all the insurgents near here have departed for the mountains.

Several hundred released Spanish prisoners arrived at Vigan and had to be looked out for. They were given rations and sent to the beach where they were embarked on our ships and sent to Manila. Most of them had been prisoners for over a year. The officers appeared to have no control over the men so I imagined they were mostly volunteer forces.

December 8, 1899

The main part of the *Newark*'s and *Princeton*'s force was ashore for four days. The march back to the coast was void of noteworthy features except the heat. The re-enforcements from the *Newark* arrived the afternoon of 6th and left the morning of the 8th.

The Officers from the *Newark* at Vigan were: Capt McCalla, Lieutenant Pratt,[29] Capt Hall,[30] U.S.M.C., Paymaster Jewett,[31] Dr. Huntington, Naval Cadet Courtney and Gunner Sheldon with the first party, and Lieut. Bryan, Naval Cadet Elson and myself, the 2nd day. The Officers from the *Princeton* were: Lieut. Stickney,[32] Lieut. McNamee[33] and Paymaster Dryer.

---

29 William V. Pratt (1869–1951) graduated from the U.S. Naval Academy in 1899. He was president of the Naval War College (1927–30) and Chief of Naval Operations (1930–33).

30 Newt H. Hall (1873–1939) was an 1895 graduate of the U.S. Naval Academy. He was stationed at the Marine Barracks, Cavite, in the Philippines, in 1899. He retired as a colonel, U.S. Marine Corps, in 1929.

31 Henry E. Jewett was born in New York and entered the Navy in 1892 from New Jersey. In 1899 he had four years of sea service to his credit.

32 Herman O. Stickney (1867–1936), U.S. Naval Academy, 1888.

33 Luke McNamee (1869–1931) graduated from the U.S. Naval Academy in 1892. He was president of the Naval War College, 1933–34.

December 9, 1899
At 5:00 P.M. we left for Aparri on the north coast.

December 10, 1899
At 3:00 P.M. arrived off Aparri and anchored about two miles of Linao Point which forms the western boundary of the river mouth. International signals were exchanged with the insurgents on shore. Captain McCalla went ashore and held a conference with General Daniel Tirona, who commanded all the military forces in the provinces of Cagayan and Isabella. The *Helena* arrived and went up the river. *Princeton* arrived.

December 11, 1899
Canet Gun Captured at Aparri
The Marine Guards of the *Newark* and *Princeton*, under the command of Capt. Hall, were landed in Aparri. Captain McCalla then formally received the surrender of General Tirona's command consisting of about 1,000 men. The garrison laid down their arms being accorded the honors of war by the marines. Two 9 cm. Canet guns, 1887 type, forming the battery on Linao Point, and several old brass field pieces were turned over to the Americans. The officers were permitted to retain their side arms. At sunset the light on Linao point was re-established.

December 12, 1899
A company of sailors under Lieut. Carter[34] and Naval Cadet Forman was sent ashore as a re-enforcement to the marine garrison.

December 13, 1899
Last night I was doing picket duty with the steam launch just inside the river mouth. My orders were to stop all boats to see that none of them carried away arms or ammunition. We stopped a number of boats, but all proved to contain fishermen who were as curious to see us as we were to see them, so we had no difficulty in getting them to come alongside. Slept all day. *Callao* arrived and anchored inside river.

December 14, 1899
The *Wheeling* arrived with a letter for Capt. McCalla from General Young, asking the Captain to send an armed force to Pamplona to cut off Gen. Tino[35] who had Gillmore[36] and the American prisoners in custody, in case he should get that far before the troops that were chasing him could overtake and capture him. A company of sixty men, under command of Lieut. H. F. Bryan, with Elson and me as chiefs of sections and Dr. Huntington, was immediately formed. The men were equipped in

---

34 James F. Carter (1869–1931), U.S. Naval Academy, 1891.

35 Manuel Tinio (1877–1924) was one of the central figures in the Philippine independence movement. He fought against the Spaniards and, later, against the Americans. At age twenty-two he was a general and engaged in guerrilla warfare before accepting U.S. rule.

36 James C. Gillmore (?–1927), U.S. Naval Academy, 1876. He retired as a commodore.

heavy marching order. The officers, except Mr. Bryan, wore blue trousers and shirts, campaign hats, leggins, no swords and no blouses. At about four o'clock in the afternoon we were put on board the *Callao* which immediately started for the mouth of the Pamplona river, 15 miles to the eastward. We had a Filipino pilot, and took two of the *Newark*'s cutters in tow. The *Callao* was very slow so we did not reach our landing place until dark. After supper on board we attempted to land in the *Newark*'s cutters, but the heavy surf and the pilot's caution that our boats would be wrecked on the beach, decided Mr. Bryan to wait until morning. So we returned to the *Callao* where we spent the night.

December 15, 1899
At daylight, Mr. Bryan and the pilot took the *Callao*'s dingy to see if we could enter the river in our boats. They found it was impossible on account of the heavy surf on the bar at the mouth. The company then embarked in the cutters and we pulled for the beach where we landed through the surf. The cutter containing the stores and ammunitions was swamped before it was unloaded. Eight men from the *Callao* and a number of natives succeeded in getting the cutters clear of the breakers after two hours work.

A few yards from the water's edge were two well made rifle pits, and about 75 yards back was a small, but deep, river. On its banks was a distillery where a number of natives were making wine from the nipa palms that abounded. We learned that to get to Pamplona we would have to cross the river which could be done on a bridge a little way up the coast. Two canoes were obtained, and in them we put the stores and ammunition with a guard, and started them up the river to the bridge where they were to wait until we arrived. Our main body started along the trail about 10:30. We had to go single file through sand and under brush. Shortly before noon we came to the bridge which proved to be a rickety bamboo structure over which one man could pass at a time. The canoes, with the advanced party were awaiting us. On crossing the bridge we found ourselves on the Rancho de Biduang where we were hospitably received by the *teniente*. The officers were given coca-nuts and eggs for lunch while the men had all the cocoa-nuts they could handle. As we ate, all the men, women and children of the rancho came to shake hands with us and watch us. Mr. Rinchon, the *teniente* placed two carts and two sleds, and four caribou at our disposal so the stores were provided for. He also gave the officers horses, which were small and poor, but nevertheless, very welcome. Near the ranch was a good road which, we were informed, went direct to Pamplona, about a league distant. Our progress was very slow owing to the continual breaking down of one of our carts. After we had gone three miles, we found that a Filipino league is not necessarily three miles, as we were on the edge of a swamp across which we would have to travel. The road here was very muddy, the men sinking up to their knees. One of the caribou insisted on lying down in a mud puddle every five or ten minutes. The swamp is crossed by several streams, which in turn, are crossed by rough bridges, on and off of which, the carts had to be lifted by the men. On reaching the farther side of the swamp we were met by the *Jefe Local* and several prominent citizens of Pamplona. They were very nervous and excited, but otherwise seemed very friendly. When a short distance from the town a brass band met us and escorted our small column to the plaza, where we arrived about five o'clock. An old convent, at present occupied by the priest, was given us as quarters. It was plenty large enough to accommodate all our party, and, in addition, Captain Hall and 25 Marines, who arrived about an hour and a half after we did. They had come from Abulug via the river and road.

December 16, 1899

The next morning we were able to look about the town and take in the situation. Pamplona is situated about six miles from the coast on the Pamplona river, a clear deep stream, easily navigable for small boats. Its population is a little over 1,000 but when we arrived there were comparatively few people in the town, most of them having moved to the ranchos upon learning of our approach. We found, later, that they were informed that the Americans killed all Filipinos—men, women and children—indiscriminately. The houses are built of bamboo with thatched roofs. The floors are raised from four to eight feet from the ground. The space thus formed is occupied by chickens, pigs, dogs, etc. The only approaches to the town are by the road through the swamp, and the river.

December 17–27

During our stay the people learned that the *Americanos* were not so bad, as they supposed, so the natives commenced moving back into their houses, and become real friendly. The *Jefe Local*, the Padre, and one of the citizens who had a sick wife (he came often to get medicine) called on us frequently. We were able to buy chickens, eggs, cocoa-nuts, pomolas, bananas, and plantins. Prices were variable, the knowledge of money being very limited. They did not understand why we wanted so many eggs, as they thought all *Americanos* had machines for making eggs. The Doctor became very popular on account of his medical aid and willingness to provide for their wants. On the whole I think we made a good impression.

Our line of communications to Aparri was open as shown by the unmolested manner in which stores and letters were exchanged. At times the *Newark* attempted to signal us with the search light, but we only succeeded in reading a part of the message. Every evening we could see the *Newark* and *Helena* (about 20 miles up the Cagayan river) signaling one another with their search lights. We received word that Tino was supposed to have 1000 men, but we did not know whether he was coming our way or not. We were five miles from the nearest mountain peak, and the range was some distance farther, so we took the river to be the pass that it was supposed Tino would use. So sentries were stationed there day and night. Twice a day squads were sent out to make a reconnaissance, but no signs of any hostile forces were seen.

The river being near, the men washed themselves and their clothes in it, and were permitted to swim at the same time. The water is very clear and pleasantly cool.

On Sunday's and Christmas, mass was held in the Cathedral, many of the men attending. The brass band furnished the accompaniment for the boys choir. This band performed the remarkable feat of playing continually for 36 hours, starting on the evening of the 24th and stopping the morning of the 26th. During this time they serenaded every house in the town.

We were beginning to think that our stay was to be indefinitely prolonged, when on the evening of the 27th, we received orders to return to ship. The pilot was sent to Abulug to obtain canoes for us to use on the river.

December 28, 1899

All hands were turned out at 4:30 A.M. and made preparations for our departure. About six the pilots returned and reported having the *cascos* ready for us. He had been up all night and showed the effects of his trip. There were four *cascos* in all, three from Abulug, and one belonging to Pamplona. All our surplus stores,

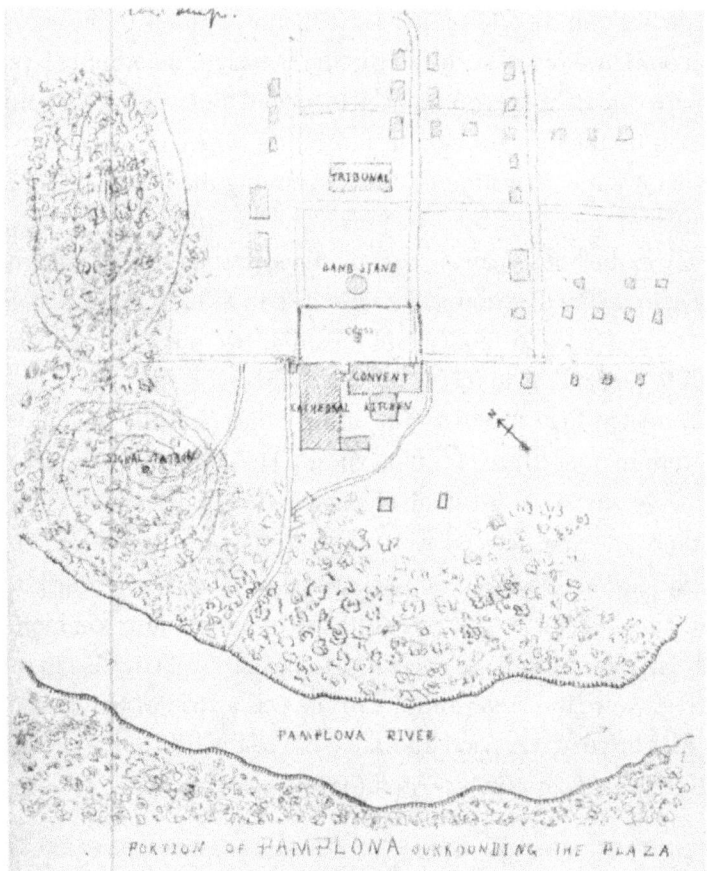

"Portion of Pamplona surrounding the plaza"

ammunition, and cooking utensils were carried to the river by the natives, and after thoroughly cleaning our quarters, and waiting a few minutes for the band, we formed in ranks and marched to the river. The four *cascos* proved amply large enough for all. I was assigned to the Pamplona *casco* with only sixteen men, this being much the smallest boat. We were rowed by six large Filipinos who proved good oarsmen. The men who pulled the Abulug *cascos* were not so fresh as mine, they having rowed from Abulug during the night.

About eight o'clock we shoved off, and as we did so the Filipinos, who had collected on the beach in large numbers, gave us three cheers, which were answered by our men. After rowing about a mile and a half down the Pamplona River we turned to the right and entered a small stream about ten yards wide and averaging ten feet in depth. This stream ran through a marsh, apparently overgrown with Nipa palms which grew to the water's edge on both sides. Now and then we passed a distillery where wine was being made from the nipa palms. We passed a mile along this narrow stream and then entered another broad stream. Whether this was the Pamplona River or not, I do not know. It is evident that the charts of this section of the island are not complete or correct. There is evidently a network of rivers running through the swamp, and I think the Pamplona and Abulug Rivers are connected in more than one place by these small winding streams. Another three miles on this river and we found ourselves in a large shallow basin with the ocean about a mile away, on our left. We were evidently in the mouth of the Abulug river proper, and, by turning to the right, we commenced to ascend the river by that name. About a mile and a half up the river brought us to Abulug, where my *casco* arrived about half past eleven. A large delegation of citizens, among them the *Jefe Local* and the Vice President, and the village brass band were at the landing to meet us. As I did not wish to stay in the hot sun any longer than necessary, I ordered the men to debark, and we marched to the tribunal behind the band. A few minutes before noon the second *casco* arrived, and about 12:15 the other two put in an appearance. The band was sent to the landing to meet each boat, and escort the men to the tribunal. The *Jefe Local* invited the officers to dine at his house, but the invitation was declined as we were anxious to start for Linao point. However, he had a table set in the tribunal and served us some very good chicken and eggs. The men having lunched at the same time, at two o'clock we were ready to start on our march. The officers had horses, and all the luggage, knapsacks, etc., were carried in caribou carts of which we had nine. My horse was a poor little animal about four feet high. The saddle was barely large enough for me to get into it; I couldn't get my feet in the stirrups as they (the feet) were too large; and the bridle was a strip of bamboo tied in the horse's mouth. The road was good and ran close to the beach, the breaking of the surf being always distinctly audible. About four o'clock we halted for our first rest.

We had marched half the distance (six miles) to Linao. The next six we did not expect to make in such good time.

Mr. Bryan sent me ahead to signal the ship we were coming. I had an hour and a half to make six miles in before dark, but my horse was so poor, he could not go faster than a slow trot, and then only when I used my heels and signal staff on him continually. When I reached Linao it was dark, and after talking Spanish for about ten minutes with some natives who knew as little about the language as I did, I succeeded in making them understand that I wanted to signal the ship and wished materials with which to make a fire. They brought me a long bamboo pole and some dried nipa leaves, which I tied on the end of the pole with strips of bamboo. A fire was lighted on the beach, and I wig-wagged "Here, Bryan," which was understood. From the ship they wig-wagged "We'll send boats for you" with the search light.

The advanced guard of the party arrived at Linao about seven, and the main body about seven-thirty. Three carts did not put in an appearance until about eight. They were detained by one of the caribou being exhausted, necessitating a transfer of stores from the one cart to the other two. About eight o'clock the steam launch, with one cutter and one whale boat in tow arrived from the ship. More boats were not sent as it was very rough outside. Half the force embarked in these boats and started for the ship, but the steam launch ran aground, and the other boats, casting off, drifted out toward the ship where they arrived at ten o'clock. The other steam launch and a whale boat were sent to get the launch off the bottom. This was accomplished about one o'clock, and at two the rest of the landing force arrived on board. At 3 A.M. we started for Vigan. We had on board, as a passenger, General Tirona. We arrived at Vigan during the afternoon. The *Zafiro* left for Manila.

January 1, 1900

The *Romulus* arrived from Manila with mail for us. The W*heeling* came in from the northward.

January 2, 1900

Capt. McCalla sent one of the old brass field pieces surrendered at Aparri to the W*heeling* to be presented to the city of that name.

The *Solace* arrived en route to Hong Kong. She stayed only a short while. The merchant steamer *San Joaquin* was at anchor a short time, and the army transport *Romulus* left for Laoag and Aparri.

January 3, 1900

The small merchant steamers *Aeolus* and *Tarlac* arrived. Had target practice during the day. At night had search light drill.

January 4, 1900

Romulus arrived and left late for Manila.

January 5, 1900

The merchant steamer *Venus*[37] arrived from Aparri. Cols Hare[38] and House and Lt. Gillmore and other Americans who were prisoners are on board. Lt. Gillmore and his men were abandoned in the mountains, and were left nothing with which to defend themselves from the savages. Two days after the abandonment the detachment of troops under Col. Hare, caught up with them. They went down the Abulug River to the town of that name, and from there overland to Aparri by the same road the *Newark*'s land force used.

January 6, 1900

The *Tarlac* left the anchorage.

January 7, 1900

The *Zafiro* arrived with coal on board for us. The Captain sent her to Aparri with orders for the *Princeton* to go to the Batan Is. and take formal possession of them.

January 9, 1900

The *Uranus* arrived with troops from Manila. The *Zafiro* returned from Aparri.

January 10, 1900

Coaling ship during morning from the *Zafiro* alongside. About eleven o'clock a fresh breeze shaping up making it necessary for the *Zafiro* to cast off.

January 13, 1900

Have been coaling from *cascos* which are loaded from the *Zafiro* there being too much wind and sea for her to come alongside. The progress during the past three days has been slow. Liquor was found in the *cascos* on the 11th, so the Capts. of these boats were placed under arrest and later sent ashore to the Capt. of the port.

January 14, 1900

The distilling ship *Iris*, Lieutenant Orchard[39] arrived and came along side. Filled up with water and took coal from her. The *Romulus* arrived.

January 15, 1900

Finished coaling from *Iris* and *Zafiro*. *Iris* hauled off and anchored near. The *Zafiro* left for Manila, the *Samar* arrived.

January 17, 1900

The *Iris* left for Hong Kong yesterday. The *Samar* left. The *San Joaquin* arrived. I went ashore for target practice with the 3-inch field piece. The targets were anchored off shore. We used schrapnel only. Small arms target practice.

---

37 *Venus* was used as an inter-island transport.

38 Luther R. Hare was born in Indiana and served with in Texas. He was promoted to colonel in the 53rd U.S. Army Infantry and retired in 1918.

39 John Orchard (?–1942) was an 1877 graduate of the U.S. Naval Academy. He retired in 1911 as a commodore.

January 18, 1900

All boats, handled by their coxswains had a sailing race this afternoon. The gig won. The *San Joaquin* left. Target practice.

January 19, 1900

The *Uranus* and *Solace* arrived. The two Canet guns taken from the battery at Aparri were sent to the *Solace* for shipment to the U.S. Target practice and search light drill.

January 20, 1900

The *Samar* arrived and left shortly afterwards to a place between here and Laoag to attempt to start a light there. The *Romulus* left the anchorage. Target practice.

January 22, 1900

The *Samar* arrived. Mustin[40] reports that the light house was in good condition but he could not find the keeper.

January 23, 1900

The *Samar* left for Manila, and the merchant steamers *San Joaquin* and *Legaspi* arrived from there. The Engineers' force had small arm target practice and boat drill.

January 24, 1900

The *Legaspi* left for Aparri.

January 26, 1900

The *Victoria*[41] arrived late at night owing to the ignorance of her pilot she ran aground to the northwestward of the anchorage. She got off with out damage. Mr. Bryan was sent to her in the steam launch and piloted her to the anchorage. She brought us mail.

January 27, 1900

The horses on the *Victoria* were unloaded one at a time in a movable stall which was lowered into a *casco*. Target practice.

January 28, 1900

Two cases of suspected small pox appeared on board. The patients are isolated on the poop. The *Samar* arrived from Manila.

January 29, 1900

Steamers *Romulus* and *Union* arrived. The telegraph line between here and Manila has been cut. General Young left on the *Samar* for a place 15 miles to the southward to see if he could get communications with Manila. The Captain sent messages asking for permission to go to Manila on account of the small pox cases on board.

---

40 Henry C. Mustin (?–1923), U.S. Naval Academy, 1896, is known as the father of naval aviation.

41 *Victoria* was chartered from the North American Steamship Company in 1899 and 1900.

January 30, 1900

Samar arrived. They were not able to communicate with Manila. In afternoon we got up anchor and started for Manila. Steaming under two boilers.

January 31, 1900

Connected third boiler during day. Passed by Corregidor shortly after sun down. Anchored off Cavite near the *Oregon, New Orlean, Monterey, Glacier, Petrel,*[42] *Wheeling, Helena,* in port.

February 1, 1900

Were placed in quarantine. Small pox patients were removed to a small gunboat which is to be used as a temporary hospital. We have no communication with the shore, but can get fresh provisions from the Captain of the Port at Manila.

February 8, 1900

During the past week the *Nashville, Princeton* and *Calamianes* arrived. We'll be taken out of quarantine on Friday, 9th.

February 11, 1900

Have been coaling ship from lighters alongside during the past three days. The *Brooklyn* arrived from Hong Kong and anchored off Manila Anchorage. Forman was detached and ordered to Mare Island.

February 12, 1900

Went to Manila this A.M. Stopped on the *Brooklyn* for lunch. Saw Fenner, Watson, Marble, Tardy,[43] McIntyre,[44] Horne,[45] Dinger.[46] Drove around Manila in a Iuelis with Dr. Huntington.

February 13, 1900

Got up anchor at 7:30. Swung ship in the bay and went to Manila for fresh provisions. Then put out to sea. *Oregon* left Cavite for Yokohama an hour ahead of us. About sun down we overtook and passed her. Have been steaming under two boilers and making 78 turns.

Portion of stay tube taken from boiler A, showing effect of contact with base feed pipe. The hold in the tube measures 1/2" by 1 3/4".

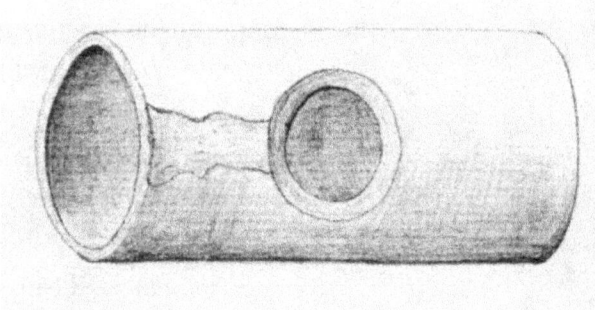

Portion of stay tube taken from boiler

---

42 USS *Petrel* (Patrol Gunboat No. 2) served with Admiral Dewey's fleet in the Philippines and remained there until 1911.

43 Walter B. Tardy (1876–1932), U.S. Naval Academy, 1898. He retired in 1918.

44 Edward W. McIntyre (1877–1931), U.S. Naval Academy, 1898. He retired in 1910.

45 Frederick J. Horne (1880–1959), U.S. Naval Academy, 1899. He retired as an admiral in 1946.

46 Henry C. Dinger (1876–1960), U.S. Naval Academy, 1898. He retired as a captain in 1930.

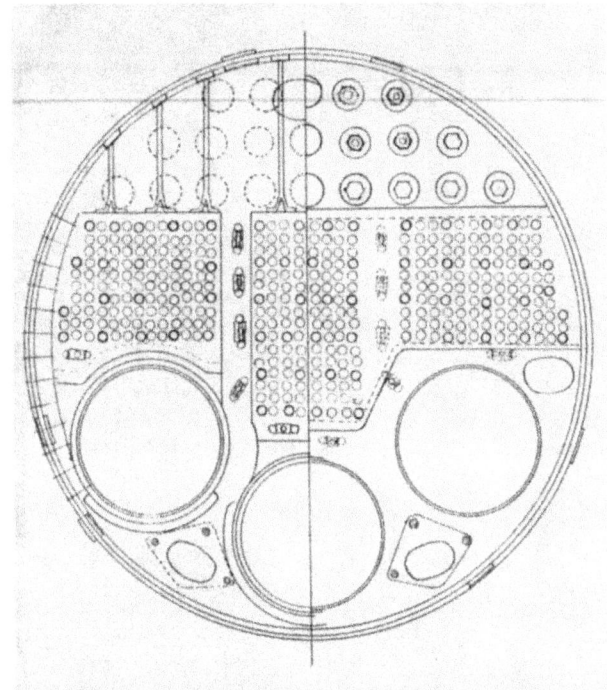

Steam boiler USS Newark

Table for steam pressure of 160 lbs., USS Newark

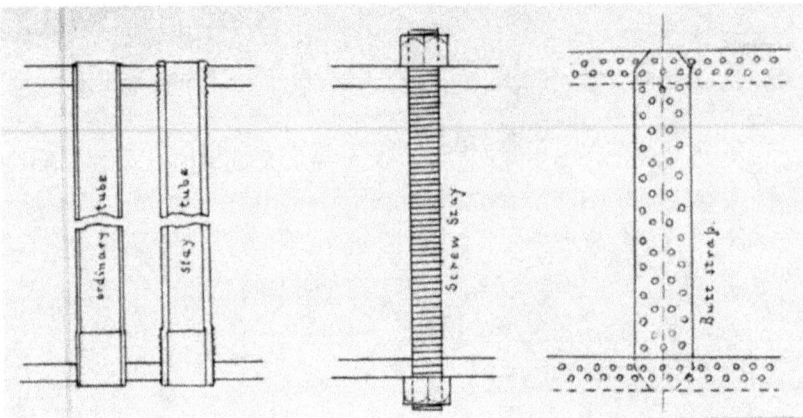

Stay tube diagram, USS Newark

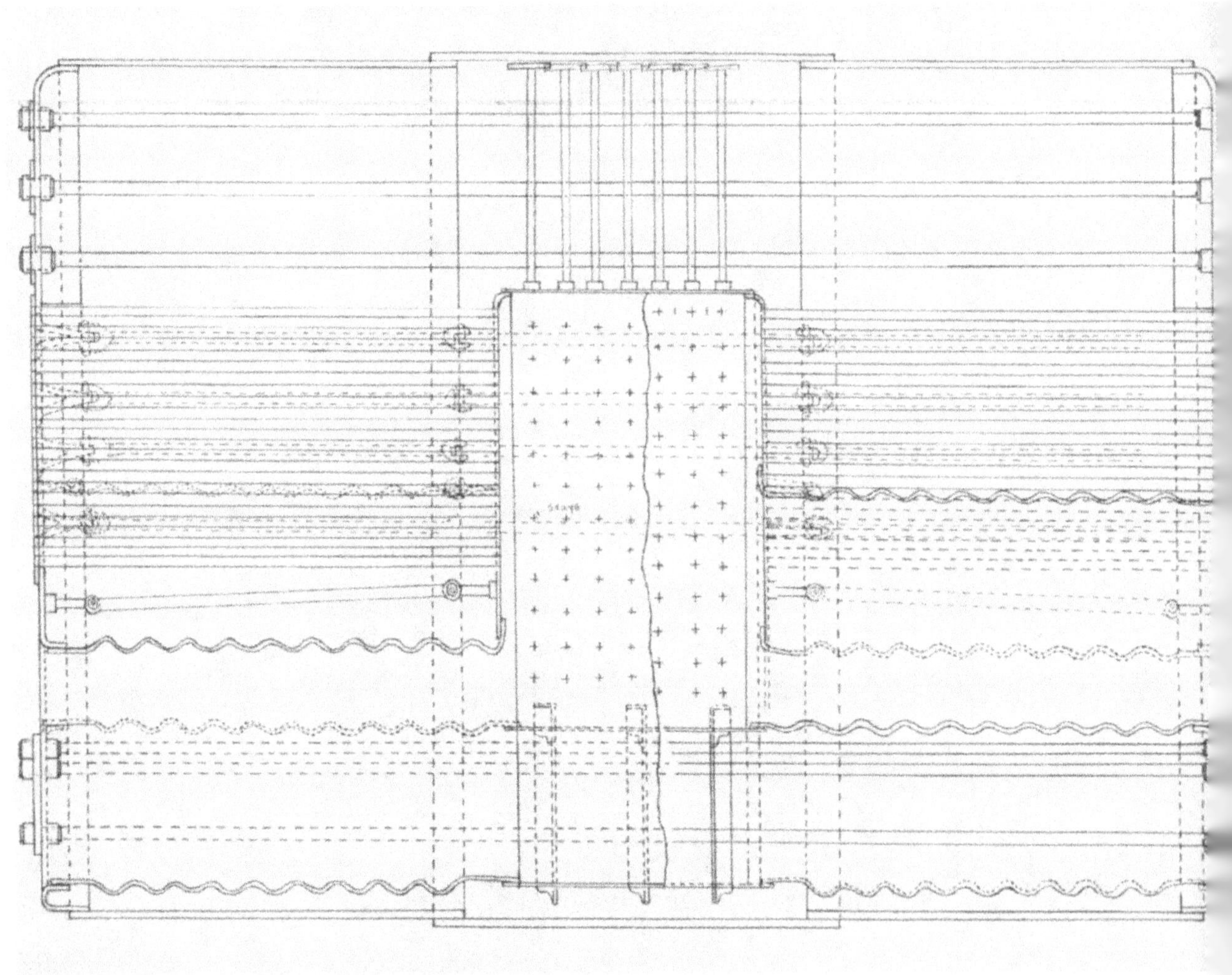

Boiler tube diag

THE PHILIPPINE ISLANDS AND CHINA

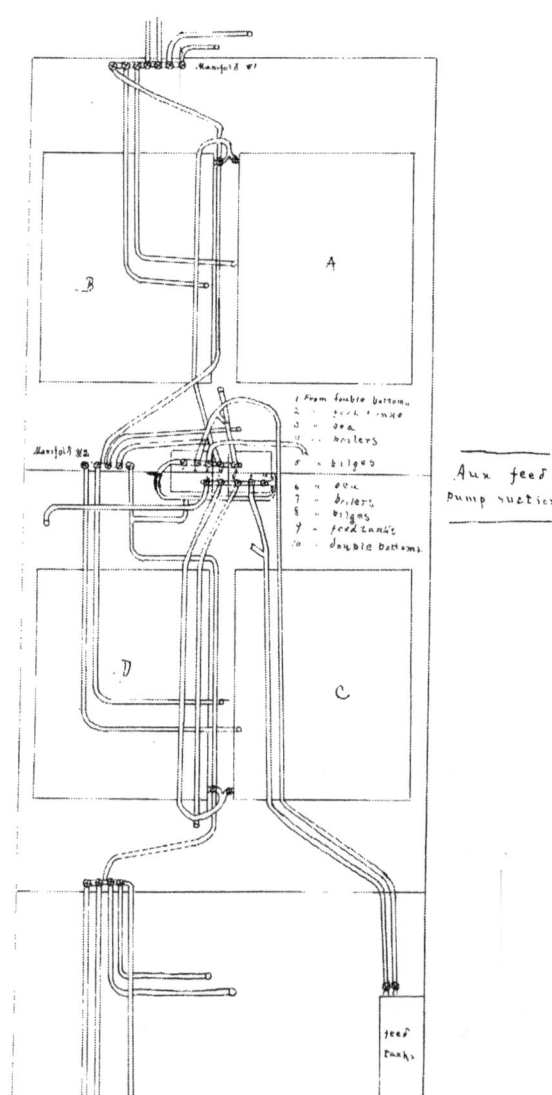

Auxillary feed pump suctions

Upon an inspection of the check valve connections to the shells of the boilers it was found that the metal of the shell around the holes for the internal feed pipes, and the bolts used to secure the flanges to the shells, were badly corroded. As this corrosion is undoubtedly due to the contact of different metals—the boiler shells being of steel; the valve, flanges, and internal feed pipes of brass; the bolts of iron,—the Chief Engineer has recommended that the internal fittings and flange connections of boilers should be of steel or iron, and has requested to be authorized to make these changes in the boilers of the *Newark*.

February 14, 1900
Had great gun target practice during the morning. The third shot fired hit the target and delayed the practice until repairs were made. The *Oregon* passed us. Arrived off Vigan in afternoon. Found the *Samar* in port.

February 21, 1900
Have been having target practice regularly during the past week. A number of merchant steamers have come and gone. The *Mindoro* arrived from Manila. Are raising the engine room hatch combing two feet.

February 22, 1900
Holiday observed on board. Dressed ship rainbow fashion.

February 28, 1900
Painted ship white: upper works spar color. Have been having regular target practice consisting of pistols, small arms and sub-calibers, day and night at stationary and movable targets.

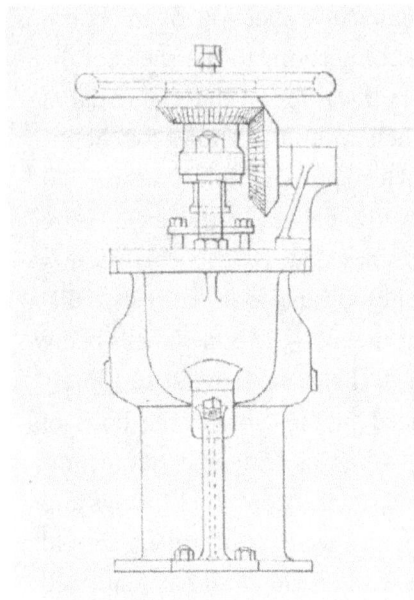
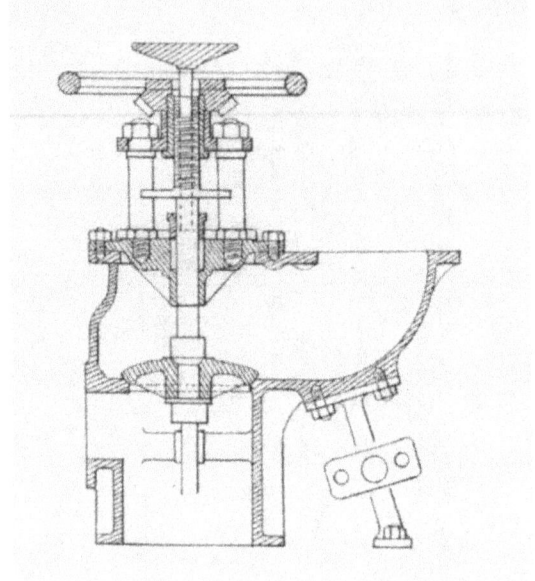

USS Newark *boiler stop valve elevation drawing*

USS Newark *boiler stop valve section drawing*

March 9, 1900

A number of steamers have been in during the past week, and the anchorage has presented a busy appearance. The beach is lined with merchandise and Army quartermaster's and commissary stores. A number of leaks were found in the boiler of the U.S.S. *Mindoro*. A gang of men from the Engineers' force of this ship was sent to make three days repairs on her, it being necessary to put a patch on the bottom and forward end of the boiler. The work was completed to day but upon the application of a cold water pressure of 80 pounds, an additional leak was found. This also requires a patch.

Word was received from Aparri that the army had a slight skirmish on Linao Point. The *Samar* has been sent there. The W*heeling* has been ordered here from Hong Kong.

This afternoon was ordered to Vigan to purchase some fine clay, if possible. Stopped at the *Mindoro* for Neichert. We succeeded in hiring a *queliz* and started for Vigan at a lively pace. When about half way the wheel on my side came off and we were dragged about 30 yards before the horses were stopped. Neither of us were hurt, and we picked up the side of the *queliz* while the driver—a boy—started to put on the wheel. Before he succeeded the horses started full speed down the road dragging the *queliz* after them. I gave the boy a dollar on account of his misfortune, and Neichert and I walked the rest of the way to Vigan. It was hot, and the road very dusty so the walking was not pleasant.

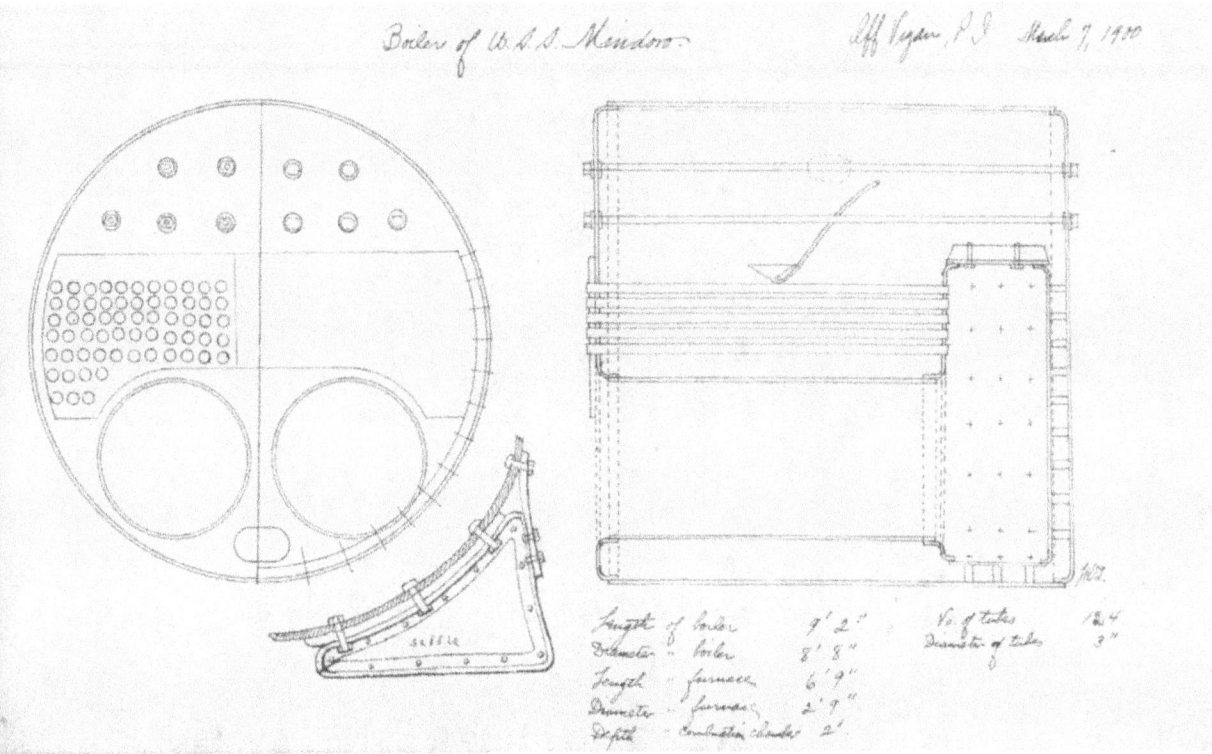

"*Boiler of USS* Mindoro, *off Vigan, P.I., March 7, 1900*"

I was not able to find any fine clay. Made a few purchases from the Army Commissary. Met Col. Hare, who was in charge of the detachment that found Lt. Gillmore. Drove down to the beach in his carriage with Lieut. Williams.[47]

March 10, 1900

The *Wheeling* arrived from Hong Kong and left shortly afterwards for Aparri. Have been continuing work on *Mindoro*'s boiler.

March 12, 1900

The *Baltimore* stopped here for a short while, en route to the north coast of the island.

March 15, 1900

Finished repairs to the *Mindoro*'s boiler. She came alongside and filled up with fresh water and then left for the north coast with our Marine Guard on board.

---

47 Clarence S. Williams (1863–1951) was an 1884 graduate of the U.S. Naval Academy. He was commander of the USS *Gwin* during the Spanish-American War and served in USS *Marblehead* with the Pacific Squadron (1899–1901). Williams was president of the Naval War College (1922–25) and Commander of the Asiatic Fleet from 1925 until 1927, when he retired.

122 THREE SPLENDID LITTLE WARS

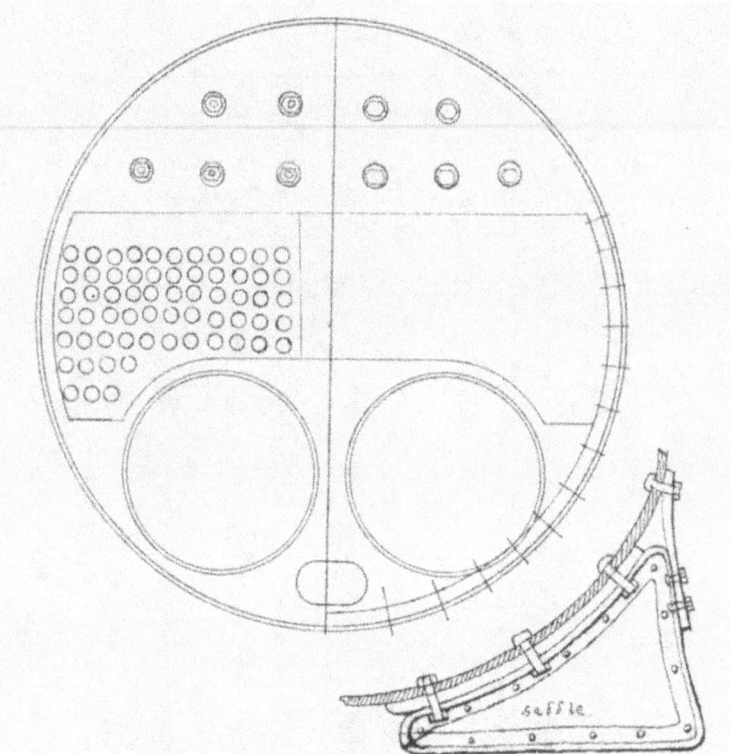

Boiler part close-up

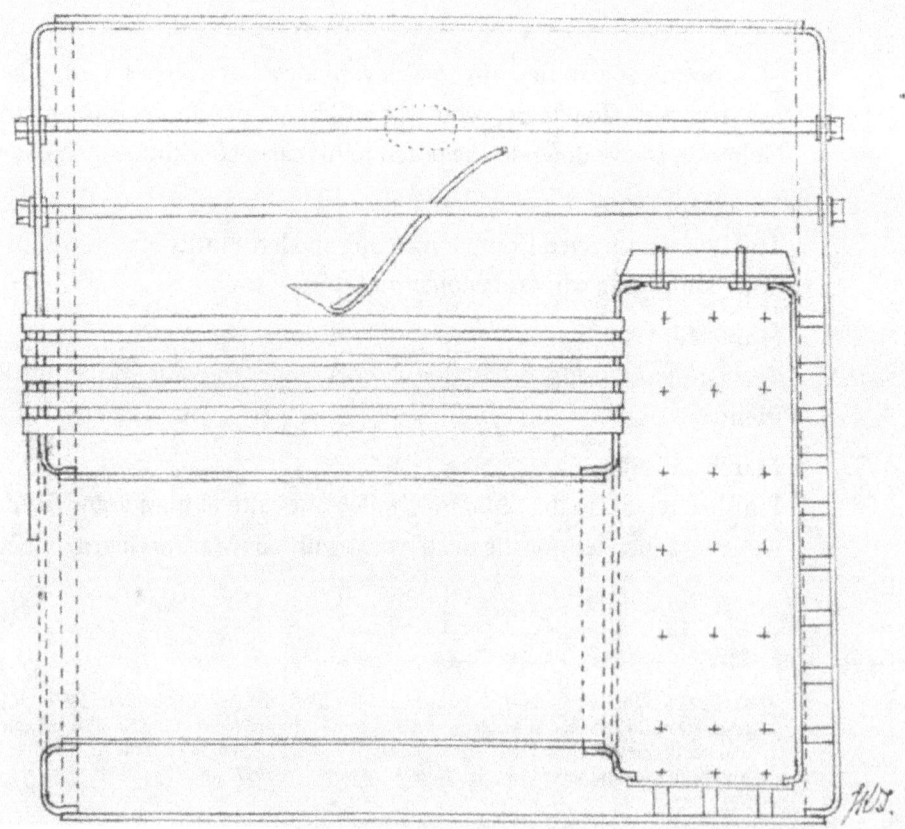

Close-up of boiler part, showing Taussig's initials

Table detail

March 16, 1900
Had great gun target practice. Concussion broke glass in Ward Room sky light.

March 17, 1900
The Army Transport *Tartar*, en route to the United States stopped long enough to take our mail. The *Newark* got under way and stood out from the anchorage, meeting the *Helena* which brought mail and stores from Manila. We passed Cape Bojeador after dark and shortly afterwards called up the *Samar* and the *Mindoro* with the searchlight. They answered with the Very, and came within hail. The *Samar* returned to Vigan and the *Mindoro* continued her trip to Aparri with us.

March 18, 1900
Arrived at Aparri early in the morning. *Wheeling* was at anchor in the river. Captain McCalla ordered her to proceed to Hong Kong via Batan Islands. Our first steam launch broke her shaft near the propeller. We are fitting a new section.

March 19, 1900
Left Aparri during night for Kanuguin Island where we arrived at daylight and anchored in Port San Rio V. harbor. This is where the *Charleston*'s crew went after the ship was wrecked. The harbor is good, and very pretty, being partially surrounded by high, thickly wooded hills. Some of the natives came to the ship in their canoes and Captain McCalla presented them with four tins of hard tack for their kindness to the *Charleston*'s Officers and crew. We remained only a short while and left for Fuga Is. where we arrived early in the afternoon and anchored in Niusa bay. Fuga is a very fertile island and is used as grazing land for cattle. The Paymaster brought three head of cattle for the officers and crew. In the evening we left for Vigan.

March 20, 1900
We arrived at Vigan at 6:30 and were securing the engines when orders came to proceed to Hong Kong immediately. We left before noon. The Captain does not know why we are ordered to Hong Kong as we thought we were going to Manila to get ready to go to Yokohama.

March 22, 1900

Sighted land at day light. Passed a great many fishing junks. While standing in to the harbor at Hong Kong passed the Italian cruiser *Liguira*,[48] outward bound. Passed the Chinese cruiser *Tai Sin*[49] [*sic*] at anchor near the dry dock. Exchanged distinguishing pennants with the *Monadnock*. Saw the *Don Juan de Austria*[50] near the dry dock. Passed the British battle ship *Victorious*[51] and cruise *Undaunted*[52] outward bound for target practice. Moored to buoy No. 2 at the man-of-war anchorage off the city. Near us are the French Flagship *D'Entrecasteaux*,[53] and H.B.M. Ships *Bonaventure*,[54] *Pigmy*,[55] *Alacrity*,[56] *Aurora*,[57] and two torpedo boat destroyers. The British Battleship *Centurion*[58] is in dry dock. There are about forty merchant steamers at anchor in the harbor. Saluted the fort and the British and French Admirals. As soon as we anchored we were surrounded by bum boats and washer men and women. Only a few were allowed on board.

The harbor is very picturesque and is a good anchorage. The man-of-war moor to buoys. There are a few docks where steamers can lie alongside. There are more docks on the Kowloon side across the harbor. The city is built along the foot and up the side of the mountain near the water's edge. The streets are clean and well kept a comparatively easy thing to do, there being no horses and carriages. Jinrickshas and chairs are used entirely for conveyance purposes. A man hauling a ricksha usually travels from six to eight miles an hour, and is able to run for some time. Chairs are carried by two men and are used for ascending the hill. The charges are twenty cents an hour (the money has one half value of U.S. currency).

March 23, 1900

The *Wheeling* arrived from the Batan Islands. I went ashore and made some purchases. Also ordered some clothes made by a Chinese Tailor. A suit of clothes costs about one half of the price in the United States. Made two calls.

---

48 *Ligura*, built in 1893, displaced 2,280 tons and had a crew of 246.

49 *Hai Shen* was built in 1897 by the Vulcan Company of Germany. The 2,950-ton steel cruiser carried 244 men and was 328 feet long, with a forty-one-foot beam.

50 *Don Juan de Austria* was built in 1875. The ship displaced 3,566 tons, was 241 feet long, and had a crew of 440.

51 HMS *Victorious*, *Majestic*-class predreadnought battleship, had a displacement of 14,900 tons, a length of 399 feet, and a beam of seventy-five feet.

52 HMS *Undaunted* (*Orlando* class) was built in 1886. The ship displaced 5,700 tons, and was three hundred feet long.

53 *D'Entrecasteaux* was built in 1896. It displaced 8,014 tons and was 394 feet long, with a beam of fifty-eight feet.

54 HMS *Bonaventure* was built in 1892. The ship displaced 436 tons, was 320 feet long, and had a beam of forty-nine feet, a draft of twenty-one feet, and a crew of 318.

55 HMS *Pigmy* was built in 1888. It was a 755-ton ship, with six four-inch guns.

56 HMS *Alacrity* was commissioned in 1886 and served for twenty-six years in the Royal Navy.

57 HMS *Aurora* was built in 1887. It was three hundred feet long, with a beam of fifty-six feet, a draft of twenty-six feet, and a crew of 497.

58 HMS *Centurion*, name ship of its class and a predreadnought battleship, displaced eleven thousand tons, was 360 feet long, and had a beam of seventy feet. It was the flagship of Sir Edward H. Seymour.

March 24, 1900

The *Zafiro* arrived from Manila en route to Shanghai. The Chinese cruiser *Hai Tein*,[59] flying the flag of a Rear Admiral anchored below the Kowloon Dock.

March 25, 1900

Commenced coaling yesterday morning taking on over 400 tons during the day. Finished this afternoon. The coal was brought from the "godowns" on the Kowloon side of the harbor and carried alongside in junks. Coalies did all the coaling including the stowing of the bunkers. The Russian battleship *Petropavlosk*[60] moored to a buoy near us. This afternoon I went ashore and took a ricksha ride with Mrs. Whiley. We walked up the hill to a road that runs along the hillside overlooking the harbor. We then road along this drive to "Happy Valley" a pretty spot between the hills. Here is the race track on one side of the road and the cemeteries on the other side. Coming home we stopped at the Convent which appeared to me to be an asylum for poor Chinese women and girls.

March 29, 1900

We expected to leave for Manila today in company with the *Monadnock*, but something is the matter with her valve gear, so we did not get off. The British gunboat *Daphine*[61] came in.

March 31, 1900

Left the anchorage at one o'clock and went to sea, picked up the *Monadnock* during the afternoon. She signalled that she could steam a short seven knots. Sea smooth.

Marked "Examined" and signed by B. H. McCalla, Captain (of the U.S.S. Newark*)*

April 3, 1900

Have had a smooth and pleasant passage. The *Monadnock* gradually increased speed to nine knots. Our 2d had great gun target practice both A.M. and P.M. Anchored off Cavite this evening. Found *Monterey, Baltimore, Petrel, Helena* and *General Alava* in port.

April 17, 1900

Have been having target practice daily except last few days while coaling ship. *Yorktown, Nevada, Basco Villalos* arrived. *Baltimore* left for Yokohama on 4th. On 14th *Newark*'s sharpshooters had competitions with *Marrila*'s crew. *Newark* won easily. At 7:00 P.M. today got under way for Yokahama. Steaming under three boilers.

---

59 *Hai-Tien* was built in 1897 at Elswick. It was 360 feet long, with a beam of forty-six and a half feet and a draft of seventeen feet; it carried two eight-inch guns.

60 *Petropavlovsk*, a Russian battleship, was built in 1894. It displaced 10,960 tons, was 367 feet long, and had a beam of sixty-nine feet.

61 *Daphne* was built in 1888. The ship displaced 1,140 tons and was 197 feet long.

April 24, 1900

At 8 A.M. arrived at Yokahama after an uneventful passage. At anchor outside the breakwater the following ships: *Brooklyn*, with flag of Admiral Remey, *Baltimore* with flag of Admiral Watson, *Oregon* with flag of Admiral Kempff,[62] *Yosemite*, *Concord*, *Albatross*, the British Battleship *Barfleur*,[63] the French cruiser *D'Entrecasteaux*, the Italian Cruiser *Calabria*,[64] and the Russian Cruiser *Admiral Korniloff*.[65] Many merchant vessels inside of breakwater.

April 26, 1900

Admiral Kempff transferred his flag from the *Oregon* to the *Newark*. It was raining hard so there was no ceremony. Lieutenant Blue, Lieutenant (J.G.) McLean,[66] and Naval Cadet Pettengill reported on board as members of Admiral Kempff's personal staff. Naval Cadets Marble[67] and Graham[68] reported for duty. Lt. Comdr. Richman[69] and Lt. Pratt were detached.

April 28, 1900

Lt. Comdr. Barton[70] relieved Lieut. Moritz[71] as Chief Engineer of the *Newark*, the latter going to the *Yosemite*. The *Brooklyn* left for Manila. The German Gunboat *Albatross*[72] arrived.

April 30, 1900

H.M.S. *Endymion*[73] arrived. The *Baltimore* flying Admiral Watson's flag left for home. She was cheered by each ship as she passed. Lt. Comdr. Bull[74] and Ensign Tozer reported for duty.

May 1, 1900

I was transferred from duty in the Engine room to duty on deck. At present there are six officers standing watch and as I just missed my turn, I have five days off, so I put in a request for four day's leave which was granted.

---

62 Louis Kempff (1841–1920) graduated from the U.S. Naval Academy in 1862. He was Senior Squadron Commander, Pacific Squadron. He was promoted to rear admiral in 1899.

63 HMS *Barfleur* (*Centurion* class), was built in 1892. Admiral Earl Beatty served in it and was wounded at Tientsin.

64 *Calabria* was built in 1894. It displaced 2,470 tons and was 249 feet long.

65 *Admiral Korniloff* was built in 1887. The ship displaced five thousand tons and was 350 feet long.

66 Ridley McLean (1872–1933), U.S. Naval Academy, 1894.

67 Ralph Marble (?–1952), U.S. Naval Academy, 1898.

68 John S. Graham (1875–1957), U.S. Naval Academy, 1898.

69 Clayton S. Richman (?–1903), U.S. Naval Academy, 1870.

70 John K. Barton (?–1921), U.S. Naval Academy, 1873.

71 Albert Moritz (?–1941), U.S. Naval Academy, 1881.

72 *Albatross* was launched in 1871 at Danzig. It became a survey ship in 1888 and was stricken from the Navy in January 1899. It was sold as a seagoing lighter and later used as a coal barge.

73 HMS *Endymion*, an *Edgar*-class cruiser, was launched in 1891. It displaced 7,350 tons and was 387 feet long.

74 James H. Bull (?–1932), U.S. Naval Academy, 1870.

May 6, 1900

Courtney and I returned from four days leave—we left on the 2nd. After going ashore we took the train for Tokio, and on arriving there put up at the Imperial Hotel. In the afternoon we took a long ricksha ride and visited some of the Temples. We saw the Government buildings and the Palace grounds. From a hill near the centre of the city we had a fine view of the surrounding country. We returned to the hotel, had dinner, and, as it was raining, hired a carriage and drove through the Yoshiwara district.

The next morning it poured down rain, so we spent several hours playing pool with three Midshipmen from H.M.S. *Endymion*. It cleared about twelve o'clock so we went to the Uyeno Station, and took the train to Nikko. We and Alger (a son of the En Sec. of war)[75] were the only ones in our section of the car. The trip to Nikko was very pleasant and interesting. At the stations there was a great racket made by the natives' wooden shoes on the paved platforms. There were always a number of men shouting out what they had to sell—beer, mineral waters, hard boiled eggs and little lunches put up in flat boxes. At Utsunomiya we changed cars, and the road now led up toward the mountains at the foot of which Nikko is situated. We arrived at Nikko about dark and found hotel rickshas waiting for us. The drive to the hotel is through the main street which is lined on both sides by Japanese shops. Many gaily colored lanterns were hanging in front of the houses, making a very picturesque appearance. The hotel, called the Kanaya House, is kept, by a Japanese in European style. We were made very comfortable, and found everything very satisfactory.

The morning of the 4th was very clear, so we had a fine view from the hill on which the hotel was built. We engaged a guide who showed us through some of the Shinto Temples and tombs of the Shoguns. These temples and tombs are built on the side of a hill which is covered with beautiful tall trees. Stone steps, many in number, lead from the road at the foot of the hill, up to the temples. The amount of work done on the temples is wonderful. Detailed wood carvings and lacquered panels abound. The Japanese Government is no longer rich enough to build such temples.

In the afternoon we took a long walk up the mountain side to Kirifuri water falls. There was not a great abundance of water in the stream so the falls were not so fine as we expected to find them.

We returned to Yokahama the next day, and reported our return on board ship.

---

75 Russell A. Alger (1836–1907) was a lawyer and businessman who made a fortune in the lumber business and served as governor and senator from Michigan. He was appointed secretary of war in 1897 in the McKinley administration and served until 1899, when he resigned due to criticism of his handling of the department during the war and his appointment of General Shafter as army commander in Cuba.

May 21, 1900

We expected to remain here some time and then go to Kobe and other Japanese ports and Chinese ports for an extended cruise, but orders have come on board to proceed to Taku, China, immediately. The *Concord* and *Bennington* which were under orders for San Francisco, and were going to leave tomorrow, got orders to proceed to Manila instead. The Admiral stayed to inspect the two gunboats before they left for the States, and had only inspected the *Concord* when the new orders came. I was a member of the Inspection Board. The *Concord* was short about forty of her complement, and some of the Officers were only recently attached to the ship, so she did not pass a very good inspection. We left this A.M. for Kobe.

May 24, 1900

The Inland Sea—Coaling the Newark at Nagasaki

We arrived at Kobe about 3 P.M. on the 22d, and stopped just long enough to take on a pilot for the Inland sea. Unfortunately, we passed through the narrower parts of the sea at night, so we did not see the scenery. However the moonlight effect at night was very pretty.

The small fishing boats dot the sea, and make it very unpleasant for steamers to keep clear of them. We passed the P.M.S.S. *China* and the C.P.S.S. *Empress of Japan.* We arrived at Nagasaki early in the morning of the 24th. The Harbor here is a fine one being completely land locked by high hills covered with verdure. Its principal drawbacks are the heat in summer, and lack of size. During the past few years Nagasaki has become a very important coaling station for vessels of all nations, and the number of ships continually there crowd the harbor very much. We commenced coaling immediately—Japanese coolies (mostly women and girls) doing the work. They coal very rapidly from lighters alongside, tossing small baskets from one to another in a long line thus keeping a continual stream of coal passing through the port.

Today being the Queen of England's[76] birthday all the men-of-war in the harbor (about ten of them) dressed ship and at noon fired a salute of 21 guns. The cannonading sounded very loud owing to the closeness of the vessels, and the high hills surrounding the bay. Courtney and I went ashore with the Captain and had tiffin with Consul and Mrs. Harris and Daughter. After tiffin Courtney and I went with the ladies to see the boat races between the boat crews from the men-of-war in harbor. The *Newark* sent a small cutter which was ruled out of the cutter race but was permitted to row with single banked boats from the Austrian and English cruisers. Of course our boat was beaten. The Austrians won all the races.

---

76 The celebration marked Queen Victoria's last birthday, as she died on 1 January 1901.

When Courtney and I started to return to the *Newark*, we saw that she was under way and going down the harbor. We though she was not going to leave until the next morning. A steam launch from the *Oregon* picked us up and went chasing after the *Newark* which was steaming slowly. We soon caught her and scrambled up the sea ladder.

XI *The Boxer Rebellion*

1900

We are off to Taku, presumably to send a guard of Marines to the Legation at Peking. We have on board 25 Marines from the *Oregon* under command of Capt. Meyers.

May 27, 1900

We arrived off Taku on the afternoon of the 27th. Near us were Chinese cruisers, and, about two miles away, the French cruiser *D'Entrecasteaux* and the French Gunboat *Surprise*.[1]

The anchorage at Taku is from twelve to fifteen miles off shore, due to the shallow water. The land is so low it cannot be seen from the anchorage unless one goes aloft; the water is a yellowish green, so on the whole "off Taku" is not an attractive place to remain at anchor.

When we arrived the French Admiral was ashore, but he returned the next day, and his two vessels put out to sea. It was rumored that he said he would not land any men to guard the French Legation at Peking, because he heard the R.R. line was in danger of being cut.

May 29, 1900

On the Landing at Taku—On the Lighter Going Up the Peiho to Tientsin—Street scene in Tientsin—Admiral Kempff and Lieut. Blue—A Chinese barber in Tientsin

On the morning of the 29th, I was awakened at five o'clock by the Captain's orderly who said, "The Captain says to get ready to go ashore right away, and be prepared to remain four or five days." The uniform was heavy marching order which meant leggings, knapsacks, haversacks, blankets, and canteens. The officers wore sword and pistol; the men rifle and belt.

On deck the sixty men who were to go were making preparations to embark. Canteens were filled, one day's ration put in each haversack, and each belt filed with 180 rounds of rifle ammunition. The remainder of the crew were busy getting the

---

NOTES 1 *Surprise* was launched in 1895. The gunboat displaced six hundred tons, was 184 long and twenty-six feet in beam, drew twelve feet, and was armed with two 3.9-inch guns. She sank on 3 December 1916.

3-inch field piece, ammunition, stores, and water in the sailing launch, and a cutter. At 7:30 the party being embarked in the above mentioned boats, we shoved off from the ship in tow of the steam cutter.

The bar at the mouth of the Peiho River has from nine to eleven feet of water on it at high tide, and a few inches to two feet at low tide, so boats can pass over it only when the tides favor. When several miles from the slip, the steam launch stuck in the mud. We lightened her by transferring some of the men into the other boats, and in this way ploughed through the soft mud for some distance but she finally stuck fast, and Ensign Wurtsbaugh, who was in charge, gave orders for the other boats to cast off and to pole ahead. We found poling very hard work, as both tide and wind were against us.

The sailing launch succeeded in making sail, but there were over fifty men in the cutter so I could not get at the sails. To add to our present discomfort a heavy wind and rain squall passed over us about this time. After poling about a mile, I threw over our anchor and waited developments. The officers and men in the launch (except the crew) hired a couple of sampans and started after us. These sampans being very light draft, and built especially for working in this shallow water, soon came up to the cutter, and one of them coming alongside I transferred enough men into it, to enable us to make sail. The wind and the tide were such now that in heading to windward we lost as much as one leg as we made on the other. The Sailing launch gave up sailing as a bad job, and anchored some distance ahead of us. Before long, the tide changed, and with it the wind so we were enabled to steer a straight course for the mouth of the river. The change of tide caused the water to rise sufficiently to permit the steam launch to get under way, so she came ahead full speed, and caught up to us just before we entered the river. The two ship's boats, and the several sampans were taken in tow and in this way we proceeded to Taku. Before reaching the landing, we passed through a large fleet of junks and fishing boats, and between the two low mud forts on either side of the river. At the landing we found the 50 Marines under the command of Capts. Meyers and Hall, who had left the *Newark* at four o'clock that morning. It was now one o'clock, as all hands turned to and ate lunch, which consisted of canned corned beef and hard tack.

The Europeans at Taku advised us to start immediately for Tientsin as it was rumored that the next day no armed foreigners would be allowed to pass the forts. For some unknown reason, the privilege of traveling on the rail-road was denied us, so a tug and a large lighter were chartered. This lighter had previously been used to carry mud so when we were sent below immediately after starting, our discomfort can easily be imagined. We remained below until all the forts were passed, and were glad when we were permitted to go on deck again. The Peiho River is a muddy winding stream varying in width from thirty to a hundred yards. The banks are low, and covered with growing rice—a very pleasant contrast to the mud banks near the mouth of the river.

We passed numbers of villages, all the houses of which are built of mud and straw. The villages—with their narrow streets, and uniform yellow coloring—are not picturesque—more over all villages look alike to me. The houses are built on the water's edge, and as we passed within a few yards of the banks, the people would run out of their houses to gaze at us.

Junks loaded with tribute rice for the Empress Dowager and merchandise; fishing boats and sampans were at anchor [or] moving up and down the river. As we passed each village there was a great scurrying among the boat owners to get in their crafts and prevent them from being washed against the bank by the waves of our two.

Many people were engaged in throwing water from the river into the irrigation troughs on the banks. This and fishing appeared to be the chief occupations.

We arrived at Tientsin at 11 P.M. When we disembarked we found a brass band and the whole foreign colony on the wharf to meet us. They had been so worked up over the possibility of a Boxer uprising, and had been looking forward so eagerly to the arrival of foreign forces, when we arrived the enthusiasm ran high. As we fell in on the wharf some one shouted, "Three cheers for Uncle Sam," and they were given with a will, all nationalities taking part. When the stores and field piece were disembarked, the band began a tune and we marked to Temperance Hall—our temporary barracks. The foreigners followed us all the way. When we entered the building another three cheers for "Uncle Sam" were given, and the crowd dispersed.

The next day, Capt. McCalla and the American counsel, Mr. Ragsdale,[2] tried to get permission to send the fifty marines to Peking, but the Chinese authorities would not allow the armed force to travel on the railroad; so we had to await further developments.

The foreign city of Tientsin was, when we arrived, a clean well policed place. The houses are of brick; the streets good and comparatively wide. Business was progressing in the liveliest manner. Along the Taku road, on which Temperance Hall is situated, there was a continuous stream of jinrickshas, carts, and peculiar Chinese wheelbarrows loaded with all kinds of merchandise. Along the bund (riverfront) loading and unloading the junks went on day and night, large gangs of coolies being employed for this purpose.

---

2 James W. Ragsdale (1848–?) was born in Indiana and attended Cornell College, Iowa. He was involved in newspaper work in Iowa and California for twenty years before joining the diplomatic service. He was consul and consul general in Tientsin from 1897 to 1908, then held similar posts at St. Petersburg, Russia, and Halifax, Nova Scotia.

May 30, 1900

During the day foreign detachments representing the British, French, German, Russian, Japanese, Italian, and Austrian marines arrived at Tientsin. It seems that the call for troops by the Ministers at Peking must have been very urgent, because when we left the *Newark* at 7:30 A.M. on the 29th, there was not another foreign warship at Taku, and on the evening of the 30th, there were over twenty foreign men-of-war, at the anchorage.

May 31, 1900

Third Class Accommodations—The Crew of the Colt Automatic and Sentry—Marine Guards of the Oregon *and* Newark *Marching to the R.R.*

The next day, May 31, the pressure brought to bear by all the powers having landing forces at Tientsin, became too great for the authorities to continue to refuse the use of the railroad, and accordingly a train was made up for the combined forces. The Americans being the first at the station, Captain McCalla demanded the right to occupy the front coaches of the train, which our force accordingly did. The American officers that went to Peking were: Captain McCalla, Paymaster Jewett, Captains Meyers and Hall of Marines, Assistant Surgeon Lippitt,[3] and Naval Cadet Courtney. Only the Marine officers and surgeon remained, the others returning to Tientsin the next day.

The force consisted of fifty marines and four sailors with a colt automatic gun. Each man had 180 rounds of ammunition in his belt, and an additional 10,000 rounds were taken along. The Allied force comprised in all about 400 men.

In the meantime, we, who were left in Tientsin, moved our quarters from Temperance Hall, to the American Board Mission Compound, where we occupied a house belonging to a missionary, then in the States. This compound, like others in Tientsin, is enclosed by a brick wall. In it is a chapel and four houses—residences of the missionaries and families. Our force consisted of fifty-four sailors with the following officers: Ensign Wurtsbaugh,[4] Gunner Sheldon, Warrant Machinist Mullinix, and myself. We had with us the 3-inch field piece with 72 rounds of schrapnel, and a colt automatic mounted on a tripod.

There was a great difference of opinion among the people of Tientsin as to whether there was really going to be any trouble, or whether it would all blow over. Rumors came very day that the Boxers were approaching with the intention of repeating the massacres of 1870. But the Imperial troops were encamped near the city and at Yang Tsun 18 miles distant. How could the Boxers attack the foreign city of

---

3 Thomas M. Lippitt, an assistant surgeon in USS *Baltimore*, had one year and one month of sea service.

4 Daniel W. Wurtsbaugh (1873–1941) graduated from the U.S. Naval Academy in 1896. He retired as a captain in 1922.

Tientsin so long as these troops were near to protect it? However there were several missionaries who were outspoken in their belief that the foreigners had more to fear from these troops, than from the Boxers.

All was quiet in Tientsin and we settle down to routine life. We had sentries at the two gates during the day, and an additional post on the Taku Road at night. We also sent patrols around certain parts of the city during the night.

We established messes for the Officers and men. Fresh meat and vegetables being available, the rations were good. When the water we brought with us from the ship was consumed, we boiled all water used for drinking purposes—as the Tientsin water is not considered wholesome.

Rumors continued to be spread concerning the approach of the Boxers. Numerous posters were posted up about the native city—a translation of one is as follows:

Sacred Edict

Issued by the Lord of Health and Happiness

The Catholic and Protestant Religions being insolent to the Gods and extinguishing sanctity, rendering no obedience to Buddhism and enraging both Heaven and Earth, the rain clouds now no longer visit us; but 8,000,000 spirit soldiers will descent from Heaven and sweep the Empire clean of all the foreigners. Then will the gentle showers once more water our land; and when the tread of soldiers and the clash of steel are heard, heralding woes to all our people, then the Buddhist Patriotic League of Boxers will be able to protect the Empire, and bring peace to all its people.

Hasten then to spread the doctrine far and wide; for if you gain one adherent to the faith your own person will be absolved from all misfortunes; if you gain five adherents to the faith your whole family will be absolved from all evils; and if you gain ten adherents to the faith your whole village will be absolved from all calamities. Those who gain us no adherents to the cause will be decapitated; for until all foreigners have been exterminated the rain can never visit us.

Those, who have been so unfortunate as to have drank water from wells poisoned by foreigners, should at once make use of the following divine prescription, the ingredients of which are to be decocted and swallowed when the poisoned patients will recover:

Dried Black Plums—half an ounce

Solanum dulcamara—half an ounce

Enconimia ulmoides—half an ounce.

The Chinese are so superstitious an edict like the above has a great effect upon them. Then also they undoubtedly feared that the Boxers would carry out their threats—one of the chief reasons of the rapid growth of the organization.

As the situation grew more serious, and as more men-of-war arrived off Taku, detachments of sailors and marines continued to arrive at Tientsin.

June 6, 1900

About June 6th the railroad line between Tientsin and Peking was cut, but the telegraph lines were (for some unknown reason) left intact. Fifty additional sailors under command of Ensign Gilpin[5] were sent from the ship. There were quartered at Temperance Hall. Definite news came that the Boxers were burning railroad stations and foreign missions, that they had murdered some missionaries and many native Christians, and that they were moving toward Tientsin.

Our vigilance was now increased—especially at night. The city was divided into sections to be guarded by the different nations, and many streets were barricaded. Our men stationed at Temperance Hall slept out in the open in rear of the building. Sentries were placed at points on the large plain there guarding all approaches to the city from that direction.

The field piece was on land—ready for action. Those of us at the compound slept near the main gate opening on the Taku road. Sentries were placed a short distance from the road to guard that approach, which is the main thoroughfare for the Chinese and foreign cities. We had benches and boxes ready to barricade the street at a moment's notice—and the cold automatic was on hand at the compound gate.

Further attempts were made to run a train through to Peking—but they met with failure—the tracks being torn up. Telegrams from Peking stated that affairs were becoming more serious—and asking for reinforcements to the Legation guards. As it began to look as if we might have to do some fighting, 10,000 additional rounds of rifle ammunition were sent from the ship.

June 9, 1900

On the evening of June 9th there was a meeting of the consels and the commanders of the several detachments to consider important news that had been received from Peking. About midnight I was awakened by Wurtsbaugh, and told to call all hands at four o'clock, have them place their effects together, get breakfast, and be ready to march to the station at six o'clock. It seems that at the meeting it was decided to send a relief column to Peking immediately. Captain McCalla had us march to the station early, so as to be sure to get in the first train. However when we reached the station we found a train there that had just arrived from Taku. In the train were the crews of H.B.M.S. *Centurion* and *Endymion*. In rear of this train there was a second with the crew of H.B.M.S. *Aurora* on board. These forces had left their ship at midnight, and were to go to Peking. Vice Admiral Sir Edward Seymour[6] was in command. After some delay, the Americans, Italians and Austrians embarked in the first train together with the English that were in it. Our men were placed in two cars; the provisions, water and ammunition in a flat car; and the American Officer[s] in that part of Admiral Seymour's baggage car that was not occupied by Admiral

---

5 Charles E. Gilpin (?–1936), U.S. Naval Academy, 1896.

6 Sir Edward Hobart Seymour (1840–1929), Admiral of the Fleet, served in the Crimean War, on the China Station, and on the west coast of Africa. He was promoted to flag rank at age forty-nine. In 1897 he was named commander in chief of the China Station and then, in 1900, Commander in Chief, Naval Forces, during the Boxer Rebellion. He retired in 1910.

Seymour's baggage. And we expected to reach Peking in two days! That is how well we, who were on the spot, understood the situation.

We, the Americans, had six days provisions with us: what the others had I do not know, but some of the detachments started with the intention of living on the country.

The train left the station early in the afternoon. Every thing along the road appeared normal for the first twenty-five miles. The country is flat, and dotted with graves. In fact all this part of China appeared to be one big grave yard. The ground was dry and sun-baked, the crops accordingly being in a very behind time condition. Villages and cities are innumerable, the plain being dotted with them as far as the eye could reach. I noticed that there were no houses standing alone—the Chinese evidently live entirely in villages and cities. The country is also unfenced—the only fences being those around the yards in the village. But the fields used as rice paddies in the wet season are divided by mud walls from two to four feet high and about a foot thick.

At Yang Tsun, the first important station outside of Tientsin, and about eighteen miles from that city, a portion of the Chinese Imperial Army, under General Neigh, was encamped. The men were well tented on the banks of the Peiho, and appeared to be in good condition. The army was protecting the track.

About seven miles beyond Yang Tsun we were brought to our first stop. Here we found a few rails and ties torn up, but they were replaced in short order, and we proceeded. However in the next five miles we were frequently brought to a stop by rails and sleepers being missing, but the repairs were soon made in each case. Towards evening we came to a long bridge spanning a part of the country that is flooded by the overflowing of the Peiho River during the rainy season. The ties at both ends of the bridge were burned, but otherwise no damage had been done.

Why the damages so far had been so slight we could not understand. It seems that the first intention of the Boxers was to keep the people in Peking from getting to Tientsin; because the right up track, was much more badly torn up than the left. The railroad being under British management, our train, of course, was on the left up track; a fortunate thing for us as we only repaired that track, and consequently saved much time and Labor. Parties from all detachments turned to and gathered the partly burned ties for fire wood. Soon camp fires were lit on both sides of the train, and supper was in order. As we ate our hard-tack and canned beef, remarks of this sort were frequently heard: "Well, tomorrow evening we will take supper in Peking"; I remember remarking as I looked down at my soiled uniform, "I'll be a pretty sight to dine with the Minister and the Ladies at the Legation": As we turned

---

7 Nieh Shih-ch'eng (1836–1900) was a Chinese general who commanded the Wuyi army that fought against the rebel forces during the Boxer Rebellion.

in on the ground someone said, "I hope there are enough beds at the Legation to go round," etc., etc.

A double line of sentries with pickets inside were placed around the train.

Under the bridge we saw the first signs of the Boxers or Chinese Soldier's work. Lying on the sand were the trunks of three bodies—the heads, arms and legs being scattered around. From the appearance of the remains, the butchering had not been done, more than twenty-four hours previous to our arrival. It was a gruesome sight, but it undoubtedly had its good effect, for it was proof that we were in the Boxers' country, and consequently, there was not a sentry who was not all ears and eyes that night.

June 10, 1900

The next morning work on the bridge was commenced at five o'clock. The British and Americans did the work—the others looked on. Our progress was very slow, and about three o'clock, when near Lofa station, we had our first experience with the Boxers. An alarm was given by someone shouting, "Man the cars." Immediately all was confusion, there being a variety of orders that made it impossible to understand what was to be done. Captain McCalla gave us orders to get under the cars, and a few moments later to form in skirmish line on the left side of the train. We then advanced, and saw before us a party of about ten Chinese, whom we at once recognized as Boxers, by their red caps, belts, and anklets, and the white and red flags they were carrying. Each one carried a huge knife or a long spear, and as they advanced towards us very slowly, making all sorts of gestures and salaams, they formed a picturesque group. It was the Boxers' belief that they were bullet proof, and they made these peculiar motions to turn the bullets aside—consequently they had nothing to fear. However I suppose that they have become convinced of the fallacy of their belief in regard to their invulnerability. These few men were fired on by about two hundred men, at about two hundred yards range, so of course all were killed in a few minutes. We then advanced in skirmish line through a village near by, but no Boxers were seen.

Towards evening we arrived at Lofa. This place is thirty-five miles from Tientsin and was a watering place for the engines. Both tracks and the switch were torn up very badly, the station was in ruins, and the water works, demolished. It was decided to repair both tracks and the switch, so any shunting that might become necessary could be accomplished. During the day two more trains from Tientsin had caught up to us, so our force now consisted of about 2100 men. The four trains stretched along the track for over a mile.

June 11, 1900

Early the next morning, a meeting of the senior officers of each detachment brought forth the following order from Vice Admiral Sir Edward Seymour, R.N., the commander of the combined forces:

At Lofa Station

Agreement made at the meeting of officers in command of forces of different nationalities on Monday 11 June.

(1.) That some further organization is required to keep up proper discipline, and be prepared in case of meeting an emergency.

(2.) That though we are a mixed force of 8 different nations, we are all united in two objects which are: (a) To open communications by railway with Peking and thus ensure the safety of our Legations and national interests at that city. (b) To assist the Chinese Government to restore peace and order in this part of China.

(3.) That in view of (1) we arrange and agree as follows:—

    a. That the senior officer of each train, whatever his nation, be treated as commander thereof.

    b. That the instructions I have addressed to that train be sent to him. He will be in easy communication with the officers commanding the forces in his train, and will at once confer with them.

    c. That whenever we stop for the night, as soon as may be after sunset, pickets and sentries be posted on the plan sent here with, unless special circumstances demand other arrangements.

    d. That whenever the trains stop, sentries of each nation be posted round the train on the same plan as for night, but only as many as seem required to control the movements of our men.

    e. That no men be allowed beyond these lines of sentries unless accompanied by or passed out by an officer of their own service, who will then be responsible for their conduct and safety.

(4.) That in order to preserve the railway as it is opened we leave, as we go on, a picket on each station on placed advised by Mr. Currie, composed from each nation in turn, according to their number, and beginning with the British as there are most of them.

(5.) That a system of signals be arranged between each train.

(6.) That when a watering place is reached, as here, arrangements as to who shall first use it be made by the commander of each train if they are alone; and if all are together by him in consultation with Captain Jellicoe—my flag captain.

(7.) That some simple system of bugle calls be considered by an officer of each nation this forenoon and when agreed on adopted for present use; also of steam whistle of the engine for the trains to show what they are about to do.

(8.) Watering the engines to be arranged by the officer commanding each train when it is required by the engine driver, or for any other work to do with the train.

(Signed) E. H. Seymour, Vice Admiral & Commander-in-Chief

The plans for sentries and pickets were never carried into effect, some circumstance always preventing. The plan placed the pickets 500 yards from the train, and the sentries 200 yards beyond these. This distance was found to be entirely too great, and both lines were drawn in so that the sentries were never more than 300 yards from the train. The last two nights the sentries were placed on top of the cars and on the platforms, as both sides of the road bed were protected by sheets of water.

The water supply was beginning to be a serious question. All the water used came from wells, and that for drinking purposes had to be boiled. But we first had to ascertain whether the wells had been poisoned by the Chinese, who invariably deserted each village before we reached it. The Chinese coolies with us never hesitated to drink the water, and as soon as we saw it did them no harm, we began to use it too. Strange to say we did not find one poisoned well. I think this was due to the fact that the villages intended to return to their homes as soon as the column passed through. The next question was concerning the amount. There were numerous wells, but only a few of them were artesan, and as it had not rained for many weeks, most of the wells had but little water in them. The third day out from Tientsin we were still at Lofa, and it became necessary to water the engines. Our tender held 4000 gallons, and as the pumping apparatus in the wells had been demolished by the Boxers, it was necessary to form a bucket line from a well thirty yards from the track. The water was hoisted by a tackle suspended form a tripod placed over the well. Although the Americans had been working on the track all day, it fell to us to water the engine of our train. The buckets were passed as fast as the water could be hoisted, but it took us six hours to fill the tank, the work being completed at midnight. It was the intention at first to limit the men to one canteen of water a day, but it was so hot and dry, it was absolutely necessary to allow more.

I do not remember ever experiencing such dry weather. Without exception everybodys' lips were parched, and most of them split. To add to the discomfort, the wind, which was hot during the day, from blowing over the dry soil, always carried a fine dust that made it impossible for us to keep clean with the limited supply of water. The nights were cold—that is cool enough to make it very uncomfortable, and while standing watch, one had to keep in motion to prevent shivering. All our men had rubber and woolen blankets, so sleeping was comparatively comfortable.

It was now seen that it was going to take at least a week longer to reach Peking. So every day, until the line was cut in our rear, a supply train was sent to Tientsin. This train was in charge of Paymaster Jewett who had a small marine guard with him. It left the trains every evening and returned the next morning. It is a significant fact that altho' this train always passed through the Chinese Army at Yang Tsun, it was never molested. We received good supplies of canned goods and mineral waters, so we lived fairly well as far as food was concerned. About 100 coolies were engaged to assist in repairing the road. Car loads of ties, rails, spikes and fish plates were brought from the railroad yard at Tientsin. By means of the switches at Lofa these cars were transferred to a place next to the engine of the first train, which came to be known as the "construction train" and was placed in charge of Captain McCalla. Admiral Seymour's car was the last one of this train.

When we left Lofa, about 100 men from H.M.S. *Endymion* were detailed as a garrison. They made their quarters in an enclosed compound that served them as a fort. Not long after they occupied it, "Fort Endymion" was painted in large letters on the wall.

Between Lofa and Lang Fang—the next station, about five miles beyond—the track was in fairly good condition. But when we reached Lang Fang we saw that the track was torn up for about a mile. The station, which was burned, is just half way from Peking and Tientsin being 40 miles from each. The water works had been treated similarly to those at Lofa. It was decided to prepare both sides of the track here also, so as to utilize it for shunting purposes. There was undoubtedly three or four days work ahead of us here.

Up to this time, the British and Americans, with the aid of the Chinese coolies, had been doing all the work on the track. The work was very hard for men not accustomed to it. It consisted chiefly in carrying ties—sometimes several hundred yards, digging out the rocky road bed for the ties, lifting the rails and putting them in place, and driving spikes. The sailors were not very successful spike drivers so most of that work was done by Chinese coolies. I doubt if a Naval force ever had to build a railroad before, and I also doubt if any force of equal size ever laid so much track per unit of time. Every other tie was placed—then one track was laid in an approximate line, and spiked down, no leveling being done nor plural line used. The other track was laid parallel by means of gauges. On looking along the relaid track it presented a snake like appearance. But it answered our purpose just as well as if we had taken more pains and more time—and time was the chief element.

When the repairs at Lang Fang were completed, a portion of the construction train was sent ahead about two miles to start repairs on the next broken stretch. I was with the working party, and was sorry for it afterwards, as I missed an exciting fight between the Boxers and our forces at Lang Fang. Nor did we know anything about the fight until after it was over, and a squad advancing along the track signalled, "The trains have been attacked in force." This was to put us on our guard in case the Boxers contemplated attacking us. Fortunately they did not, as only half of us were armed, and we were not prepared to repel an attack, so that we would have been taken by surprise. When we returned to the station that evening I saw the results of the fight and heard the stories told by different people who took part in it. It seems that the fighting ability of the Boxers had not been appreciated, nor was it thought for a moment that they would make a bold attack in force, so the train was not properly picketed. The Boxers had no fire arms, but were armed with spears and large knives. They passed through a village near the track and through an orchard very near the station, and were advancing in the double time down the track before they were discovered. Several Italians who had been surprised in the village were fleeing before them, but they were evidently too frightened to give an alarm. The cry "man the cars" was given, and was obeyed by a great many, who were then unable to fire on the Boxers who were advancing straight down the track. A few American and British officers rushed to the head of the train and soon had a number of men around them. The Boxers were nearly to the train when the first shots were fired by our men, and in many cases hand to hand conflict ensued. Captain McCalla took his orderly's rifle and shot down several men, while a number of officers used their revolvers with good effect. One British officer stuck his sword in a Boxer's mouth. The mob continued to advance until a gatling gun was brought on the scene and turned loose. This seems too much for the enemy who turned around and fled, leaving 102 dead on the field. Our loss was five Italians who had been surprised in the neighboring village.

When I looked at the dead Boxers I could easily see how reports of casualties were usually exaggerated. It looked to me as if there were at least 500 of them but the count showed only 102—a great disappointment. The Italians were buried at the station—detachments of all nations attending the funeral.

A large collection of knives, spears and banners were taken from the dead Boxers. These were going to be kept as curios and souvenirs. One of the banners had printed on it in Chinese, ideographs. "Death to all foreigners: by order of the Government." We did not take this seriously but considered it a Boxer scheme to obtain new numbers to their faith. Our train ran back to Lofa to see if the garrison in Fort Endymion was all right. When we arrived, the dead Boxers lying in the field showed that there had been a fight there also, with the result of about 100 Boxers killed.

Our attempts to communicate with Peking were not very successful. Of course it would have been impossible for a foreigner to get to the Legations, and not one of the Chinese with us could be persuaded to make the attempt. At Peking they were more successful, but although several messengers were sent to us, only one put in an appearance. He was an old Chinaman who had long been employed at the American Legation. He came through from village to village disguised as a rag-picker and delivered his message which was from Mr. Squires,[8] the Secretary to the American Legation. The message said that the Legations were in a critical condition, and urged us to advance as rapidly as possible. The same messenger was entrusted with a note to our Minister, telling of our progress and whereabouts.

Our plan now was to continue repairing the road to Anting, about fifteen files beyond and twenty-five miles from Peking, and from there make a forced marched to Peking. A party of British Marines were sent ahead to reconnoiter and give warning of the vicinity of any Boxers. The construction train then pushed ahead, repairing the road as rapidly as possible. The other trains remained at Lang Fang on account of the watering facilities.

This part of the track was very much torn up, and in some place the road-bed removed. A small, single span bridge was completely down. We raised the spans by using rails for levers, and chocking up with ties until high enough.

---

8 Herbert Goldsmith Squiers (1859–1911) served in the U.S. cavalry from 1877 to 1891 and then joined the diplomatic service. He served as secretary to the legation in Peking in 1898 and was chief of staff to Sir Claude Macdonald during the siege of Peking (1900–1901). He was envoy extraordinary and minister plenipotentiary to Cuba (1902–1905) and to Panama (1906–10).

Our policy from now on was to burn every village that showed signs of harboring Boxers,—and we found a number of them which made very good blazes. We also sent all foraging expeditions to kidnap mules, horses and carts, that might be useful on the march from Anting. The Americans got one horse and five mules, which afterwards were very useful.

June 16, 1900

About three miles from Anting we came to a village where the track was very badly torn up for a long distance. The British marines who preceded us found a number of Boxers here, and killed many of them at the village inn. In the inn yard we found many ties, fish plates and spikes. The village was burned.

While repairing this break, Captain McCalla received orders from Admiral Seymour to return to Lang Fang. We put back immediately, and on arriving learned that the track had been torn up in our rear near Yang Tsun, so that our line of supplies and communications had been cut. The supply train reported that the Chinese Army was no longer at Yang Tsun.

June 16, 1900

That evening, July [June] 16, the construction train put back as near Yang Tsun as the torn up condition of the track would allow. The next morning we began to repair the track again, but this time we were working towards Tientsin. The Admiral was anxious to get the train to the station before night and then water the engine, but the track was so badly damaged, our attempt failed. The next day we started in again on the repairs, and a small detachment was sent a short way ahead to ascertain the extent of the damages. On their return they reported that the tracks were torn up as far as they could see. So now there was no doubting the fact that the Imperial Troops had stopped protecting the road, and it looked as if they were the ones who had destroyed it, before leaving the station. That afternoon, the 18th, the three trains that were at Lang Fang returned to Yang Tsun, bringing with them about forty wounded. They reported that they were attacked in the morning by a large body of Boxers, supported by Imperial troops. The enemy were defeated with a loss of about 500, but the allies lost several killed and the above mentioned number of wounded. It was the first time, fire arms were employed against us. Captain Von Usedom,[9] of the German Navy, who was the senior officer at Lang Fang, knew that the Chinese army had taken part in the engagement, because several Imperial banners were captured. Seeing that it would now be futile to try to make Peking and went to hold Yang Fang, he had ordered the trains there and at Lofa to put back to Yang Tsun. A meeting of senior officers was held, and it was decided to abandon the trains and start for Tientsin the next day. Although Yang Tsun is only eighteen

---

9 Guido von Usedom (1854–1925) joined the Imperial Navy in 1871. He was promoted to captain in 1899, rear admiral in 1905, and vice admiral in 1908. He retired in 1911 with the rank of admiral.

miles from Tientsin by rail, and about thirty by the river, it was decided to follow the river, as we had no means of carrying the wounded overland. The Germans had seized three junks which were used to convey the wounded and part of the stores, and the Americans captured several small boats in which were placed water beakers, knapsacks, and blankets.

June 19, 1900

The morning of the 19th found all detachments busy preparing to move. Nothing was to be carried excepting what was absolutely necessary. Our horse was given to Admiral Seymour, Captain McCalla rode one donkey, and the other donkeys were used as pack animals to carry water and stores, and the ammunition for the 3-inch field gun. Each American carried 180 rounds of rifle ammunition in his belt, and 70 rounds in his haversack. The haversacks were filled with hard tack and canned goods. The Americans took along the 3-inch field piece, and Colt automatic, and the British had two nine pounders.

Admiral Seymour complimented the Americans by detailing us the advanced guard and Captain McCalla organized us as follows: First a point of three marine sharpshooters—1st Sergeant in charge; a distance of 100 yards in support of 10 marines with Paymaster Jewett in charge; another 100 yards and a reserve of 20 men with me in charge; 100 yards and the main body hauling the field piece, and as infantry, with Ensigns Wurtsbaugh and Gilpin and Cadet Courtney, Gunner Sheldon was in charge of the Colt automatic.

The British were next to us, but I do not know the order of the other detachments. I think the Austrians and Italians formed the rear guard, as I do not remember seeing them on the return march.

At noon on the 19th, the Americans started on the return march to Tientsin. It was decided to follow the left bank of the river so the force crossed on the bridge, the field piece being ferried across on a junk. As each of the other detachments formed, we advanced to make room for them in our rear, and it was not until four o'clock that all detachments were clear of the trains and ready to move. Our progress, at first, was very slow, the bugle frequently sounding "the halt," for apparently no reason. We learned later, however, that the junks were giving a great deal of trouble owing to the inexperience of the men handling them. They had to be poled and hauled from the banks, so they frequently ran aground until the navigators became more expert. That night found us only a few miles from the trains, and we camped in an open space, having the river on one side for protection. After the sentries were posted we turned in on the ground, for the usual three hours' sleep—it being impossible to get more, owing to the arrangement of watches. The night passed without noteworthy instances, the only disturbances being the very frequently hee-hawing of the mules.

June 20, 1900

At six in the morning we were again underway, and made fairly rapid progress until about ten. The advanced guard was resting in the shade waiting for the column to close up, when the point reported a body of men advancing on the road. Captain McCalla sent me with a few men to reconnoiter. By passing through a recently deserted village on our left I saw that the body of men consisted of a force of about 200, who judging from the great number of banners they carried, were evidently Boxers. Our field piece was brought up in a hurry and planted in the middle of the road, all our men except the gun's crew being deployed as skirmishers on either side. Some of us had a mud wall for protection—others were lying down in the open. Owing to a slight rise in the road ahead of us we could see only the Boxers banners. For some time we did not know whether they had fire arms or not, but when they came to within 800 yards they opened on us with about thirty rifles—evidently all they had—but the bullets flew high over our heads. As we did not return the fire, they advanced slowly until within 570 yards, when a shot from our field piece caused them to halt. Two more shots, and not a Boxer was to be seen, they having disappeared in a village a short distance in their rear. We had no casualties, and if the Chinese had any they carried them along as we came across no killed or wounded when we advanced across the open space and through the village into which the enemy had disappeared. Strange to see this village was deserted—the Boxers evidently being scared by the field gun. The country being flat and interlined with mud walls, together with the numerous villages and thousands of grave mounds so that it was easy to defend, but very hard for the party on the offensive.

The Boxers took up their position in the next village and again opened fire, but this time as we advanced. They were soon put to flight but only went as far as the next village, which was a very short distance away. Although we saw very few Chinese, we were brought to a temporary stop at every village, by these thirty or forty rifles that always opened on us. They also had two jingals that threw a projectile that made a very nasty sound as it whistled over our heads. These projectiles always went so high we began to regard them as a joke, but towards evening, our gunner's mate who was some distance in the rear with the Colt automatic was struck in the leg with one of them which took out a big piece of his calf. The projectile was a large bolt nut! We had to charge through a number of villages, and several times the Admiral found it necessary to send flanking parties across the river to drive the Boxers out of the villages on that bank.

Late in the afternoon we were brought to a halt at a village a short distance from the river. The rifle fire of the enemy was suddenly augmented, and instead of only thirty or forty rifles, we heard volleys—ragged ones—as if from a hundred or more. All the Americans were now on the skirmish line which was gradually strengthened by the British, French, and Japanese. Our field gun and the British nine pounders were put into action, but the ragged volleys continued. It suddenly dawned on us that although the volleys were increased, we heard no more whistling bullets overhead than previously. The Japanese Captain was the first to solve the problem, which he did by uttering the single word "fire-crackers." The order was given to fix bayonets followed by the order "charge." The whole line—Americans, British, French, Japanese, advanced on the double, all yelling at the top of their voices. We passed through the village—not a Chinaman was seen. Firecrackers were added to the list of defensive fire arms by eight nations. The line continued to advance through the next village, as it was desired to hold these two villages as protections for our camp which was to be pitched in the open space between them.

The order was passed to burn these two villages, and small firing parties were dispatched to start the conflagration. Before long both villages were burning brightly, and we encamped with a feeling of security as we were nearly surrounded by the river and the burning villages. The camp was a fine sight.

June 21, 1900

All hands were called at four o'clock, but it was six before we got started. In front of us was a mile of open plain with a city—Pietsang—on the farther side. The city is built on both sides of the river. We crossed the plain unmolested, but as we approached the houses, we could see, with the aid of the glasses, a number of men in a grove of trees to the left. As we were about to enter the city along the river bank a sharp musketry fire was opened on us from a point in the river bed where it made a sharp turn to the right. This fire, which was much heavier and more rapid than the day before was supplemented by some large guns that threw shrapnel. Although the Chinese shot high, we were brought to a halt and took whatever cover could be found.

Admiral Seymour saw that in order to dislodge the enemy (we were now quite sure that we were no longer dealing with Boxers only, but also had the Chinese army against us) he would have to dispatch a force across the river, and continue the advance on both sides. The Russians, Germans and Japanese were ferried across the river; the Americans, English, and French remaining on the original side; and the Austrians and Italians continuing as rear guard. As soon as the Russians reached the other bank a heavy schrapnel fire was directed at them, and they were forced to take shelter behind some joss houses. As soon as the Germans were across they stretched out in skirmish line to the right, and the advance commenced on both sides. We kept close to the river, keeping under cover of the houses, when possible, and firing on the Chinese whenever we saw them, which was seldom. Bullets and shell were flying thick, but they continued to pass over us. As we advanced the enemy slowly retreated and finally made a stand about five hundred yards beyond the edge of the city. We were held in check for some time, as it was seen that we would have to charge, as they remained so well covered—it was impossible to drive them out by shooting. We covered the five hundred yards between us and the Chinese, in stages of about fifty yards, the Chinese in the mean time retreating and taking up a strong position behind another mud wall, while we used the one they had just abandoned as a breastwork. Our casualties were one or two killed, and several wounded. The Chinese undoubtedly greatly outnumbered us—probably 3 for 1 at least, judging from the empty cartridges they left behind them. From now on I could not see what was going on across the river.

It again became necessary to dislodge the Chinese from their new position, and this was done by advancing in stages with fixed bayonets. For two hours we continued our rushing tactics, the Chinese repeatedly leaving one position for a new one several hundred yards in their rear. Our casualties were few, and theirs were not much heavier, as they kept so well under cover, but they could not stand up to the bayonet.

Our skirmish line was made up of Americans, British and French, indiscriminately mixed. It was very difficult to make the Frenchmen understand orders—the one cease firing especially—as when the once got started it seems the height of their ambition to shoot as rapidly as possible, whether [there] was anything to shoot at or not. Once I got on the wall we were using for a covering, to signal the men to stop firing—and a Frenchman shot right between my legs. I cussed him out in English, which I am afraid he did not understand—I did not have time to think up my French. However, there never was any hesitancy in obeying the order to advance, the line always moving forward on the double until the next cover was reached.

In two hours we covered about two miles, and we were beginning to think that we were not going to have so hard a time after all. We were advancing along one side of a raised road which afforded good cover, and the Chinese now took a position farther on under cover of the same road where it made a sharp turn to the right. Here they made a determined stand, and for a while we were checked. Then suddenly the Chinese cavalry, about three hundred strong, appeared on our left-flank deployed as skirmishers. They opened fire on us with their carbines, but the range was too great, and we could see the little puffs of dust made by the bullets striking the ground some distance short. The field pieces which were a short distance in our rear were hauled up on top of the road and opened on the enemy in front, but the bullets flew so thick they were brought under cover of the road again, and opened up on the cavalry which appeared timid about approaching. The first shot fired by our 3-inch fell among the horsemen and caused them to split, and two more shots scattered them and put them to flight. The cavalry did not bother us again. If we continued to advance along the road we would soon lose the benefit of its protection on account of the turn, unless we crossed over, so this was the next step to be accomplished.

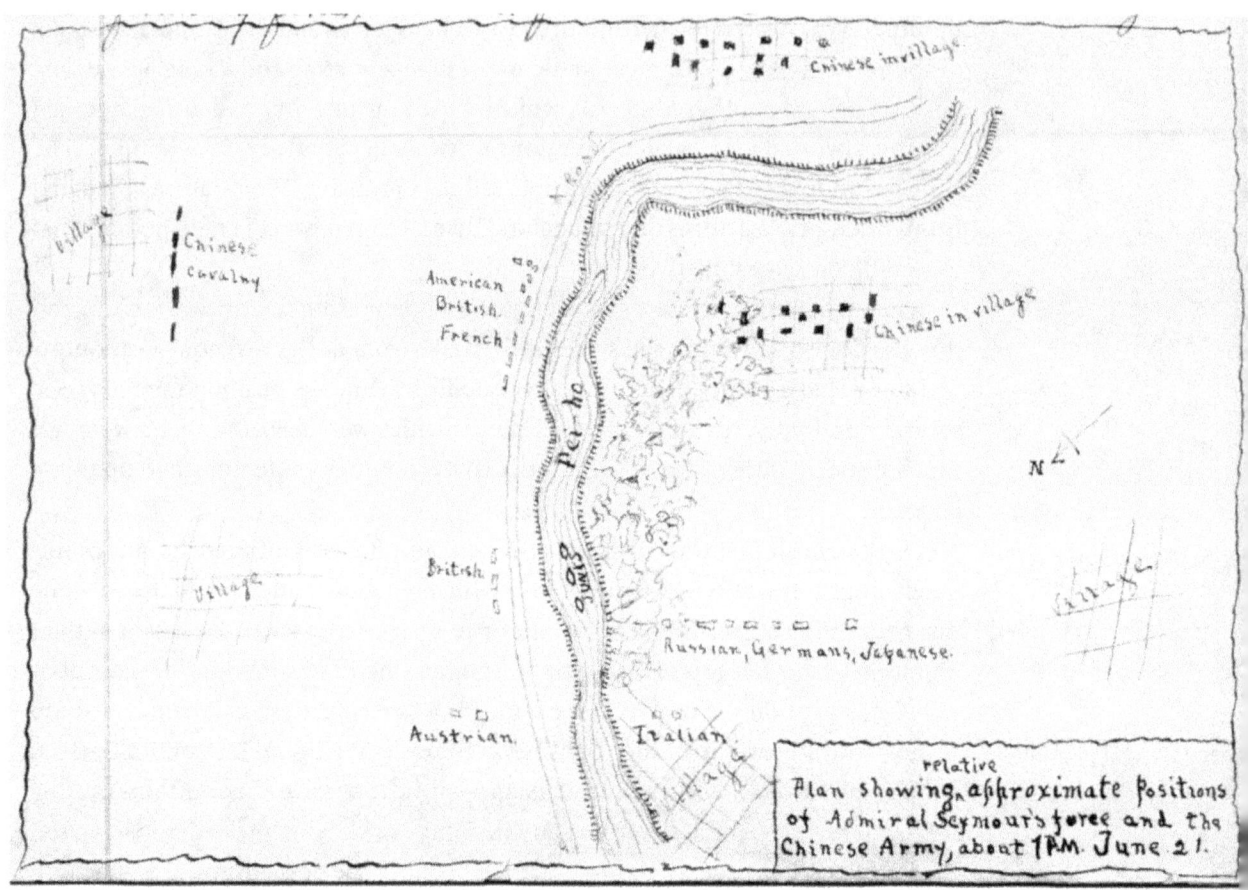

Locations of various armies during the battle

As the men who had been dragging the field piece were tired out, Captain McCalla ordered that my sections should change places with them. Before the charge was completed, Captain McCalla and Paymaster Jewett with a few men crossed over the road. In a few moments I was following, and as I gained the top of the road I saw our men lying down about twenty yards ahead of me. Although the bullets were flying thick I was never so surprised in my life when I felt a blow in my right hip that knocked me down.

My first impulse was to get under cover, and as I was the only person on top of the road at the time, no one saw me fall, so I managed to slide down the other embankment, and thought I was undercover—which I found out afterwards was a mistake. I couldn't get up so there wasn't anything to do but to wait until someone came across me. In a few minutes an English Midshipmen with a few men went by on the double, and I asked him to give me a hand, but he went on as he had orders to re-enforce the firing line. A few minutes more and a British Lieutenant and two sailors picked me up and carried me to a small depression in the ground, not far away.

In a few moments more wounded and several killed were brought to the same place. This was the first time we encountered casualties of any importance. It seems that we, on our side of the river, advanced more rapidly than the force on the other side, so that when we crossed the road, the Chinese whom we supposed the Germans and Russians had driven back were on our flank and opened up on us as soon as we were exposed to their fire. So when I slid off the road, I slid towards this flanking force, and was fortunate not to have been hit again.

After driving the enemy from their positions a halt was called for a little lunch and some much needed rest. Captain McCalla asked me if I was badly hurt, and I told him, "No," that I thought a bullet hit a stone which flew up striking me in the hip and bruising it badly. The several killed were buried on the spot, and when the advance moved on the wounded were left in charge of a few men until the junks came along, when we were to be placed on them. In about an hour I noticed that I was bleeding a little and upon examining my wound I discovered that the bullet had passed through my thigh. In two or three hours we were carried on improved stretchers to the junks, which were very crowded so that places had to be made for us. My billet was on top of a lot of stores, necessitating a moving every time stores were needed. However I was perfectly indifferent as to what was going on, and although bullets were flying I paid no attention to them, and do not remember much of what went on during the remainder of the day. In fact a great deal of the happenings from then on, I learned through hearsay. That afternoon the column continued to move forward, the fighting being similar to that done in the morning.

As there was no American doctor with us (Dr. Lippitt was in Peking and Dr. Russell[10] was sick on board ship), the British doctors tended to the American wounded. As there were so many casualties, the Dr. did not get to me until about six in the evening. All they could do for me was to set my leg (I did not know it was broken until the Dr. told me) and wrap a bandage around it. No splint was to be had. That night morphine was injected in my arm to allay the pain.

The column camped for the night and were not disturbed.

June 22, 1900
Early in the morning the advance commenced again, and the Chinese opened fire as soon as the movement commenced. The day passed very much as the previous day. Bullets and shell continually passed over the junks and several bullets hit the one I was in. In turning a bend in the river, the junk ahead of mine ran aground, and for some time was exposed to a heavy fire. It was got out of range by several British sailors who jumped overboard and shoved it to a place of safety. However before this could be done, two of the wounded were hit with bullets, and the junk was struck by a shell causing it to sink later on. The wounded had to be crowded into the other

---

10 Averley W. Russell, Jr., was appointed surgeon in 1895.

junks. Camp was made early in the afternoon so as to give the men much needed rest, before an intended night march when it was hoped the column would be able to reach Tientsin without further resistance, as the Chinese never had given any trouble at night.

June 23, 1900

At 2 A.M. camp was broken and the forward movement commenced. For a short distance the column was unopposed, and we began to think our hopes were realized, but we were doomed to disappointment, as before long the Chinese showed that they were on the lookout for us, and commenced firing. During the remainder of the night very little progress was made, and it began to look as if another long day of continual fighting was ahead of us.

About 9 A.M. there was a sudden let up in the firing, and for a short time the column advanced unopposed. We were approaching a number of buildings surrounded by a wall and moat. The head of the column was nearly past the farther wall, when two Chinamen hailed Admiral Seymour asking who we were and where we were going. The interpreter answered that we were peaceful foreigners going to Tientsin. The Chinese leisurely disappeared, and instantly a heavy fire was opened on the column. Our men returned the fire and took cover wherever it afforded. It became evident that we must take the place. So a large flanking party, under the command of Major Johnstone,[11] Royal Marines, was sent out with orders to make a wide detour and thus surprise the enemy. The movement proved entirely successful and at a pre-arranged signal the charge was made from the two directions, and the surprised Chinamen became utterly routed, leaving the compound in possession of the foreigners. A hasty inspection was made and those with us who knew the country said we had captured the Hsiku Arsenal. As the inspection uncovered an immense supply of arms and ammunition it was decided to occupy the Arsenal until a relief force was sent from Tientsin. Several rooms were cleared out and all the wounded were brought from the junks and placed on boards on the floor of the arsenal building.

This Arsenal proved to be an undreamed of discovery. The Chinese government had been secretly laying up arms and ammunition in this place until it was simply stacked with the most modern implements of defense and offense, the value of which amounted to millions of dollars. There were powder magazines with both black and smokeless powder, thousands upon thousands of Winchester, Mauser, and Manlichen rifles and carbines, hundreds of thousands of rounds of ammunition for these rifles, swords by the hundreds, and field guns, siege guns and larger guns enough to equip armies and forts. That this place was so easily taken was really

---

11 James R. Johnstone (1859–?) was promoted to major on 1 May 1894.

marvellous. All detachments were set to work fortifying the place, so that before many hours the Admiral considered it able to withstand the attacks of many thousands of Chinese. As enough rice was captured to last two weeks, for the present we felt secure.

All the wounded officers were placed in a large room which contained numerous field and siege guns, and boxes of ammunition stacked to the ceiling. On my left was a Russian Lieutenant, and on my right a German Lieutenant, while near my feet was a British midshipman. The Russian could not speak any English, but the German spoke quite fluently so we were able to carry on a conversation on the subject of being relieved, and to compliment one another—he commenting on the magnificent bravery of the Americans—and I telling him how finely the Germans were organized and how beautifully they maneuvered. He had with him a picture of his wife and two children which he showed me with great pride.

Shortly after dark it was determined to send a small detachment through to Tientsin so as to report our whereabouts and condition. The attempt was unsuccessful as we were so completely surrounded by the Chinese it was impossible to get through. Later several rockets were fired but they evidently were not seen as we received no answer. In fact we were not sure that the foreigners still held Tientsin.

June 24, 1900
The next day the Chinese fired schrapnel at us continually and several men were wounded. No attack was made however, probably on account of the dust storm that was raging. In fact outside, it was blinding, while inside the building where the wounded were it found its way through the windows which had no glass in them. The wooden shutters had to be left open so as to give light. All of us got very dirty, but it did no good to wash, as in a few minutes the effects of the water were lost. The doctors found a splint among the Chinese medical stores in the arsenal, and, after it had been bandaged to my leg I was very much more comfortable.

That night other rockets were fired, and this time an answer was made from Tientsin, so we looked for a speedy relief.

June 25, 1900
On the morning of the 25th a count of dust was seen approaching from the Tientsin side. Rumors immediately began to spread, and one minute some one would come in and say a relief was approaching, and the next minute some body else would say it was Chinese cavalry. We were left in suspense for about half an hour when word was brought that there was no longer any doubt as to the identity of the approaching troops—they were our relief. The American portion of this relief column consisted

of a battalion of Marines under command of Major Waller,[12] and a few sailors under command of Lieutenant N. E. Irwin.[13] We learned from them that they had succeeded in reaching Tientsin a few days before after a hard march and much fighting in which they had a number of casualties. They had set out to relieve us about 1 A.M. and met with little resistance, but unfortunately went astray on account of lack of knowledge of the roads and our exact whereabouts, so they did not reach the arsenal until much later than they expected to.

It was decided to leave for Tientsin that afternoon. We would have to go overland as it would be impossible to follow the river which flowed through the native city and had a couple of forts on its banks for defense. So as many men as could be employed were put to work on making stretchers for the wounded. Fortunately the French had brought their hammocks with them, and when we abandoned the train they were stowed in the bottom of one of the junks, and now proved to be just the things that were needed. Paymaster Jewett got a stretcher for me that belonged to Welsh Frishers who were in the relieving force.

As ammunition was found that would fit all the rifles except the Lee, which the Americans carried, all the detachments filled their belts, and the Americans threw away their rifles with a sigh of relief (they had given any amount of trouble and proved a very poor weapon) and supplied themselves with Marliches. Arrangements were made for firing the arsenal as soon as we abandoned it. About four o'clock the procession started. As there were over a hundred wounded who had to be carried, the original Seymour column was nearly entirely employed to do the carrying, while the relief force was counted on to do any fighting that might be necessary. Six men were assigned to a stretcher—four to carry and two for relief. As the stretchers soon became very heavy they were frequently placed on the ground so that the carriers could rest, and consequently the progress was very slow. At dusk, when we halted for the night we were about two miles from the arsenal, and the dense columns of smoke that were rising showed us that the Chinese were losing an immense amount of war stores.

For four days I had not eaten a thing, and did not feel hungry until I saw some of the men eating cheese and ham, and took a piece of each when offered me. I do not know where the luxuries came from, but they were very strong, and I think had a great deal to do with my upset internal condition that followed. When the doctor came around I told him my leg was bleeding, and he seemed disappointed as he hoped the wound would heal up without any separation taking place. But nothing

---

12 Littleton W. T. Waller (1856–1926) served in the U.S. Marine Corps from 1880 until his retirement as a major general in 1920. He saw action in the Spanish-American War and commanded marines in China, Cuba, Mexico, and Haiti during the first two decades of the twentieth century. He was honored for his participation in the battle of Tientsin.

13 Noble Irwin (1869–1937) was an 1891 graduate of the U.S. Naval Academy. He retired in 1933 as a rear admiral.

could be done until we reached Tientsin. That night the wind blew hard, stirring up the dust and making it very uncomfortable.

June 26, 1900
At 3 A.M. we were under way again but our progress was necessarily slow. As there were legs to my stretcher I did not feel the inconvenience of being frequently placed on the ground, but for those who had broken legs and were being carried on the improvised stretchers, the frequent change of position caused by the picking up and setting down of the stretchers must have been very painful. After sun rise it became very warm, and the carriers had a hard time of it. About ten o'clock we came to what was left of the railroad station—a ruin with a few walls left standing. All the houses in the neighborhood showed the effects of shell fire. When we crossed the pontoon bridged across the Peiho leading to the foreign settlement, the bund presented a very different appearance from the time we saw it last, 16 days before. All the business houses were closed, and many of them showed marks from shells. Not a stroke of work was going on, nor was a Chinaman to be seen. The city seemed deserted save for a few civilians and now and then a detachment of foreign troops.

The American wounded were taken to the house of Mr. Drew,[14] an American and Commissioner of Customs. Here we were given hot soup and toast which was very welcome. The American mission hospital was being prepared to accommodate so many wounded, and as soon as it was ready we were moved there. This place was on the Taku road near where we had been previously quartered, but at present was outside of the lines held by the foreigners.

The people of Tientsin, who had just been relieved from a siege, did all in their power to make the wounded comfortable. The ladies and men assisted the three lady missionary doctors, the ladies doing duty by day, and the men by night. After being washed four or five times—(I was very dirty having had only a blanket over me for some time and my clothing consisting of one sock and a hat)—I was lifted from the stretcher and placed on a bed. In the evening Dr. McNamara[15] from the *Endymion,* came to examine my wound. I was given chloroform, and learned the next morning that the doctor had cut out the wound and removed a great deal of puss, besides several pieces of bone and bullet, and some gravel which had worked its way in. That day Dr. McNamara had to return to the *Endymion,* so I was left in charge of Dr. Wilson, a civilian, and the lady doctors.

---

14 Edward Bangs Drew (1843–1928) was born in Orleans, Massachusetts. He received a bachelor's degree from Harvard University in 1863 and a master's in 1868. From 1865 to 1906, he served in various posts in China. In 1896, he was secretary of the embassy in special mission of Li Hung-Chang to the United States. During the Boxer Rebellion he was Commissioner, Chinese Imperial Maritime Customs at Tientsin. Fluent in Chinese, he received several commendations from the imperial government.

15 Eric D. MacNamara was a surgeon in the Royal Navy.

June 28, 1900
On the 28th Dr. Kennedy[16] of the *Yorktown* arrived and all the American wounded were placed under his charge. The same day, my father came from Taku to see me.

As the buildings occupied by us were outside the Allies lines, they were constantly under fire from snipers in the neighboring Chinese houses, making it dangerous for people to move about the compound, and on the Taku road nearby. So it was determined to move the wounded to the American Consulate, and I was carried—bed and all—to that place, about a mile distant. Later it was decided to move the men to a vacated building—formerly a bank—but I was left in the consulate under the kind and good care of the Ragsdale family.

July 4, 1900
I remained here until the 4th of July, when, owing to the shells and bullets that were falling dangerously near, it was determined to move the wounded to Taku, where an improvised Naval hospital in charge of Dr. Decker[17] of the *Monocacy* was organized. So again I was picked up—bed and all—and carried to the river where I was placed on a British tug, just as it started. Corporal Sinclair of the Marines, belonging to the *Yorktown*'s guard, was detailed to accompany me as a nurse.

The trip down the river was an uncomfortable one, as it rained hard nearly all the time. When we arrived at Taku it was dark and as the gangway of the *Monocacy* was not wide enough for my bed to pass, I was moved into a Russian hospital where I remained that night and part of the next day. This hospital was crowded with Russian enlisted men, and was not an attractive place. However, they were very nice to me, and I was offered a ration at breakfast time, but declined, preferring the egg sent from the *Monocacy*. In the afternoon I was placed on a junk and towed down the river to Taku where I was moved to the improvised Naval Hospital there.

July 25, 1900
While at Taku the weather was very hot, and as the flies were very annoying during the day, and the mosquitoes more so at night, I was glad when on the 25th of July I was moved on board the *Solace*. All of the wounded in the hospital and those of the Army who were wounded at Tientsin on the 13th, were also placed on board the *Solace*.

July 29, 1900
The *Solace* left Taku on the 29th and arrived at Nagasaki on the 1st of August. My Mother, who had been waiting in Nagasaki for over a month moored on board and was allowed to remain until we reached Yokohama, which was on the 9th, we

---

16 Robert M. Kennedy was a passed assistant surgeon. He had four years and ten months of sea service at this time.

17 Corbin J. Decker was a surgeon in the Navy with five years' sea service and seven years' shore duty.

having been delayed at Nagasaki until the 6th so that the Army wounded could be moved to the Transport *Thomas*.[18]

The hospital at Yokohama is very comfortable and although the weather was warm, I had a south west room which nearly always caught the breeze.

Mid-September, 1900

About the middle of September I sat up for a few hours each day in a chair although the wound was still open and had to be dressed every day. After I had been sitting up for a week I was operated upon to take out some pieces of bone that commenced to bother me. I was given chloroform, and the doctor removed several pieces of bone and several pieces of bullet which were scatter about. After the operation I was allowed to use crutches a little each day and go out driving the hospital carriage which was hired with money sent by the U.S. Red Cross Society to be used for the comfort of the sick and wounded from China.

The Japanese people were very attentive to us in the hospital. Representatives of the Emperor and Empress, the Governor of Kanagawa, the Mayor of Yokohama, and a number of other dignitaries called to see us. And all of them brought presents including such things as writing paper, handkerchiefs, fans, cigars and cigarettes.

November 4, 1900

Last night I attended the ball given at the Imperial Hotel, Tokio, in honor of the Emperor of Japan's birthday. Many high Japanese officials were present, several Princes and Princesses being in attendance. There being but few foreign men-of-war at Yokohama, there were not many foreign officers there. The place was so crowded very little space was given up to dancing. After the Imperial party arrived, the doors were locked and no one was allowed to depart until after they left. An extensive supper was served.

November 11, 1900

Yesterday afternoon the Emperor and Empress of Japan gave their annual fall garden party to celebrate the blooming of the Chrysanthemums. Foreign residents of Japan unless high officials are not invited, and only a limited number of visitors, who obtain invitations through their Ministers at Tokio can attend. The invitations to Japanese are restricted to high officials. On the card of admittance that came with the invitation was a request that frock coats be worn. Mother, Mrs. Spratling, Paymaster and Mrs. O'Leary[19] and I went to Tokio in the afternoon train. At the station we took rickshas and rode to the palace ground—a rather long and cold ride. The palace grounds are very extensive and artistically arranged in true Japanese style. The maples which had just turned red and yellow were particularly noticeable for

---

18 *Thomas* was chartered from the Atlantic Transportation Company in 1898 for use as an Army transport.

19 Charles R. O'Leary was appointed from Pennsylvania. His was an assistant paymaster in USS *Machias*.

their beauty. Small spaces were allotted for the Chrysanthemums. These spaces were nearly surrounded by small sheds which were built to protect the plants from inclement weather. A great deal of attention is paid by the gardeners to the cultivation of the flowers with the results there are many varieties of all colors, all sizes and all forms—with plants with one large bloom to plants with several hundred small blooms. The chief feature of the exhibition was a plant with 800 blooms, which is said to be the largest number of blooms ever grown on one plant. After nearly every body was frozen to death the Emperor and Empress with the court attendants put in an appearance.

The Emperor and the Princes were dressed in the service uniforms of generals in the Army. The Empress and court ladies wore European dress. A few foreigners, among them Admiral[20] and Mrs. Beardslee, were introduced to the Emperor. The affair wound up with a luncheon in the open.

---

20 Lester A. Beardslee (1836–1903) entered the U.S. Naval Academy in 1850 and graduated in 1856. He was a member of Commodore Matthew Perry's expedition to Japan in 1853 and served in the Civil War, where he took part in the bombardment Charleston, South Carolina, in 1863. He commanded U.S. naval forces in the Pacific Station from 1894 to 1897. Beardslee was in Japan in 1900–1901 to petition the Japanese to erect a monument at Kurihama, where Perry first landed. He was successful, and the monument was dedicated on 14 July 1901.

XII *Duty in USS Nashville and USS Culgoa*

1900–1901

December 24, 1900

On December 9th telegraphic orders from the Admiral to Dr. Harmon said to send me to the *Nashville* for duty. The next day I was detached from the hospital and ordered to proceed to Nagasaki and report to the Commanding Officer of the U.S.S. *Nashville*[1] for duty on board that vessel. Mother and I made preparations for leaving and left on the Pacific Mail Steamer "*China*," Captain Seabury.

The passage to Nagasaki was pleasant, but the weather a trifle cold to thoroughly enjoy the scenery of the Inland Sea. We stopped a few hours in Kobe and took a ride around the city in Rickshas. We arrived in Nagasaki on the 13th, and I immediately reported on board the *Nashville,* of which vessel, Commander N. E. Niles,[2] USN, was in command. As the Dr. at the hospital wrote a letter to Captain Niles saying I should not stand watch for several months, I was assigned the duties of Assistant Navigator. The *Nashville*'s engines were undergoing a thorough overhauling so we remained in Nagasaki until January 23rd. As Nagasaki has not very much of a European population, after a short time in port it became monotonous, there being nothing to do ashore excepting to play billiards and bowl, both of which we did a great deal of. Many foreign men-of-war came in—usually to coal and make repairs. My duties consisted of finding the error of and rating the chronometers and finding the deviations of the Standard Compass. The former I did by taking double altitudes of the sun and comparing a chronometer with the telegraph signal at the post office; the latter I did by taking azimuths as the ship swung at her buoy.

NOTES 1 USS *Nashville* (Patrol Gunboat No. 7) supported the U.S. Army in its campaign against the Filipino insurgents in 1900. It transported U.S. forces to China during the Boxer Rebellion and remained at Taku until allied forces ended the siege at Peking.

2 Nathan E. Niles (1847–1930) was an 1868 graduate of the U.S. Naval Academy. He commanded *Nashville* on the Asiatic and European stations, 1900–1903. He was promoted to rear admiral in 1908.

The officers of the *Nashville* were: Comdr. N. E. Niles, Lieut's. J. H. Oliver,[3] M. A. Anderson (Ch. Engn.),[4] R. H. Jackson,[5] Lieut's. (J.G.) D. V. H. Allen,[6] A. M. Cook,[7] Ensign K. G. Castleman,[8] Naval Cadet C. L. Arnold,[9] Assist. Surgeon E. Thompson,[10] Assist. Paymr. C. J. Cleborne,[11] Warrant Machinist James Will, Paymaster's Clerk, G. Southgate. We left yesterday for Manila.

February 2, 1901

We arrived at Cavite yesterday after a smooth and pleasant run. Nothing unusual occurred. We steamed at about 11 knots. At Cavite we found the *Newark, Manila, Isla de Cuba*,[12] *Glacier, Culgoa,* and the *Vicksburg,* and *Wilmington,* the latter two vessels being recently arrived from the States. The *Nashville* is to relieve the *Yorktown* off the Northwest coast of Luzon.

February 4, 1901

Yesterday I received orders detaching me from the *Nashville* and ordering me to report to the Commanding Officer of the U.S.S. *Culgoa* for duty on board that vessel. This morning I reported to Lieut. Comdr. J. C. Fremont[13] who is in command of the *Culgoa*.

The *Culgoa* is one of the three refrigerating vessels belonging to the Navy and employed in carrying frozen beef and mutton, and ice from Australia to Manila. These vessels make about two trips a year, running on a schedule so that one of them is always at Cavite with fresh meat on board. The *Culgoa* originally belonged to the Blue Anchor Line and ran between Liverpool and Sydney. She was bought during the war with Spain and left England under the Danish flag and was re-transferred to the American flag while at sea.

The *Culgoa* has two holds forward intended for carrying a general cargo, and two refrigerating holds aft for carrying the ice and frozen meat. At present the lower forward hold is filled with coal for ballast and the upper hold is used for living purposes of the men.

---

3 James H. Oliver (?–1928), U.S. Naval Academy, 1877.

4 Martin A. Anderson (?–1926) was an 1881 graduate of the U.S. Naval Academy. He retired as a commander in 1905.

5 Richard H. Jackson (1866–1971) was an 1887 graduate of the U.S. Naval Academy. He retired in 1930.

6 David V. H. Allen (1870–1944), U.S. Naval Academy, 1892.

7 Allen M. Cook (1870–1941), U.S. Naval Academy, 1893.

8 Kenneth G. Castleman (1876–1954), U.S. Naval Academy, 1896.

9 Clarence Lamont Arnold (1878–1967) was a 1900 graduate of the U.S. Naval Academy. He retired as a captain in 1930 and was recalled to active duty during World War II.

10 Edgar Thompson was an assistant surgeon in USS *Celtic*.

11 Cuthbert J. Cleborne was an assistant paymaster in *Nashville*. He was appointed from the state of New Hampshire.

12 *Isla de Cuba* was a Spanish gunboat, built in 1896, captured by the U.S. Navy in 1898, and commissioned in 1900. During the Philippine Insurrection, it was a supply ship and patrol boat. Its activities in the islands contributed materially to the defeat of the insurgents.

13 John C. Fremont (1851–1911), U.S. Naval Academy, 1872, was the son of the famous explorer and senator of the same name. He was promoted to rear admiral in 1910.

We leave on the 9th for Sydney, but are to stop at a number of places among the Islands to deliver meat to the Navy and Army.

February 6, 1901

The *Kentucky* arrived this afternoon from the States. She is a powerful, and impressive looking vessel.

February 9, 1901

On the 9th we left Cavite for Sydney via a number of ports in the Philippines. Our first stop was on the 10th when we arrived at Batangas early in the morning. We stayed just long enough to give the Army what meat they wanted, and then started for Salinas where we anchored about two o'clock. We saw nothing of the Army here so at six we put to sea. On the 12th we arrived at Ilo Ilo, going to the anchorage by the south channel. We saw the small gun boats *Paragua* and *Leyte* here, and from the former got a pilot Captain Sueh, a Spaniard, who stayed with us and was of great service during the remainder of our itinerary in the Philippines. As I had the day's duty, I did not get ashore.

February 13, 1901

On the morning of the 13th we were again under way and left the anchorage by the North channel. The rain set in hard during the afternoon making it necessary for us to anchor, which we did about four o'clock near the island of Balubadiangan. We remained here until early the next morning and then left for Cebu where we arrived during the forenoon.

February 14, 1901

We entered by the north channel. We found the *Princeton, Petrel* and *Calamianies* in port, and the *Villalobos* and *Pampanga* came in during the day.

While at anchor we were entertained by six native children—four boys and two girls—who came to the ship in a canoe. They dived for pennies, and in order to induce us to throw the money, they did some fancy numbers in the singing and dancing line. Their greatest triumph however, was when the four boys stood up in the bottom of the canoe and went through the manual of arms in obedience to the orders of the smallest boy given in English. They then went through the drill while treading water and later, when we invited them on board ship, went through their whole repertoire on the deck. We gave them some Lowney's candies which they ate with great enjoyment.

February 16, 1901

We left Cebu on the afternoon of the 16th and the next day hove to off Kagayan. We saw nothing of our army there, but a number of Filipinos in uniform were moving about, so the Captain did not deem it advisable to send a boat in, and we left immediately for Nisamis. This place is at the head of a long narrow inlet that is dotted with reefs. We did not go very far up the inlet because, although there is plenty of water, we would have difficulty in turning round owing to the lack of room.

The Paymaster went in the whaleboat to the port to see if they wanted any meat. Owing to the strong wind and tide the boat did not get back to the ship until after dark, it having taken them two and a half hours to make five miles, half of which distance was with the tide and wind, and the other half against it. At six o'clock we were under way again and the next forenoon arrived at Zamboanga, getting underway again the same afternoon. At 8:00 the next morning, the 19th, we arrived at Polok. There is a very good harbor here and the station is in charge of the Navy. A small detachment of Marines is on duty here. We landed Lieut. Hollcombe[14] with some material for repairing a dry dock for small gunboats that the Spaniards had allowed to fall into ill repair. The *Isla de Cuba* was in port. From Polok we went to Jolo on the island of Sulu. We arrived there on the afternoon of the 21st.

February 21, 1901
After dark we had night signal exercise with the Army.

On the 22nd all hands were allowed to go ashore to witness the athletic sports held by the Army. The events were well contested and exciting, the prizes being money.

At 10:30 A.M. on the twenty-third we left for Sydney, via Thursday Island, where we will pick up a pilot.

March 10, 1901
The run from the Philippines to Australia is through the Sulu Sea, Celebes Sea, Banka Strait, Molucca Passage, Pitt Passage, Banda Sea and Arafura Sea. The course lies close to parts of Celebes and near Boura, Ceram, Ambon, Bick Is., and numerous small islands. We arrived at the Goode Island anchorage off Thursday Island on the morning of March 2nd, and after taking on board Pilot Thompson of the Torres Strait Pilot Association, left the same afternoon for Sydney.

Albany Pass is the first point of interest. It is a narrow passage about three miles long between the main land and a small island. There is plenty of water, but a strong current sets through, changing with the tide. For two days the course runs through reefs—some always showing and some above water only at low tide. The channel lies quite close to these reefs in certain places. Most of them are marked with large square black beacons, that are easily picked up in the day time, but can not be seen at night unless there is bright moon light. So when if running at night certain land marks (small islands) cannot be picked up, it becomes necessary to anchor. The reef recedes from the shore after two days and for two days the course is comparatively open, the main land usually being in sight and now and then a small island. Then

---

14 John H. L. Holcombe (?–1906), U.S. Naval Academy, 1878.

the Northumberland and Whitsunday passages are traversed and the course lies open from Brisbane to Sydney. The distance from Thursday Island to Sydney is 1800 miles. The pilotage costs £50. The weather was marked by strong winds and heavy rains, making it very unpleasant, and at times very difficult to pick up land and lights. Early in the morning of March 10th we picked up the South Head Sydney light 30 miles away, and shortly after day light entered Port Jackson, stopping first to take on board a local pilot. After passing through the Heads, we stopped to take on the Health Officer.

Sydney, Australia
April–May, 1901

Sydney is situated on the south bank of Port Jackson, an inlet of the South Pacific that forms one of the finest harbors in the world. Its fine shipping facilities undoubtedly give it the right to the claim of being the busiest port in the Southern Hemisphere. For many miles the depth of water in the harbor is ample for vessels of the largest tonnage. The tides average 3 1/3 feet and in the fair way the flood and ebb is almost imperceptible. The harbor is land-locked, not even the opening between the Heads being visible from any part of Sydney. Along the shores of the harbor, the New South Wales Government has constructed over 16,000 feet of wharfage, the major part having a depth alongside ranging from 25 to 30 feet at low tide. The private wharves are of about equal extent, the depth of water varying from 20 to 35 feet. The bottom of the harbor is even, soft and free from currents, making good holding ground for vessels at anchor.

The dock accomodations of Sydney comprise the two Government docks on Cockatoo Is., and Mort's Dock in Balmain. The latter company is now building a new dry dock that will accommodate the largest vessels. Of the Government docks the Southerland Dock is 600 feet long by 84 feet, and will take a vessel drawing 32 feet; the Fitzroy dock is 470 feet long by 59 feet and will take a ship drawing 21 1/2 feet. The Mort's dock is 410 by 66 feet, and will accommodate vessels with a drought of 19 feet. The light house and tug service are very good. Coaling is done from colliers of from 500 to 1100 tons.

Sydney was incorporated as a city in 1842. Since then it has grown to be a metropolis of nearly 500,000 inhabitants while the total number of inhabitants in the city and suburbs surrounding Port Jackson is in the neighborhood of 1,000,000. The business portions of the city are crowded during business hours, but on Sunday and holidays, and after business hours, many of the streets in this section are nearly deserted. This is because the people live in the suburbs that fringe the bay and stretch along the Paramatta River and Botany Bay.

The streets of Sydney are fairly wide and generally well paved. On the principal business streets the side walks are not of sufficient width to allow the crowds of people that are shopping to walk up and down comfortably.

Port Jackson, Sidney, Australia

The Town Hall is a large brown sand stone building of good proportions and pleasing aspect. Its floor dimensions are 166 1/2 by 85 feet; its height 65 feet and the height of its tower, 200 feet. The post-office is another larger brown stone building being conspicuous for its Italian façade of colonnaded granite and sandstone, and its tower 250 feet high. Among the other noticeable edifices are the University buildings, the two Cathedrals, the public offices of the Colonial Secretary, Land and Works, the Museum, and Hospital. Strange to say the two best office buildings in the city belong to American Companies—the Mutual Life

Insurance Association and the Equitable Life Assurance Association, both of New York.

The city is by no means regularly laid out, as it was not built originally on any fixed plans, but has grown up from year to year as settlement progressed without much forethought in the laying out of the streets. Consequently we find crooked and blocked streets in many sections of town.

One of the chief attractions of Sydney is the Botanical Garden. The gardens are situated on the water front in what is known as Farm Cove. While the immediate purpose of the gardens is to serve as a collecting place for plants and botanical specimens from all over the world, the gardens also serve as a public park under almost perfect conditions.

Other parks and pleasure grounds are Hyde Park, the Sydney Domain, Moore Park, and Centennial Park.

The Sydney and Suburban Trainway lines are under the direction and control of the Government Railway Commissioners. Those of greatest extent are steam trainways. Two lines, however, are worked upon the cable system, and one on the electric. The trainway fares are worked on what is know as the "zone" system, the greater bulk of the fares paid being by penny tickets, the average being about a penny a mile.

The postal and telegraph services are also in the hands of the Government. Although the postal rates to foreign countries are at the regular standard, the internal rates are unusually high, it costing two pence to send a letter anywhere beyond the limits of New South Wales. The average time for the mails to reach London from Sydney is 24–34 days, but the new American service via San Francisco, promises to cut this time down to 30 days.

Sydney has a splendid cab system that is a great convenience. A cab can always be found near at hand. The rates are 1 shilling per quarter of an hour (for two) for the first hour, and 9 pence per quarter hour afterwards.

The theatres, race courses, rowing and yachting are the chief forms of amusement, but association foot ball and cricket are also played. Few bicycles are seen in the streets.

May 1, 1901

>Intelligence Report on Fortifications of Sydney Harbor, and the Military Organization of New South Wales.
>
>U.S.S. *Culgoa,*
>
>Sydney, N.S.W.,
>
>May 1, 1901
>
>Sir:—
>
>1.   In obedience to your order of April 1, 1901, I have the honor to submit the following report.

2. Batteries, gun-pits, etc., are distributed along the bluffs at the entrance to the harbor, and immediately inside the heads, forming a double line of defense, which undoubtedly is very effective on account of the natural advantages afforded. Many of these batteries are concealed by trees and brush so that they cannot be seen by vessels entering the harbor. The exact types and calibres of the guns installed could not be ascertained, but many of the guns are old muzzle loading smooth bores and rifles of large calibre. There are a number of 5" breech loading rifles also.

3. The most important batteries are distributed as follows:—On the Inner South Head a battery facing seaward, and one near Camp Cove facing the harbor: On Middle Head two batteries facing the harbor entrance: On Georges Head a battery facing the harbor entrance: a large battery on Shark Point: Extensive batteries and gun-pits on Bradley Head. The batteries are manned by the permanent artillery forces, and regular target practice is carried out annually.

4. At Chowder Bay the submarine mine station is located. This is fitted out with extensive mines of modern types, together with the necessary appurtenances. The mines are in charge of a permanent force known as the Submarine Miners. A practical course in laying mines is carried out during two weeks in April of each year. A vessel to be used solely for laying and taking in the mines is under construction.

5. Each colony of Australia has its own military organizations. They are very much alike and consist generally of a permanent force, a partially paid force, and volunteers. Some of the officers have Royal commissions, and some hold only Colonial commissions issued by the Governor of the colony. Colonials, on the recommendation of the Governor of a colony, have the privilege of taking examinations for a Royal commission, provided they have seen active service in the field, or served more than 15 months in a local military organization.

6. The military organization of New South Wales, although more extensive than that of the other colonies, may be taken as a fair example. The whole military department is placed under the control of the Chief Secretary as Minister for Defense. The present establishment of the forces is as follows:—

Headquarters staff	85
Lancers	499
Mounted Rifles	387
Cavalry	638
Artillery	1174
Engineers	63
Infantry—Permanent	24
Volunteers	2563
Partially paid	2734
Army Service Corps	134
Cadets	10
TOTAL	8842

The distribution of the Artillery throughout the colony is as follows:—

Sydney	834
Northern district	137
South coast district	87

The distribution of Infantry through the Colony is as follows:—

Sydney and suburbs	2456
Southern district	428
Western district	638
Southwestern district	60
Northern District	724
South coast district	119

The Engineers, Cavalry, etc., are distributed throughout the Colony in about the same proportions.

Very Respectfully,
(signed) J. K. Taussig,
Naval Cadet, U.S. Navy.
The Commanding Officer

This journal was submitted for review to the commanding officer of USS Culgoa:

Respectfully submitted

J. K. Taussig,

Naval Cadet

U.S. Navy

The reviewer commented and signed:

An Excellent Journal

Approved

J C Fremont

Commander, U.S.N.

Culgoa

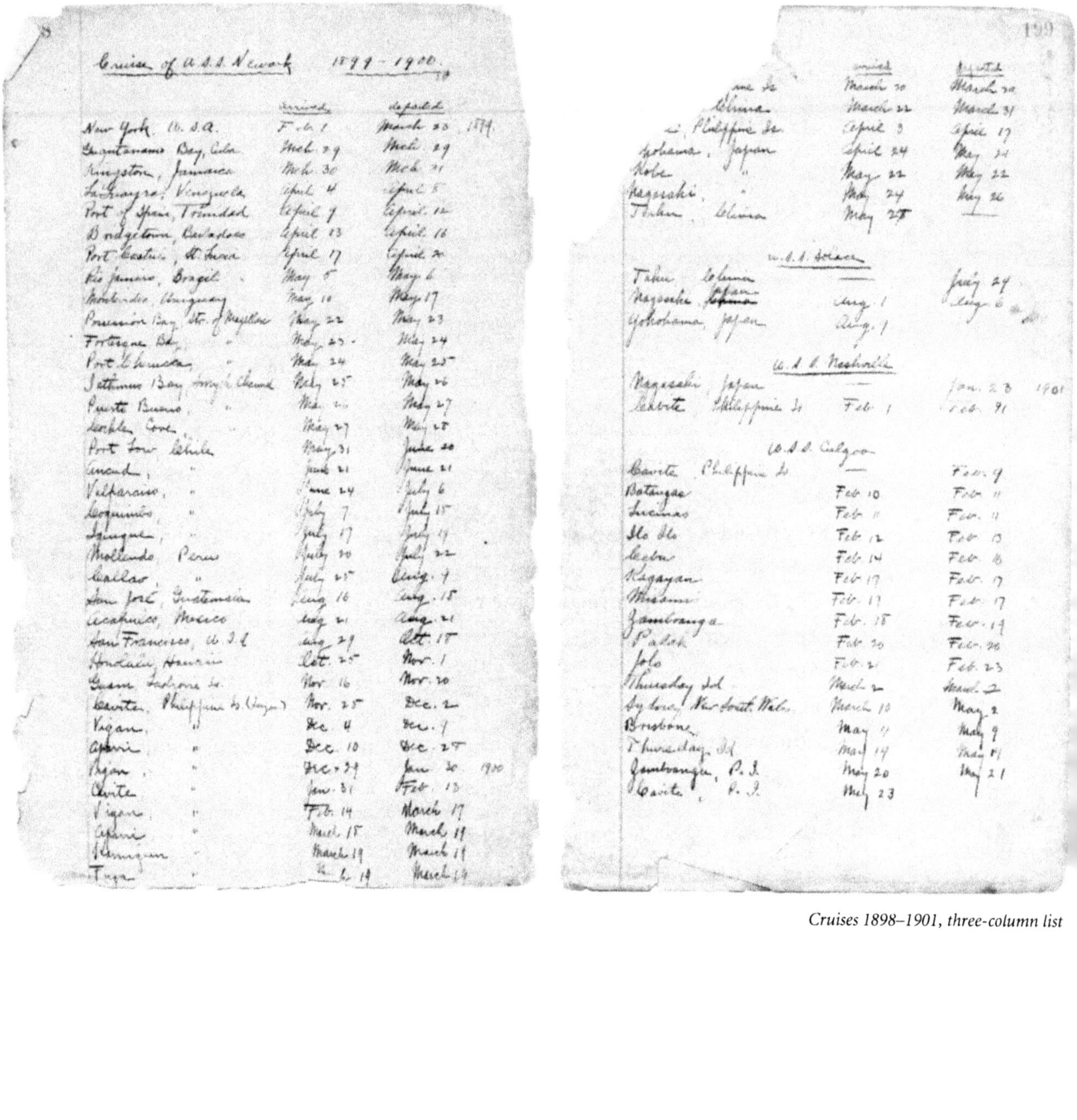

Cruise of U.S.S. Newark 1899–1900.

	arrived	departed
New York, U.S.A.	Feb. 1	March 23 1899
Guantanamo Bay, Cuba	Mch. 29	Mch. 29
Kingston, Jamaica	Mch. 30	Mch. 31
La Guayra, Venezuela	April 4	April 5
Port of Spain, Trinidad	April 7	April 12
Bridgetown, Barbados	April 13	April 16
Port Castries, St. Lucia	April 17	April 20
Rio Janeiro, Brazil	May 5	May 6
Montevideo, Uruguay	May 10	May 17
Possession Bay, St. of Magellan	May 22	May 23
Fortescue Bay, "	May 23	May 24
Port Churruca, "	May 24	May 25
Isthmus Bay, Smyth Channel	May 25	May 26
Puerto Bueno, "	May 26	May 27
[illegible] Cove, "	May 27	May 28
Port Low, Chile	May 31	June 20
Ancud, "	June 21	June 21
Valparaiso, "	June 24	July 6
Coquimbo, "	July 7	July 15
Iquique, "	July 17	July 19
Mollendo, Peru	July 20	July 22
Callao, "	July 25	Aug. 9
San José, Guatemala	Aug. 16	Aug. 18
Acapulco, Mexico	Aug. 21	Aug. 21
San Francisco, U.S.A.	Aug. 29	Oct. 15
Honolulu, Hawaii	Oct. 25	Nov. 1
Guam, Ladrone Is.	Nov. 16	Nov. 20
Cavite, Philippine Is. (Luzon)	Nov. 25	Dec. 2
Vigan, "	Dec. 4	Dec. 9
Aparri, "	Dec. 10	Dec. 25
Vigan, "	Dec. 29	Jan. 30 1900
Cavite	Jan. 31	Feb. 13
Vigan, "	Feb. 14	March 17
Aparri, "	March 18	March 19
[illegible]	March 19	March 19
[illegible]	[illegible] 19	March 19

199

	arrived	departed
[illegible] Is.	March 20	March 20
[illegible] China	March 22	March 31
[illegible], Philippine Is.	April 3	April 17
Yokohama, Japan	April 24	May 20
Kobe "	May 22	May 22
Nagasaki "	May 24	May 26
Taku, China	May 28	—

U.S.S. Solace

	arrived	departed
Taku, China	—	July 24
Nagasaki, ~~China~~ Japan	Aug. 1	Aug. 6
Yokohama, Japan	Aug. 1	

U.S.S. Nashville

	arrived	departed
Nagasaki, Japan		Jan. 23 1901
Cavite, Philippine Is.	Feb. 1	Feb. 9

U.S.S. Culgoa

	arrived	departed
Cavite, Philippine Is.	—	Feb. 9
Batangas	Feb. 10	Feb. 11
Lucinas	Feb. 11	Feb. 11
Ilo Ilo	Feb. 12	Feb. 13
Cebu	Feb. 14	Feb. 16
Cagayan	Feb. 17	Feb. 17
Misamis	Feb. 17	Feb. 17
Zamboanga	Feb. 18	Feb. 19
Pollok	Feb. 20	Feb. 20
Jolo	Feb. 21	Feb. 23
Thursday Isl.	March 2	March 2
Sydney, New South Wales	March 10	May 2
Brisbane	May 4	May 9
Thursday Isl.	May 14	May 14
Zamboanga, P.I.	May 20	May 21
Cavite, P.I.	May 23	

Cruises 1898–1901, three-column list

INDEX

Abra Province, Philippines, 105
Abulug, Philippines, 110–12
Acapulco, Mexico, 94
Agaña, Guam, 100
Aguadores, Cuba, xv–xvi, 24–25, 45, 61
Alger, Russell A., 127
Allen, David V. H., 158
Allen, Robert S., xix
Altares, Cuba, 19
Ambon, 160
American Campaign Medal, xx
American Defense Service Medal, xx
Ancud, Chile, 81–84
Anderson, Martin A., 158
Andes, 69
Andrade, Ignacio, 70–71
Annapolis, Md., xv, xx
Anting, China, 142–43
Aparri, Philippines, xv, 108, 113–15, 120–21, 123
Arafura Sea, 160
Arequipa, Peru, 88–90
Army, U.S., xvi–xvii, 6–7, 9, 23, 61–62, 159–60
Arnold, Clarence Lamont, 158
Atlantic Fleet, xvii
Atlantic Ocean, 80
Australia, xvii, 158, 160, 164

Bahamas, 56
Bailey, Simon I., 90
Balmain, Australia, 161
Balubadiangan, 159
Banda Sea, 160
Banka Strait, 160
Barbados, 72–73, 75
Barker, Albert S., 54
Barton, John K., 126
Bataan Province, Philippines, xv
Batan Islands, 114, 123–24
Batangas, Philippines, 159
Bayly, Louis, xviii
Beardslee, Lester A., 156
Beatty, David, xvi
Bick Island, 160

Blanco y Erenas, Ramón, 54
Bloch, Claude C., 98
Blue, Victor, 23, 126, 131
Bojeador, Cape, 123
Bolivia, 88
Boone, Charles, 73, 75, 80, 99
Boston Fruit Co., 50
Botany Bay, 161
Boura, 160
Boxer Rebellion, xvi–xvii, xix, 133
Boxers, xvi, 134–38, 140–43, 145–46
Bridgetown, Barbados, 72–73, 75
Brisbane, Australia, 161
Brooklyn Navy Yard, 74
Bryan, Henry, 82–83, 107–109, 113, 115
Buchanan, Allen, 4, 22–23
Buchanan, William I., 79
Buenos Aires, Argentina, 78
Bull, James H., 126
Bureau of Navigation, xviii

Cabras Island, 99
Cagayan Province, Philippines, xv, 108
Caimanera, Cuba, 53
Callao, Chile, 85, 91–92
Camiguin (Kanuguin) Island, 123
Cape Verde Islands, 55
Capeheart, Edward E., 46–47
Caracas, Venezuela, xv, 69–70, 72
Caribbean Sea, xv
Carter, James F., 108
Castleman, Kenneth G., 158
Catlin, Albertus W., 20
Cavayan, Philippines, 105
Cavite, Philippines, xv, 103, 116, 158–59
Cayo Smith, 48
Cebu, 159
Celebes, 160
Celebes Sea, 160
Ceram, 160
Cervera y Topete, Pascual, xv, 32, 64, 68
Chadwick, French, 36, 74
Cherucca, Port, 80–81

Chile, xv, 80, 87, 92
Chile River, 89
Chiloé Island, 81, 83
China, xvi, xix, 137, 139
China Relief Expedition Medal, xvi
Cienfuegos, Cuba, 54
Clark, Charles E., 54
Cleborne, Cuthbert J., 158
Clyde Line, 7
Cockatoo Island, 161
Concepción, Chile, 83
Cook, Allen M., 158
Coquimbo, Chile, 85–87
Corregidor, 116
Courtney, Charles S., 4, 23, 67, 70, 73, 75, 79, 99–100, 107, 127–29, 134, 144
Crosstide, Cape, 80
Cuba, xv, 6, 9, 55, 67
Cuban Pacification Medal, xx
Curaçao, 68
Cutler, William G., 82–83
Cuzco, Peru, 88

Daiquirí, Cuba, xvi, 19, 21, 41
Daniels, Josephus, xviii
Danville, Va., 3
Day, George C., 82–83
Decker, Corbin J., 154
Destroyer Division 8, xviii
Dinger, Henry C., 116
Distinguished Service Medal, xviii, xx
Dole, Sanford, 99
Doyle, James, 48, 50
Dresden, Germany, xvii
Drew, Edward Bangs, 153
DuBose, William G., 25

Elson, Herman J., 75, 87, 89–90, 93, 107–108
Empress Dowager, xvi, 133
Equitable Life Assurance Association, 163
Escuintla, Guatemala, 93
Europe, 53

Farragut, David, 95
Fenner, Edward B., 4, 22–23, 116
Filipinos, 106, 110, 112
Flores Island, 78
Forman, Charles W., 67–68, 75, 86–87, 108, 116
Fortescue Bay, 80
France, xviii
Fremont, John C., xvii, 158, 165
Frio, Cape, 77
Froward, Cape, 80
Fuga Island, 123

García Íñiguez, Calixto, 22
Gillmore, James C., 108, 114, 121
Gilpin, Charles E., 136, 144
Goode Island, 160
Goodrich, Caspar F., 19–21, 54, 68, 74, 93, 95
Graham, John S., 126

Great Inagua Island, 15
Great White Fleet, xvii
Guaicanec Island, 82–83
Guam, xv, 99, 103
Guantanamo, Cuba, 16, 27, 41–42, 49, 54–55, 64
Guantanamo Bay, xvii, 67
Guatemala City, Guatemala, 92–93
Guayacan, Chile, 86

Hall, Newt H., 107
Hare, Luther R., 114, 121
Harper's Weekly, 52
Harvard Law School, 61
Harvard Observatory, 89–90
Havana, Cuba, xv–xvi, 10, 21, 54
Hawaii, xv
Helm, Frank P., 50
Helmer, Margaret Philip, xix
Hobson, Richmond, 37, 42
Holcombe, John H. L., 160
Hong Kong, 113–14, 116, 120–21, 123–24
Honolulu, Hawaii, 98, 103
Horn, Cape, xvii
Horne, Frederick J., 116
Hsiku Arsenal, 150
Hunker, John J., 4–6, 10, 13, 21
Huntington, Elon O., 87, 93, 100, 107–108, 116

Iloilo, Philippines, 159
Iquique, Chile, 87–88
Irvine, Calif., xx
Irwin, Noble, 152
Isabela Province, Philippines, xv, 108
Isle of Pines, 54

Jackson, Port, 161
Jackson, Richard H., 158
Jacksonville, Fla., 3
Jamestown, R.I., xix
Japan, xvi
Jellicoe, John, xvi, 139
Jewett, Henry E., 107, 134, 140, 144, 148, 152, 155
Johnson, Alfred W., 67–68, 70, 75, 94–95
Johnstone, James R., 150
Jolo, Philippines, 160
Jones, Hilary P., xviii

Kagayan, Philippines, 159
Kanagawa Prefecture, Japan, 155
Kempff, Louis, xvi, 126, 131
Kennedy, Robert M., 154
Key West, Fla., 3, 23, 48, 52–53
Kingston, Jamaica, 67–68
Kline, George W., 6, 16
Knefler, Ellen, xvii
Kobe, Japan, 128, 157
Kosmos Line, 86
Kowloon, 124–25

La Guayra, Venezuela, 68–71
La Serena, Chile, 86
Lackey, Henry E., 4, 23, 34–35, 62

Lang Fang, China, 141–43
Laoag, Philippines, 113, 115
Latimer Clark Muirhead mine, 48
Leahy, William D., 98
Leary, Richard P., 100
Legion of Merit, xx
Leigh, Richard H., xix
Lima, Peru, 91–92
Limanche, Chile, 87
Linao, Philippines, 112–13, 120
Lippitt, Thomas M., 134
Liverpool, Australia, 158
Lofa station, 138, 140–43, 159
London, United Kingdom, 163
Long, John D., 55
Lota, Chile, 83
Low, William L., 98
Luzon, xv, 104–105, 158

MacNamara, Eric D., 153
Magellan, Strait of, 79
Major, Samuel I. M., 4–5, 21–22
Mallory Line, 7
Manila, Philippines, 94–95, 98–99, 107, 113–16, 119, 123, 125–26, 128, 158
Manila Bay, 103
Manzanillo, Cuba, 54
Marble, Frank, 46
Marble, Ralph, 116, 126
Mare Island, 94–95, 98, 116
Mare Island Navy Yard, xv
Marine Corps, U.S., xvi, 53–54, 108, 110, 131–34, 152, 154, 160
Massachusetts, xix
Maxim-Nordenfelt gun, 46
Maxim-Nordenfelt machine guns, 47
Maysi, Cape, 16, 56, 67
McCalla, Bowman H., xvi, 95, 97, 105, 107–108, 113, 123, 125, 133–34, 136, 138, 140, 142–45, 148–49
McGraw-Hill, xx
McIntyre, Edward W., 116
McKay, Charles Edmund, 6
McLean, Ridley, 126
McNamee, Luke, 107
McNiter, Mr., 93
Meiggs, Henry, 88
Mentz, George W., 17
Merchants and Miners Transportation Company, 7
Miami, Fla., 3
Miles, Nelson A., 41, 45
Mobile, Ala., 7, 55
Mohun, Philip V., 91
Mollendo, Peru, 88, 91
Molucca Passage, 160
Moncrief, George B., 83
Montevideo, Uruguay, xv, 75, 77–79
Morgan, Gunner, 47
Morgan Line, 7
Moritz, Albert, 126
Morro Castle, Havana, Cuba, xvi, 37

Morro Castle, Santiago de Cuba, Cuba, 16, 22, 27, 45–47, 62
Mustin, Henry C., 115
Mutual Life Insurance Association, 162

Nagasaki, Japan, 128, 154–55, 157
Naval War College, xviii–xix
Navy, U.S., xvi, xviii–xx, 21, 42, 46, 62, 64, 72, 159–60
Netherlands East Indies, xix
New South Wales, Australia, xvii, 161, 163–64
New York City, N.Y., xv–xvi, 45, 55–56, 61, 67, 74, 86–87, 93, 163
Newport, R.I., xviii–xix
Nieh Shih-ch'eng, 137
Nikko, Japan, 127
Niles, Nathan E., 157–58
Nisamis, Philippines, 159
Norfolk, Va., 49, 52
Norfolk Naval Base, xix
Norfolk Navy Yard, xvii, xix

O'Leary, Charles R., 155
Oliver, James H., 158
Orchard, John, 114
Order of Saint Michael and Saint George, xviii
Organ Mountains, 78

Pacific Ocean, 80
Paget, Alfred W., 36
Pamplona, Philippines, xv–xvi, 108–12
Panama, 92
Parramatta River, 161
Patagonia, 80
Pearl Harbor, Hawaii, xix
Pearson, Drew, xix
Peiho River, 131–132, 137, 153
Peking, China, xvi, 131, 133–37, 139–43
Perrill, Harlan P., 74
Peru, xv, 92
Pettengill, George T., 98, 126
Philippines, xv–xvii, xix, 98, 159–60
Pietsang, China, 146
Pilot Island, 81
Pimo, Peru, 88
Piti, Guam, 100–101
Pitt Passage, 160
Pizarro, Francisco, 92
Plant Line, 7
Playa del Este, Cuba, 39
Polok, 160
Port Castries, Saint Lucia, 73–75
Port Low, Chile, 82
Port of Spain, Trinidad, 71–72
Possession Bay, 79
Pratt, Alfred A., 96
Pratt, William V., 107, 126
Puerto Bueno, 81
Puerto Rico, 53
Punta Arenas, Chile, 80
Purple Heart, xvi

Queenstown, Ireland, xviii
Quellón, Chile, 82–83

Ragsdale, James W., 133
Red D Line, 69
Remey, George Collier, 3–4, 126
Richman, Clayton S., 126
Rio de Janiero, Brazil, 75, 77–78
Río de la Plata, 78
Roosevelt, Franklin D., xviii–xix
Royal Marines, 142, 150
Royal Navy, xviii
Russell, Averley W., Jr., 149

Salinas, Philippines, 159
Sampson, William, 27, 30–31, 34, 41–42, 45–46, 50, 56, 67–68, 70, 72, 74
Sampson Medal, xx
San Bernardino Straits, 101
San Diego, Calif., 94
San Francisco, Calif., xv, xvii, 92, 94, 98–99, 103, 128, 163
San José de Guatemala, Guatemala, 92–93
San Lorenzo Island, 91
San Luis de Apra Harbor, 99
San Salvador, 56
Santiago Bay, xv–xvi
Santiago de Cuba, Cuba, xv, 16, 21–25, 27, 34, 39, 41–42, 45–46, 48, 53, 56, 61–62, 64, 68
São Roque, Cape, 77
Sarmiento, Mount, 80
Second Nicaraguan Campaign Medal, xx
Seymour, Edward Hobart, xvi, 136–140, 143–44, 146, 150
Shafter, William, 11, 16, 20–21, 27, 36, 41, 46, 48, 62
Shanghai, China, 125
Sheldon, Clifford H., 86, 89, 107, 134, 144
Sherman, Emily Whitney, xix–xx
Shinto temples, 127
ships
    Acme, 55
    Admiral Korniloff, 126
    Adula, 39
    Aeolus, 113
    HMS *Alacrity*, 124
    Alamo, 7
    Albatross (American), 126
    Albatross (German), 126
    USS *Albay*, 104
    Alleghany, 7
    USS *Alliance*, 71
    Almirante Cochrane, 85
    Almirante Oquendo, 29–30, 34, 54, 63
    Almirante Simpson, 85
    Alvarado, 46
    America, 52–53
    Amiral Rigault de Genouilly, 42
    USS *Ammen*, xvii
    USS *Amphitrite*, xvii
    USS *Annapolis*, 4–5, 11, 13–15, 19–21
    Aquidaban, 77
    Arausus, 7
    HMS *Aurora*, 124, 136
    Australia, 99
    USS *Badger*, 54–55, 98
    USS *Baltimore*, 103–104, 121, 125–26
    USS *Bancroft*, 15, 21
    HMS *Barfleur*, 126
    Barrozo, 77
    Basco, 105
    Basco Villalos, 125
    USS *Bennington*, 104, 128
    Berkshire, 7
    HMS *Blake*, 64
    Blanca Enclada, 85
    HMS *Bonaventure*, 124
    USS *Boston*, 94–95
    Breakwater, 7
    USS *Brooklyn*, 16, 29–32, 41, 46, 55, 63–64, 68, 74, 98, 116, 126
    USS *Brutus*, 99–100
    Calabria, 126
    USS *Calamianes*, 104, 116, 159
    USS *Callao*, 104, 108–109
    USS *Castine*, 9–11, 14–15, 19, 104
    USS *Celtic*, xvii, 41–42, 53, 104
    HMS *Centurion*, 124, 136
    USS *Charleston*, 104, 123
    Cherokee, 7
    USS *Chicago*, xix
    China, 128, 157
    USS *Cincinnati*, 50
    City of Key West, 3
    City of Washington, 10
    USS *Cleveland*, xviii
    Clinton, 10
    USS *Columbia* (AG 9), xviii
    USS *Columbia* (C 2), 41
    Comal, 7
    Concho, 7
    USS *Concord*, 104, 126, 128
    Constitution, 91
    Cristobal Colon, 29–32, 63–64
    USS *Culgoa*, xvii, 104, 157–58, 165
    Cumberland, 10
    D. H. Miller, 7
    Daphne, 125
    D'Entrecasteaux, 124, 126, 131
    USS *Detroit*, 14–15, 19, 68
    USS *Dixie*, 41, 53
    USS *Dolphin*, 45
    Don Juan de Austria, 124
    USS *Eagle*, 15, 67
    Empress of Japan, 128
    HMS *Endymion*, 126–27, 136, 140, 153
    USS *Fanning*, xviii
    USS *Fern*, 50
    HMS *Flora*, 78
    USS *Florida*, 9
    USS *Foote*, 15
    USS *Frolic*, 53

Furor, 29
USS *Gardoqui*, 105
General Alava, 125
USS *Glacier*, 104, 116, 158
USS *Gloucester*, 25, 29–30, 41, 61–64
USS *Great Northern*, xviii
Gussie, 7, 10
Hai Shen (Tai Sin), 124
Hai-Tien, 125
USS *Hartford*, 95, 97
USS *Harvard*, 39, 64
USS *Hawk*, 48
USS *Helena*, 9–11, 14–15, 19, 104, 108, 110, 116, 123, 125
Hornet, 10–11, 13–15
USS *Idaho*, xix
HMS *Indefatigable*, 73
Independence, 97
USS *Indiana*, 14–16, 19, 27, 29–30, 41, 50, 55–56, 62–64, 68, 74
Infanta Maria Teresa, 29–30, 54, 63
USS *Iowa*, xix, 16, 29–32, 52, 55, 64, 94
USS *Iris*, 104, 114
Irizaba, 6–7
Iroquois, 7
USS *Iroquois*, 99
Isla de Cuba, 158, 160
USS *Joseph K. Taussig*, xx
USS *Kansas*, xvii
Kentucky, 159
Knickerbocker, 10, 19
Laura, 10
Leander, 92
USS *Lebanon*, 23, 39
Legaspi, 115
Leona, 7
USS *Leonidas*, 53
Leyte, 159
Ligura, 124
USS *Little*, xviii
Louisiana, 24
USS *Maine*, xv, 77
USS *Manila*, 104, 158
USS *Manileno*, 104
USS *Manning*, 15–16
USS *Marblehead*, 39, 50, 52, 68, 73–74, 91–92, 98
USS *Mareveles*, 105
Maria Theresa, 32, 34, 64
USS *Marietta*, 71
Marrila, 125
USS *Maryland*, xix
Mascotte, 4
USS *Massachusetts*, 16, 27, 34, 41–42, 53, 55, 62, 64, 74–75
Mateo, 20
Matteawan, 7
USS *Mayflower*, 53
USS *Merrimac*, 36–37, 45
Merritt, 54
Mexico, 49

Miami, 7, 9
USS *Mindoro*, xvi, 105, 119–21, 123
USS *Monadnock*, 104, 124–25
USS *Monocacy*, 104, 154
USS *Montana*, xix
USS *Monterey*, 104, 116, 125
USS *Montgomery*, 50
Morgan, 7, 10
Morrie, 10
Mortera, 49
USS *Nashville*, xvii, 116, 157–58
Naushan, 104
USS *Nero*, 104
Nevada, 125
USS *Nevada*, xix
USS *New Orleans*, 16, 19, 41, 77, 116
USS *New York*, xv, 4, 6, 16, 22–25, 29–32, 34, 41–42, 45–48, 50, 52, 55, 62–64, 68, 71–72, 74
USS *Newark*, xv–xvii, 25, 27, 41, 54, 61, 64, 71–75, 81, 83, 86, 91–92, 95–97, 99, 104–105, 107–110, 114, 123, 125–26, 128–29, 132, 134, 158
Newport, 10
USS *Niagara*, 39, 52–53
Ohio, 99
USS *Olivette*, 7, 10, 20, 22
USS *Oregon*, 16, 22, 27, 29–32, 34, 39, 41–42, 54–55, 62–64, 104–105, 116, 119, 126, 129, 131, 134
USS *Osceola*, 14–16
HMS *Pallas*, 34, 73
USS *Pampanga*, 104, 159
Panay, 104
Papin, 84–85
USS *Paragua*, 104, 159
USS *Petrel*, 104, 116, 125, 159
Petropavlovsk, 125
Philadelphia, 69
USS *Philadelphia*, 95
HMS *Pigmy*, 124
Pilcomayo, 84
Pisagua, 83
Plutón, 29
USS *Princeton*, 104–105, 107–108, 114, 116, 159
HMS *Proserpine*, 73
USS *Ranger*, 95
Reina de los Angeles, 49
Reina Mercedes, 37, 45
Relay, 92
USS *Resolute*, 32, 53, 63–64
Riachuelo, 77
Rio Grande, 7
USS *Rogers Ericsson*, 15, 63
Romulus, 113–15
USS *Samar*, 104, 114–16, 119–20, 123
Samoset, 52
San Joaquin, 113–15
San Juan, 49, 53
Saratoga, 7
USS *Scorpion*, 19, 54
Seguranca, 7, 11, 16, 20–21
Seneca, 7, 20

USS *Solace*, 98, 113, 115, 154
USS *Southery*, 49
St. Louis, 16, 19–21, 54
St. Paul, 41, 54
Staffa, 45
Stillwater, 7
USS *Supply*, 52–53
Surprise, 131
USS *Suwanee*, 25, 47, 61
Tarlac, 113–14
Tartar, 123
USS *Terror*, 49
USS *Texas*, xvii, 16, 29–31, 41, 50, 52, 63–64, 68, 73–74
Thomas, 155
USS *Topeka*, xvii
USS *Trenton*, xviii
Tupy, 77
USS *Unadilla*, 98
HMS *Undaunted*, 124
Union, 115
Uranus, 114–15
USS *Urdaneta*, 105
Venus, 114
USS *Vesuvius*, 22, 34
Vicksburg, 158
Victoria, 115
HMS *Victorious*, 124
Vigilancia, 7
Villalobos, 159
USS *Vixen*, 22, 24, 29, 31
Vizcaya, 29–31, 63
USS *Vulcan*, 39, 52
USS *Wadsworth*, xvii
USS *Wasp*, 15
USS *Wheeling*, 104, 108, 113, 116, 120–21, 123–24
Whitney, 7
USS *Wilmington*, 39, 158
USS *Winslow*, 4
USS *Wompatuck*, 15, 19–20
USS *Yale*, 23, 41
USS *Yankee*, 49, 53
USS *Yorktown*, xvii, 104, 125, 154, 158
USS *Yosemite*, 99–100, 126
Yucatan, 7
USS *Zafiro*, 99–100, 104, 113–14, 125
Zeeland, 74
Zostous, 104
shoguns, 127
Siboney, Cuba, xvi, 21–25, 27, 36, 41–42, 61–62
Sigsbee, Charles D., 73
Silver Life Saving Medal, xvii
Simpson, George W., 91
smallpox, 116
Smyth Channel, 81
South America, 80
Spain, xv
Spanish Campaign Medal, xx
Spanish-American War, xvi–xvii, 3, 90
Squiers, Herbert Goldsmith, 142

Stark, Harold R., xix
Staunton, Sidney A., 36, 74
Stickney, Herman O., 107
Sulu, 160
Sulu Sea, 160
Sydney, Australia, xvii, 158–61, 163–65

Taku, China, xvi, 128, 131–32, 134–36, 154
Talcahuano, Chile, 81
Tambo Valley, 88
Tampa, Fla., xvi, 4–5, 9–10
Tampa, Port, 4–6, 9–10
Tardy, Walter B., 116
Taussig, Charles, xvi, 25, 61
Taussig, Edward D., xvii
Taussig, Hawley, 93
Taussig, Joseph K., Jr., xix–xx
Taussig, Joseph Knefler, xv–xx
Taussig, Lulie Johnston, xix
Taylor, Henry C., 13–14
Thompson, Edgar, 158
Thursday Island, 160–61
Tientsin, China, xvi, 131–38, 140–41, 143–44, 150–54
Tilley, Benjamin F., 10
Tingo, Peru, 89–90
Tinio, Manuel, 108, 110
Tirona, Daniel, 108, 113
Tokyo, Japan, 127, 155
Tomb, William, 67, 71
Tompkins, John T., 14–15
Tompkinsville, N.Y., 67
Tozer, Ensign, 126
Treasury Department, xvii
Trinidad, 71, 73
Tropic of Cancer, 14
typhoid fever, 101

United States, xv, xvii, 78, 123–24
U.S. Fleet, xviii
U.S. Naval Academy, xv, xvii, 3
U.S. Naval Institute *Proceedings*, xx
Usedom, Guido von, 143
Utsunomiya, Japan, 127

Valparaiso, Chile, 73, 75, 79, 84–86
Victory Medal, xx
Vigan, Philippines, xv–xvi, 105–107, 113, 119–20, 123
Viña del Mar, Chile, 84
Vreeland, Charles, xvii

W. R. Grace & Co., 86, 91
Waikiki, 99
Waller, Littleton W. T., 152
Walsh, David I., xix
Ward Line, 6–7
Washington, D.C., xvii, xix
Watson, John C., 41, 116, 126
Wichart, John W., 50
Williams, Clarence S., 121
Wilson, Woodrow, xviii
Withington, Fredric S., xix

World War I, xvii
World War II Victory Medal, xx
Wurtsbaugh, Daniel W., 132, 134, 136, 144

Yang Tsun, China, xvi, 134, 137, 140, 143
yellow fever, 41, 45

Yokohama, Japan, 98, 116, 123, 125–27, 154–55
Yokohama Harbor, xvii
Young, Samuel B. M., 105, 108, 115

Zamboanga, Philippines, 160
Zeigemeier, Henry J., 4

NAVAL WAR COLLEGE HISTORICAL MONOGRAPH SERIES

1. *The Writings of Stephen B. Luce,* edited by John D. Hayes and John B. Hattendorf (1975).

3. *Professors of War: The Naval War College and the Development of the Naval Profession,* Ronald Spector (1977).

4. *The Blue Sword: The Naval War College and the American Mission, 1919–1941,* Michael Vlahos (1980).

5. *On His Majesty's Service: Observations of the British Home Fleet from the Diary, Reports, and Letters of Joseph H. Wellings, Assistant U.S. Naval Attaché, London, 1940–1941,* edited by John B. Hattendorf (1983).

7. *A Bibliography of the Works of Alfred Thayer Mahan,* compiled by John B. Hattendorf and Lynn C. Hattendorf (1986).

8. *The Fraternity of the Blue Uniform: Admiral Richard G. Colbert, U.S. Navy, and Allied Naval Cooperation,* Joel J. Sokolsky (1991).

9. *The Influence of History on Mahan: The Proceedings of a Conference Marking the Centenary of Alfred Thayer Mahan's The Influence of Sea Power upon History, 1660–1783,* edited by John B. Hattendorf (1991).

10. *Mahan Is Not Enough: The Proceedings of a Conference on the Works of Sir Julian Corbett and Admiral Sir Herbert Richmond,* edited by James Goldrick and John B. Hattendorf (1993).

11. *Ubi Sumus? The State of Naval and Maritime History,* edited by John B. Hattendorf (1994).

12. *The Queenstown Patrol, 1917: The Diary of Commander Joseph Knefler Taussig, U.S. Navy,* edited by William N. Still, Jr. (1996).

13. *Doing Naval History: Essays toward Improvement,* edited by John B. Hattendorf (1995).

14. *An Admiral's Yarn,* edited by Mark R. Shulman (1999).

15. *The Memoirs of Admiral H. Kent Hewitt,* edited by Evelyn M. Cherpak (2004).

www.ingramcontent.com/pod-product-compliance
Lightning Source LLC
Chambersburg PA
CBHW082120230426
43671CB00015B/2759